SCRUMstudy
Targeting success

A Guide to the

SCRUM BODY OF KNOWLEDGE

(SBOK™ Guide)

2013 Edition

A Comprehensive Guide to Deliver Projects using Scrum

Library of Congress Cataloging-in-Publication Data

A Guide to the Scrum Body of Knowledge (SBOK™ Guide) – 2013 edition

Includes bibliographical references and index.
ISBN: 978-0-9899252-0-4

1. Scrum Framework. I. SCRUMstudy™. II. *SBOK™ Guide*

2013950625

ISBN: 978-0-9899252-0-4

Published by:
SCRUMstudy™, a brand of VMEdu, Inc.
410 N 44th Street, Suite 240
Phoenix, Arizona 85008 USA
Phone: +1-480-882-0706
Fax: +1-240-238-2987
Email: sbok@scrumstudy.com
Website: www.scrumstudy.com

10 9 8 7 6 5 4 3 2

PREFACE

A Guide to the Scrum Body of Knowledge (SBOK™ Guide) provides guidelines for the successful implementation of Scrum—the most popular Agile product development and project delivery methodology. Scrum, as defined in the *SBOK™ Guide,* is a framework which is applicable to portfolios, programs, or projects of any size or complexity; and may be applied effectively in *any* industry to create a product, service, or other result.

The *SBOK™ Guide* was developed as a standard guide for organizations and professionals who want to implement Scrum, as well as those already doing so who want to make needed improvements to their processes. It is intended for use as a reference and knowledge guide by both experienced Scrum and other product or service development practitioners, as well as by persons with no prior experience or knowledge of Scrum or any other project delivery methodology.

The *SBOK™ Guide* draws from the combined knowledge and insight gained from thousands of projects across a variety of organizations and industries. In addition, contributions have been made by experts who have taught Scrum and project delivery courses to more than 400,000 professionals in 150 countries. Its development has truly been a collaborative effort from a large number of experts in a variety of disciplines. In particular, I would like to thank the seventeen co-authors and subject matter experts and the twenty-eight reviewers who greatly contributed to the creation of the *SBOK™ Guide*.

Wide adoption of the *SBOK™ Guide* framework should help standardize how Scrum is applied to projects across organizations globally, as well as significantly help to improve their Return on Investment. Additionally, it should promote greater thought and deliberation regarding the application of Scrum to many types of projects, which will in turn contribute towards expanding and enriching the body of knowledge and consequently future updates to this guide.

Although the *SBOK™ Guide* is a comprehensive guide and framework for delivering projects using Scrum, its contents are organized for easy reference, regardless of the reader's prior knowledge on the subject. I hope each reader will learn from and enjoy it as much as the many authors and reviewers learned from and enjoyed the process of collating the collective knowledge and wisdom contained within it.

Tridibesh Satpathy,

Lead Author, *SBOK™ Guide*

TABLE OF CONTENTS

LIST OF FIGURES

LIST OF TABLES

1. INTRODUCTION

A Guide to the Scrum Body of Knowledge (SBOK™ Guide) provides guidelines for the successful implementation of Scrum—the most popular Agile project management and product development methodology. It provides a comprehensive framework that includes the principles, aspects, and processes of Scrum.

Scrum, as defined in the *SBOK™ Guide*, is applicable to the following:

- Portfolios, programs, and/or projects in *any* industry
- Products, services, or any other results to be delivered to stakeholders
- Projects of any size or complexity

The term "product" in the *SBOK™ Guide* may refer to a product, service, or other deliverable. Scrum can be applied effectively to any project in any industry—from small projects or teams with as few as six team members to large, complex projects with up to several hundred team members.

This first chapter describes the purpose and framework of the *SBOK™ Guide* and provides an introduction to the key concepts of Scrum. It contains a summary of Scrum principles, Scrum aspects and Scrum processes. Chapter 2 expands on the six Scrum principles which are the foundation on which the Scrum framework is based. Chapters 3 through 7 elaborate on the five Scrum aspects that must be addressed throughout any project: organization, business justification, quality, change, and risk. Chapters 8 through 12 cover the 19 Scrum processes involved in carrying out a Scrum project. These processes are part of the five Scrum phases: Initiate; Plan and Estimate; Implement, Review and Retrospect; and Release. These phases describe in detail the associated inputs and outputs of each process, as well as the various tools that may be used in each process. Some inputs, tools, and outputs are mandatory and are indicated as such; others are optional depending on the specific project, organizational requirements, and/or guidelines set forth by the organization's Scrum Guidance Body (SGB). Finally, Appendix A contains an overview of *The Agile Manifesto* (Fowler and Highsmith, 2001) and a discussion of various Agile methods for those who want more information about Agile.

This chapter is divided into the following sections:

1.1 Overview of Scrum

1.2 Why Use Scrum?

1.3 Purpose of the *SBOK™ Guide*

1.4 Framework of the *SBOK™ Guide*

1.5 Scrum vs. Traditional Project Management

1.1   Overview of Scrum

A Scrum project involves a collaborative effort to create a new product, service, or other result as defined in the Project Vision Statement. Projects are impacted by constraints of time, cost, scope, quality, resources, organizational capabilities, and other limitations that make them difficult to plan, execute, manage, and ultimately succeed. However, successful implementation of the results of a finished project provides significant business benefits to an organization. It is therefore important for organizations to select and practice an appropriate project management methodology.

Scrum is one of the most popular Agile methodologies. It is an adaptive, iterative, fast, flexible, and effective methodology designed to deliver significant value quickly and throughout a project. Scrum ensures transparency in communication and creates an environment of collective accountability and continuous progress. The Scrum framework, as defined in the *SBOK™ Guide*, is structured in such a way that it supports product and service development in all types of industries and in any type of project, irrespective of its complexity.

A key strength of Scrum lies in its use of cross-functional, self-organized, and empowered teams who divide their work into short, concentrated work cycles called Sprints. Figure 1-1 provides an overview of a Scrum project's flow.

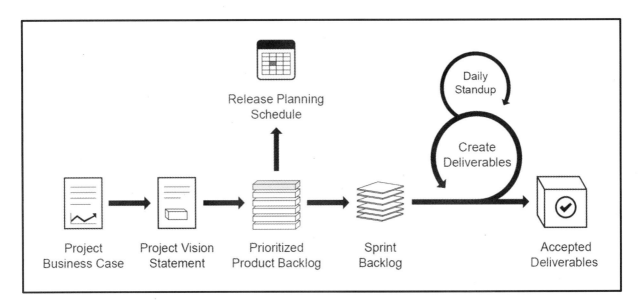

Figure 1-1: Scrum Flow for one Sprint

The Scrum cycle begins with a Stakeholder Meeting, during which the Project Vision is created. The Product Owner then develops a Prioritized Product Backlog which contains a prioritized list of business and project requirements written in the form of User Stories. Each Sprint begins with a Sprint Planning Meeting during which high priority User Stories are considered for inclusion in the Sprint. A Sprint generally lasts between one and six weeks and involves the Scrum Team working to create potentially shippable Deliverables or product increments. During the Sprint, short, highly focused Daily Standup Meetings are conducted where team members discuss daily progress. Toward the end of the Sprint, a Sprint Review Meeting is held during which the Product Owner and relevant stakeholders are provided a demonstration of the Deliverables. The Product Owner accepts the Deliverables only if they meet the predefined Acceptance Criteria. The Sprint cycle ends with a Retrospect Sprint Meeting where the team discusses ways to improve processes and performance as they move forward into the subsequent Sprint.

1.1.1 Brief History of Scrum

In the mid 80's, Hirotaka Takeuchi and Ikujiro Nonaka defined a flexible and all-inclusive product development strategy where the development team works as a unit to reach a common goal. They described an innovative approach to product development that they called a holistic or "rugby" approach, "where a team tries to go the distance as a unit, passing the ball back and forth." They based their approach on manufacturing case studies from various industries. Takeuchi and Nonaka proposed that product development should not be like a sequential relay race, but rather should be analogous to the game of rugby where the team works together, passing the ball back and forth as they move as a unit down the field. The rugby concept of a "Scrum" (where a group of players form together to restart the game) was introduced in this article to describe the authors' proposal that product development should involve "moving the Scrum downfield".

Ken Schwaber and Jeff Sutherland elaborated on the Scrum concept and its applicability to software development in a presentation at the Object-Oriented Programming, Systems, Languages & Applications (OOPSLA) conference held in 1995 in Austin, Texas. Since then, several Scrum practitioners, experts, and authors have continued to refine the Scrum conceptualization and methodology. In recent years, Scrum has increased in popularity and is now the preferred project development methodology for many organizations globally.

1.2 Why Use Scrum?

Some of the key benefits of using Scrum in any project are:

1. **Adaptability**—Empirical process control and iterative delivery make projects adaptable and open to incorporating change.

2. **Transparency**—All information radiators like a Scrumboard and Sprint Burndown Chart are shared, leading to an open work environment.

3. **Continuous Feedback**—Continuous feedback is provided through the *Conduct Daily Standup,* and *Demonstrate and Validate Sprint* processes.

4. **Continuous Improvement**—The deliverables are improved progressively Sprint by Sprint, through the *Groom Prioritized Product Backlog* process.

5. **Continuous Delivery of Value**—Iterative processes enable the continuous delivery of value through the *Ship Deliverables* process as frequently as the customer requires.

6. **Sustainable Pace**—Scrum processes are designed such that the people involved can work at a sustainable pace that they can, in theory, continue indefinitely.

7. **Early Delivery of High Value**—The *Create Prioritized Product Backlog* process ensures that the highest value requirements of the customer are satisfied first.

8. **Efficient Development Process**—Time-boxing and minimizing non-essential work leads to higher efficiency levels.

9. **Motivation**—The *Conduct Daily Standup* and *Retrospect Sprint* processes lead to greater levels of motivation among employees.

10. **Faster Problem Resolution**—Collaboration and colocation of cross-functional teams lead to faster problem solving.

11. **Effective Deliverables**—The *Create Prioritized Product Backlog* process and regular reviews after creating deliverables ensures effective deliverables to the customer.

12. **Customer Centric**—Emphasis on business value and having a collaborative approach to stakeholders ensures a customer-oriented framework.

13. **High Trust Environment**—*Conduct Daily Standup* and *Retrospect Sprint* processes promote transparency and collaboration, leading to a high trust work environment ensuring low friction among employees.

14. **Collective Ownership**—The *Approve, Estimate, and Commit User Stories* process allows team members to take ownership of the project and their work leading to better quality.

15. **High Velocity**—A collaborative framework enables highly skilled cross-functional teams to achieve their full potential and high velocity.

16. **Innovative Environment**—The *Retrospect Sprint* and *Retrospect Project* processes create an environment of introspection, learning, and adaptability leading to an innovative and creative work environment.

1.2.1 Scalability of Scrum

To be effective, Scrum Teams should ideally have six to ten members. This practice may be the reason for the misconception that the Scrum framework can only be used for small projects. However, it can easily be scaled for effective use in large projects. In situations where the Scrum Team size exceeds ten people, multiple Scrum Teams can be formed to work on the project. The *Convene Scrum of Scrums* process facilitates coordination among the Scrum Teams, enabling effective implementation in larger projects.

Large or complex projects are often implemented as part of a program or portfolio. The Scrum framework can also be applied to manage even programs and portfolios. The logical approach of the guidelines and principles in this framework can be used to manage projects of any size, spanning geographies and organizations. Large projects may have multiple Scrum Teams working in parallel making it necessary to synchronize and facilitate the flow of information and enhance communication. The *Convene Scrum of Scrums* is the process ensuring this synchronization. The various Scrum Teams are represented in this meeting and the objectives are to provide updates about progress, discuss challenges faced during the project, and coordinate activities. There are no set rules regarding the frequency of these meetings. The factors determining the frequency are the amount of inter-team dependency, size of the project, level of complexity, and recommendations from the Scrum Guidance Body.

1.3   Purpose of the *SBOK™ Guide*

In recent years, it has become evident that organizations which use Scrum as their preferred project delivery framework consistently deliver high Returns on Investment. Scrum's focus on value-driven delivery helps Scrum Teams deliver results as early in the project as possible.

The *SBOK™ Guide* was developed as a means to create a necessary guide for organizations and project management practitioners who want to implement Scrum, as well as those already doing so who want to make needed improvements to their processes. It is based on experience drawn from thousands of projects across a variety of organizations and industries. The contributions of many Scrum experts and project management practitioners have been considered in its development.

The *SBOK™ Guide* is especially valuable:

- to Scrum Core Team members including:
    - Product Owners who want to fully understand the Scrum framework and particularly the customer or stakeholder-related concerns involving business justification, quality, change, and risk aspects associated with Scrum projects.
    - Scrum Masters who want to learn their specific role in overseeing the application of Scrum framework to Scrum projects.
    - Scrum Team members who want to better understand Scrum processes and the associated tools that may be used to create the project's product or service.
- as a comprehensive guide for all Scrum practitioners working on Scrum projects in any organization or industry.
- as a reference source for anyone interacting with the Scrum Core Team, including but not limited to the Portfolio Product Owner, Portfolio Scrum Master, Program Product Owner, Program Scrum Master, Scrum Guidance Body, and Stakeholders (i.e., sponsor, customer, and users).
- as a handbook for any person who has no prior experience or knowledge of Scrum framework but wants to learn more about the subject.

The content of the *SBOK™ Guide* is also helpful for individuals preparing to write the following SCRUMstudy™ certification exams:

- Scrum Developer Certified (SDC™)
- Scrum Master Certified (SMC™)
- Agile Expert Certified (AEC™)
- Scrum Product Owner Certified (SPOC™)
- Expert Scrum Master (ESM™)

1.4   Framework of the *SBOK™ Guide*

The *SBOK™ Guide* is broadly divided into the following three areas:

1. **Principles** covered in chapter 2, expand on the six principles which form the foundation on which Scrum is based.

2. **Aspects** covered in chapters 3 through 7 describe the five aspects that are important considerations for all Scrum projects.

3. **Processes** covered in chapters 8 through 12 include the nineteen Scrum processes and their associated inputs, tools, and outputs.

Figure 1-2 illustrates the *SBOK™ Guide* framework, which shows that principles, aspects, and processes interact with each other and are equally important in getting a better understanding of the Scrum framework.

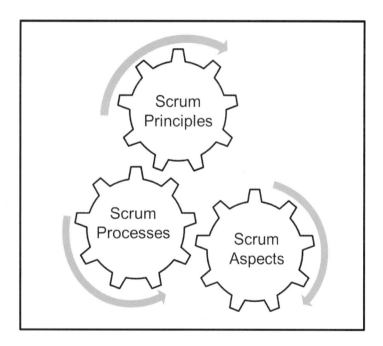

Figure 1-2: *SBOK™ Guide* **Framework**

1.4.1   How to Use the *SBOK™ Guide*?

The *SBOK™ Guide* can be used as a reference and knowledge guide by both experienced Scrum and other product and service development practitioners, as well as by persons with no prior experience or knowledge of Scrum or project management methodology. The contents are organized for easy reference by the three Scrum Core Team roles: Scrum Master, Product Owner, and Scrum Team.

The chapters covering the six Scrum principles (chapter 2) and five Scrum aspects (chapter 3 through 7) include a Roles Guide. This guide provides direction regarding the relevance of each section in the chapter to the Scrum Core Team roles.

In order to facilitate the best application of the Scrum framework, the *SBOK™ Guide* has clearly differentiated mandatory inputs, tools, and outputs, from non-mandatory or optional ones. Inputs, tools, and outputs denoted by asterisks (*) are mandatory while others with no asterisks are optional. It is recommended that those being introduced to Scrum focus primarily on the mandatory inputs, tools, and outputs, while more experienced practitioners should read the entire process chapters.

1.4.2   Scrum Principles

Scrum principles are the core guidelines for applying the Scrum framework and should mandatorily be used in all Scrum projects. The six Scrum principles presented in chapter 2 are:

1. Empirical Process Control
2. Self-organization
3. Collaboration
4. Value-based Prioritization
5. Time-boxing
6. Iterative Development

Figure 1-3 illustrates the six Scrum principles.

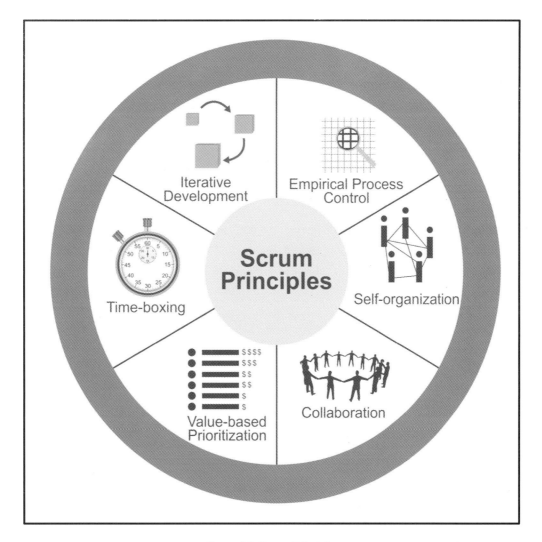

Figure 1-3: Scrum Principles

Scrum principles can be applied to any type of project in any organization and must be adhered to in order to ensure effective implementation of the Scrum framework. Scrum Principles are non-negotiable and must be applied as specified in the *SBOK™ Guide*. Keeping the principles intact and using them appropriately instills confidence in the Scrum framework with regard to attaining the objectives of the project. The Scrum aspects and processes, however, can be modified to meet the requirements of the project or the organization.

1. **Empirical Process Control**—This principle emphasizes the core philosophy of Scrum based on the three main ideas of transparency, inspection, and adaptation.

2. **Self-organization**—This principle focuses on today's workers, who deliver significantly greater value when self-organized and this results in better team buy-in and shared ownership; and an innovative and creative environment which is more conducive for growth.

3. **Collaboration**—This principle focuses on the three core dimensions related to collaborative work: awareness, articulation, and appropriation. It also advocates project management as a shared value-creation process with teams working and interacting together to deliver the greatest value.

4. **Value-based Prioritization**—This principle highlights the focus of Scrum to deliver maximum business value, from early in the project and continuing throughout.

5. **Time-boxing**—This principle describes how time is considered a limiting constraint in Scrum, and used to help effectively manage project planning and execution. Time-boxed elements in Scrum include Sprints, Daily Standup Meetings, Sprint Planning Meetings, and Sprint Review Meetings.

6. **Iterative Development**—This principle defines iterative development and emphasizes how to better manage changes and build products that satisfy customer needs. It also delineates the Product Owner's and organization's responsibilities related to iterative development.

1.4.3   Scrum Aspects

The Scrum aspects must be addressed and managed throughout a Scrum project. The five Scrum aspects presented in chapter 3 through 7 are:

1

1.4.3.1   Organization

Understanding defined roles and responsibilities in a Scrum project is very important for ensuring the successful implementation of Scrum.

Scrum roles fall into two broad categories:

1. **Core Roles**—Core roles are those roles which are mandatorily required for producing the project's product or service. Individuals who are assigned core roles are fully committed to the project and are ultimately responsible for the success of each project iteration and of the project as a whole.

   These roles include:

   - The **Product Owner** is the person responsible for achieving maximum business value for the project. He or she is also responsible for articulating customer requirements and maintaining business justification for the project. The Product Owner represents the Voice of the Customer.

   - The **Scrum Master** is a facilitator who ensures that the Scrum Team is provided with an environment conducive to complete the project successfully. The Scrum Master guides, facilitates, and teaches Scrum practices to everyone involved in the project; clears impediments for the team; and, ensures that Scrum processes are being followed.

   - The **Scrum Team** is the group or team of people who are responsible for understanding the requirements specified by the Product Owner and creating the Deliverables of the project.

2. **Non-core Roles**—Non-core roles are those roles which are not mandatorily required for the Scrum project and may include team members who are interested in the project. They have no formal role in the project team and may interface with the team, but may not be responsible for the success of the project. The non-core roles should be taken into account in any Scrum project.

Non-core roles include the following:

- **Stakeholder(s),** which is a collective term that includes customers, users, and sponsors, frequently interface with the Scrum Core Team, and influence the project throughout the project's development. Most importantly, it is for the stakeholders that the project produces the collaborative benefits.

- **Scrum Guidance Body** (SGB) is an optional role, which generally consists of a set of documents and/or a group of experts who are typically involved with defining objectives related to quality, government regulations, security, and other key organizational parameters. This SGB guides the work carried out by the Product Owner, Scrum Master, and Scrum Team.

- **Vendors**, including external individuals or organizations, provide products and/or services that are not within the core competencies of the project organization.

- **Chief Product Owner** is a role in bigger projects with multiple Scrum Teams. This role is responsible for facilitating the work of multiple Product Owners, and maintaining business justification for the larger project.

- **Chief Scrum Master** is responsible to coordinate Scrum-related activities in large projects which may require multiple Scrum Teams to work in parallel.

Figure 1-4 illustrates the Scrum Organization structure.

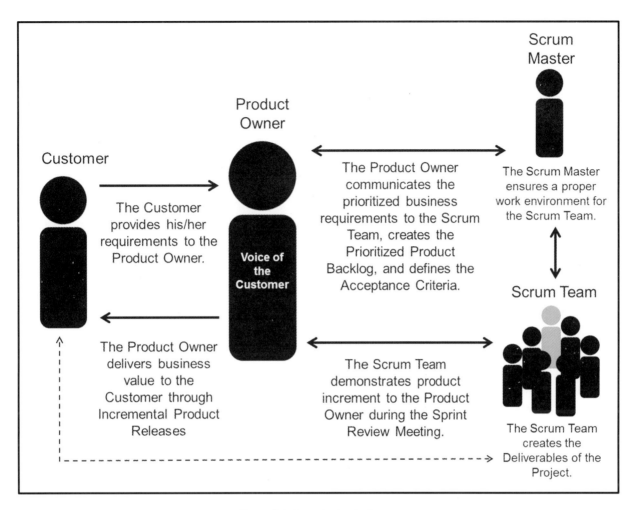

Figure 1-4: Organization in Scrum

The Organization aspect of Scrum also addresses the team structure requirements to implement Scrum in programs and portfolios.

1.4.3.2 Business Justification

It is important for an organization to perform a proper business assessment prior to starting any project. This helps key decision makers understand the business need for a change or for a new product or service, the justification for moving forward with a project, and its viability.

Business justification in Scrum is based on the concept of Value-driven Delivery. One of the key characteristics of any project is the uncertainty of results or outcomes. It is impossible to guarantee project success at completion, irrespective of the size or complexity of a project. Considering this uncertainty of achieving success, Scrum attempts to start delivering results as early in the project as possible. This early delivery of results, and thereby value, provides an opportunity for reinvestment and proves the worth of the project to interested stakeholders.

Scrum's adaptability allows the project's objectives and processes to change if its business justification changes. It is important to note that although the Product Owner is primarily responsible for business justification, other team members contribute significantly.

1.4.3.3   Quality

In Scrum, quality is defined as the ability of the completed product or deliverables to meet the Acceptance Criteria and achieve the business value expected by the customer.

To ensure a project meets quality requirements, Scrum adopts an approach of continuous improvement whereby the team learns from experience and stakeholder engagement to constantly keep the Prioritized Product Backlog updated with any changes in requirements. The Prioritized Product Backlog is simply never complete until the closure or termination of the project. Any changes to the requirements reflect changes in the internal and external business environment and allow the team to continually work and adapt to achieve those requirements.

Since Scrum requires work to be completed in increments during Sprints, this means that errors or defects get noticed earlier through repetitive quality testing, rather than when the final product or service is near completion. Moreover, important quality-related tasks (e.g., development, testing, and documentation) are completed as part of the same Sprint by the same team—this ensures that quality is inherent in any deliverable created as part of a Sprint. Such deliverables from Scrum projects, which are potentially shippable, are referred to as 'Done.'

Thus, continuous improvement with repetitive testing optimizes the probability of achieving the expected quality levels in a Scrum project. Constant discussions between the Scrum Core Team and stakeholders (including customers and users) with actual increments of the product being delivered at the end of every Sprint, ensures that the gap between customer expectations from the project and actual deliverables produced is constantly reduced.

The Scrum Guidance Body may also provide guidelines about quality which may be relevant to all Scrum projects in the organization.

1.4.3.4   Change

Every project, regardless of its method or framework used, is exposed to change. It is imperative that project team members understand that the Scrum development processes are designed to embrace change. Organizations should try to maximize the benefits that arise from change and minimize any negative impacts through diligent change management processes in accordance with the principles of Scrum.

A primary principle of Scrum is its acknowledgement that a) stakeholders (e.g., customers, users, and sponsors) change their mind about what they want and need throughout a project (sometimes referred to as "requirements churn") and b) it is very difficult, if not impossible, for stakeholders to define all requirements during project initiation.

Scrum projects welcome change by using short, iterative Sprints that incorporate customer feedback on each Sprint's deliverables. This enables the customer to regularly interact with the Scrum Team members, view deliverables as they are ready, and change requirements if needed earlier in the Sprint.

Also, the portfolio or program management teams can respond to Change Requests pertaining to Scrum projects applicable at their level.

1.4.3.5   Risk

Risk is defined as an uncertain event or set of events that can affect the objectives of a project and may contribute to its success or failure. Risks that are likely to have a positive impact on the project are referred to as opportunities, whereas threats are risks that could affect the project in a negative manner. Managing risk must be done proactively, and it is an iterative process that should begin at project initiation and continue throughout the project's lifecycle. The process of managing risks should follow some standardized steps to ensure that risks are identified, evaluated, and a proper course of action is determined and acted upon accordingly.

Risks should be identified, assessed, and responded to based on two factors: the probability of each risk's occurrence and the possible impact in the event of such occurrence. Risks with a high probability and impact value (determined by multiplying both factors), should be addressed before those with a relatively lower value. In general, once a risk is identified, it is important to understand the risk with regard to the probable causes and the potential effects if the risk occurs.

1.4.4   Scrum Processes

Scrum processes address the specific activities and flow of a Scrum project. In total there are nineteen processes which are grouped into five phases. These phases are presented in chapters 8 through 12 of the *SBOK™ Guide*, as shown in Table 1-1.

Chapter	Phase	Processes
8	Initiate	1. Create Project Vision 2. Identify Scrum Master and Stakeholder(s) 3. Form Scrum Team 4. Develop Epic(s) 5. Create Prioritized Product Backlog 6. Conduct Release Planning
9	Plan and Estimate	7. Create User Stories 8. Approve, Estimate, and Commit User Stories 9. Create Tasks 10. Estimate Tasks 11. Create Sprint Backlog
10	Implement	12. Create Deliverables 13. Conduct Daily Standup 14. Groom Prioritized Product Backlog
11	Review and Retrospect	15. Convene Scrum of Scrums 16. Demonstrate and Validate Sprint 17. Retrospect Sprint
12	Release	18. Ship Deliverables 19. Retrospect Project

Table 1-1: Summary of Scrum Processes

These phases describe each process in detail including their associated inputs, tools, and outputs. In each process, some inputs, tools, and outputs are mandatory (those with an asterisk [*] after their names), while others are optional. Whether to include the optional inputs, tools, and/or outputs depend on the particular project, organization, or industry. Inputs, tools, and outputs denoted as mandatory are important for the successful implementation of Scrum in any organization.

1.4.4.1 Initiate

1. *Create Project Vision*—In this process, the Project Business Case is reviewed to create a Project Vision Statement that will serve as the inspiration and provide focus for the entire project. The Product Owner is identified in this process.

2. *Identify Scrum Master and Stakeholder(s)*—In this process, the Scrum Master and Stakeholders are identified using specific Selection Criteria.

3. *Form Scrum Team*—In this process, Scrum Team members are identified. Normally the Product Owner has the primary responsibility of selecting team members, but often does so in collaboration with the Scrum Master.

4. *Develop Epic(s)*—In this process, the Project Vision Statement serves as the basis for developing Epics. User Group Meetings may be held to discuss appropriate Epics.

5. *Create Prioritized Product Backlog*—In this process, Epic(s) are refined, elaborated, and then prioritized to create a Prioritized Product Backlog for the project. The Done Criteria is also established at this point.

6. *Conduct Release Planning*—In this process, the Scrum Core Team reviews the User Stories in the Prioritized Product Backlog to develop a Release Planning Schedule, which is essentially a phased deployment schedule that can be shared with the project stakeholders. Length of Sprint is also determined in this process.

1.4.4.2 Plan and Estimate

7. *Create User Stories*—In this process, User Stories and their related User Story Acceptance Criteria are created. User Stories are usually written by the Product Owner and are designed to ensure that the customer's requirements are clearly depicted and can be fully understood by all stakeholders. User Story Writing Exercises may be held which involves Scrum Team members creating the User Stories. User Stories are incorporated into the Prioritized Product Backlog.

8. *Approve, Estimate, and Commit User Stories*—In this process, the Product Owner approves User Stories for a Sprint. Then, the Scrum Master and Scrum Team estimate the effort required to develop the functionality described in each User Story, and the Scrum Team commits to deliver the customer requirements in the form of Approved, Estimated, and Committed User Stories.

9. *Create Tasks*—In this process, the Approved, Estimated, and Committed User Stories are broken down into specific tasks and compiled into a Task List. Often a Task Planning Meeting is held for this purpose.

10. *Estimate Tasks*—In this process, the Scrum Core Team, in Task Estimation Meetings, estimate the effort required to accomplish each task in the Task List. The result of this process is an Effort Estimated Task List.

11. *Create Sprint Backlog*—In this process, the Scrum Core Team holds Sprint Planning Meetings where the group creates a Sprint Backlog containing all tasks to be completed in the Sprint.

1.4.4.3   Implement

12. *Create Deliverables*—In this process, the Scrum Team works on the tasks in the Sprint Backlog to create Sprint Deliverables. A Scrumboard is often used to track the work and activities being carried out. Issues or problems being faced by the Scrum Team could be updated in an Impediment Log.

13. *Conduct Daily Standup*—In this process, everyday a highly focused, Time-boxed meeting is conducted referred to as the Daily Standup Meeting. This is the forum for the Scrum Team to update each other on their progress and any impediments they may be facing.

14. *Groom Prioritized Product Backlog*—In this process, the Prioritized Product Backlog is continuously updated and maintained. A Prioritized Product Backlog Review Meeting may be held, in which any changes or updates to the backlog are discussed and incorporated into the Prioritized Product Backlog as appropriate.

1.4.4.4   Review and Retrospect

15. *Convene Scrum of Scrums*—In this process, Scrum Team representatives convene for Scrum of Scrums (SoS) Meetings in predetermined intervals or whenever required to collaborate and track their respective progress, impediments, and dependencies across teams. This is relevant only for large projects where multiple Scrum Teams are involved.

16. *Demonstrate and Validate Sprint*—In this process, the Scrum Team demonstrates the Sprint Deliverables to the Product Owner and relevant stakeholders in a Sprint Review Meeting. The purpose of this meeting is to secure approval and acceptance from the Product Owner for the Deliverables created in the Sprint.

17. *Retrospect Sprint*—In this process, the Scrum Master and Scrum Team meet to discuss the lessons learned throughout the Sprint. This information is documented as lessons learned which can be applied to future Sprints. Often, as a result of this discussion, there may be Agreed Actionable Improvements or Updated Scrum Guidance Body Recommendations.

1.4.4.5   Release

18. *Ship Deliverables*—In this process, Accepted Deliverables are delivered or transitioned to the relevant stakeholders. A formal Working Deliverables Agreement documents the successful completion of the Sprint.

19. *Retrospect Project*—In this process, which completes the project, organizational stakeholders and Scrum Core Team members assemble to retrospect the project and identify, document, and internalize the lessons learned. Often, these lessons lead to the documentation of Agreed Actionable Improvements, to be implemented in future projects.

1.5   Scrum vs. Traditional Project Management

Table 1-2 summarizes many of the differences between Scrum and traditional project management models.

	Scrum	Traditional Project Management
Emphasis is on	People	Processes
Documentation	Minimal—only as required	Comprehensive
Process style	Iterative	Linear
Upfront planning	Low	High
Prioritization of Requirements	Based on business value and regularly updated	Fixed in the Project Plan
Quality assurance	Customer centric	Process centric
Organization	Self-organized	Managed
Management style	Decentralized	Centralized
Change	Updates to Productized Product Backlog	Formal Change Management System
Leadership	Collaborative, Servant Leadership	Command and control
Performance measurement	Business value	Plan conformity
Return on Investment (ROI)	Early/throughout project life	End of project life
Customer involvement	High throughout the project	Varies depending on the project lifecycle

Table 1-2: Scrum vs. Traditional Project Management

2. PRINCIPLES

2.1 Introduction

Scrum principles are the foundation on which the Scrum framework is based. The principles of Scrum can be applied to any type of project or organization, and they must be adhered to in order to ensure appropriate application of Scrum. The aspects and processes of Scrum can be modified to meet the requirements of the project, or the organization using it, but Scrum principles are non-negotiable and must be applied as described in the framework presented in *A Guide to the Scrum Body of Knowledge (SBOK™ Guide)*. Keeping the principles intact and using them appropriately instills confidence to the user of the Scrum framework with regard to attaining the objectives of the project. Principles are considered to be the core guidelines for applying the Scrum framework.

Principles, as defined in the *SBOK™ Guide*, are applicable to the following:

- Portfolios, programs, and/or projects in *any* industry
- Products, services, or any other results to be delivered to stakeholders
- Projects of any size or complexity

The term "product" in the *SBOK™ Guide* may refer to a product, service, or other deliverable. Scrum can be applied effectively to any project in any industry—from small projects or teams with as few as six team members to large, complex projects with up to several hundred team members.

This chapter is divided into the following sections:

2.2 Roles Guide—This section outlines which section or subsection is most relevant for each of the core Scrum roles of Product Owner, Scrum Master, and Scrum Team.

2.3 Empirical Process Control—This section describes the first principle of Scrum, and the three main ideas of transparency, inspection, and adaptation.

2.4 Self-organization—This section highlights the second principle of Scrum, which focuses on today's workers, who deliver significantly greater value when self-organized and this results in better team buy-in and shared ownership; and an innovative and creative environment which is more conducive for growth.

2.5 Collaboration—This section emphasizes the third principle of Scrum where product development is a shared value-creation process that needs all stakeholders working and interacting together to deliver the greatest value. It also focuses on the core dimensions of collaborative work: awareness, articulation, and appropriation.

2.6 Value-based Prioritization—This section presents the fourth principle of Scrum, which highlights the Scrum framework's drive to deliver maximum business value in a minimum time span.

2.7 Time-boxing—This section explains the fifth principle of Scrum which treats time as a limiting constraint. It also covers the Sprint, Daily Standup Meeting, and the various other Sprint-related meetings such as the Sprint Planning Meeting and Sprint Review Meeting, all of which are Time-boxed.

2.8 Iterative Development—This section addresses the sixth principle of Scrum which emphasizes that iterative development helps to better manage changes and build products that satisfy customer needs.

2.9 Scrum vs. Traditional Project Management—This section highlights the key differences between the Scrum principles and traditional project management (Waterfall model) principles and explains how Scrum works better in today's fast-changing world.

2.2   Roles Guide

All the sections in this chapter are important for all the Scrum Core Team roles—Product Owner, Scrum Master, and Scrum Team. A clear understanding of the Scrum principles by all stakeholders is essential to make Scrum framework a success in any organization.

2.3   Empirical Process Control

In Scrum, decisions are made based on observation and experimentation rather than on detailed upfront planning. Empirical process control relies on the three main ideas of transparency, inspection, and adaptation.

2.3.1   Transparency

Transparency allows all facets of any Scrum process to be observed by anyone. This promotes an easy and transparent flow of information throughout the organization and creates an open work culture. In Scrum, transparency is depicted through the following:

- A Project Vision Statement which can be viewed by all stakeholders and the Scrum Team
- An open Prioritized Product Backlog with prioritized User Stories that can be viewed by everyone, both within and outside the Scrum Team
- A Release Planning Schedule which may be coordinated across multiple Scrum Teams
- Clear visibility into the team's progress through the use of a Scrumboard, Burndown Chart, and other information radiators
- Daily Standup Meetings conducted during the *Conduct Daily Standup* process, in which all team members report what they have done the previous day, what they plan to do today, and any problems preventing them from completing their tasks in the current Sprint

- Sprint Review Meetings conducted during the *Demonstrate and Validate Sprint* process, in which the Scrum Team demonstrates the potentially shippable Sprint Deliverables to the Product Owner and Stakeholders

Figure 2-1 summarizes the concept of transparency in Scrum.

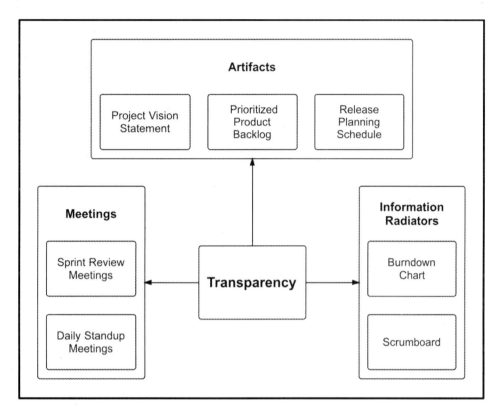

Figure 2-1: Transparency in Scrum

2.3.2   Inspection

Inspection in Scrum is depicted through the following:

- Use of a common Scrumboard and other information radiators which show the progress of the Scrum Team on completing the tasks in the current Sprint.
- Collection of feedback from the customer and other stakeholders during the *Develop Epic(s)*, *Create Prioritized Product Backlog*, and *Conduct Release Planning* processes.
- Inspection and approval of the Deliverables by the Product Owner and the customer in the *Demonstrate and Validate Sprint* process.

Figure 2-2 summarizes the concept of inspection in Scrum.

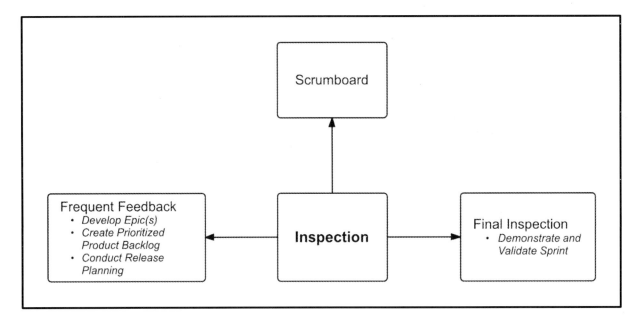

Figure 2-2: Inspection in Scrum

2.3.3   Adaptation

Adaptation happens as the Scrum Core Team and Stakeholders learn through transparency and inspection and then adapt by making improvements in the work they are doing. Some examples of adaptation include:

- In Daily Standup Meetings, Scrum Team members openly discuss impediments to completing their tasks and seek help from other team members. More experienced members in the Scrum Team also mentor those with relatively less experience in knowledge of the project or technology.
- Risk identification is performed and iterated throughout the project. Identified risks become inputs to several Scrum processes including *Create Prioritized Product Backlog*, *Groom Prioritized Product Backlog*, and *Demonstrate and Validate Sprint*.

- Improvements can also result in Change Requests, which are discussed and approved during the *Develop Epic(s)*, *Create Prioritized Product Backlog*, and *Groom Prioritized Product Backlog* processes.
- The Scrum Guidance Body interacts with Scrum Team members during the *Create User Stories*, *Estimate Tasks*, *Create Deliverables*, and *Groom Prioritized Product Backlog* processes to offer guidance and also provide expertise as required.
- In the *Retrospect Sprint* process, Agreed Actionable Improvements are determined based on the outputs from the *Demonstrate and Validate Sprint* process.
- In Retrospect Project Meeting, participants document lessons learned and perform reviews looking for opportunities to improve processes and address inefficiencies.

Figure 2-3 summarizes the concept of adaptation in Scrum.

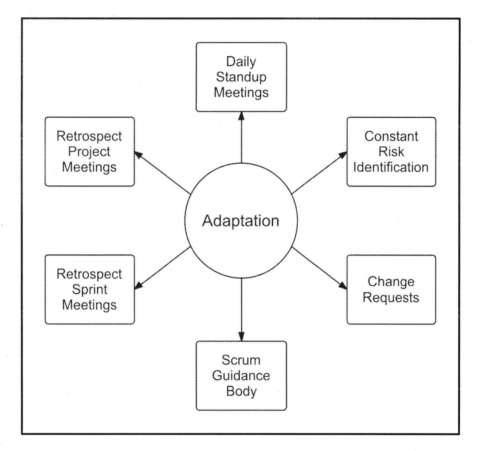

Figure 2-3: Adaptation in Scrum

With other methods, like the traditional Waterfall model, considerable planning needs to be done in advance and the customer generally does not review product components until near the end of a phase, or the end of the entire project. This method often presents huge risks to the project's success because it may have more potential for significantly impacting project delivery and customer acceptance. The customer's interpretation and understanding of the finished product may be very different from what was actually understood and produced by the team and this may not be known until very late in the project's development.

Figure 2-4 demonstrates an example of these challenges.

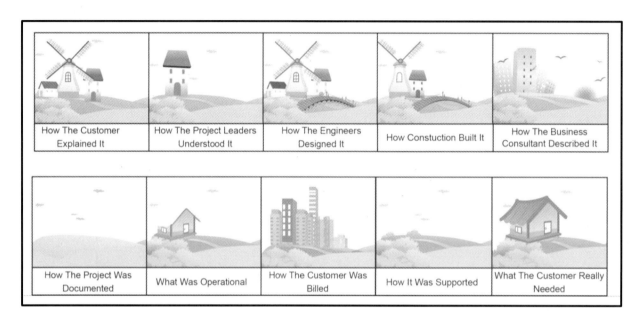

Figure 2-4: Challenges in Traditional Project Management

2.4   Self-organization

Scrum believes that employees are self-motivated and seek to accept greater responsibility. So, they deliver much greater value when self-organized.

The preferred leadership style in Scrum is "servant leadership", which emphasizes achieving results by focusing on the needs of the Scrum Team. See section 3.10.3 for a discussion of various leadership and management styles.

2.4.1   Benefits of Self-organization

Self-organization as an essential principle in Scrum leads to the following:

- Team buy-in and shared ownership
- Motivation, which leads to an enhanced performance level of the team
- Innovative and creative environment conducive to growth

Self-organization does not mean that team members are allowed to act in any manner that they want to. It just means that once the Product Vision is defined in the *Create Project Vision* process, the Product Owner, Scrum Master, and Scrum Team get identified. Also the Scrum Core Team itself works very closely with relevant Stakeholder(s) for refining requirements better as they go through the *Develop Epic(s)* and *Create User Stories* process. Team expertise is used to assess the inputs needed to execute the planned work of the project. This judgment and expertise are applied to all technical and management aspects of the project during the *Create Deliverables* process.

Although prioritization is primarily done by the Product Owner who represents the Voice of Customer, the self-organized Scrum Team is involved in task breakdown and estimation during the *Create Tasks* and *Estimate Tasks* processes. During these processes, each team member is responsible for determining what work he or she will be doing. During the execution of a Sprint, if team members need any help with completing their tasks, Scrum addresses this through the regular interaction mandatory with the Daily Standup Meetings. The Scrum Team itself interacts with other teams through the Scrum of Scrums (SoS) Meetings and can look for additional guidance as required from the Scrum Guidance Body.

Finally, the Scrum Team and Scrum Master work closely to demonstrate the product increment created during the Sprint in the *Demonstrate and Validate Sprint* process where properly completed deliverables are accepted. Since the Deliverables are potentially shippable, (and the Prioritized Product Backlog is prioritized by User Stories in the order of value created by them), the Product Owner and the customer can clearly visualize and articulate the value being created after every Sprint; and Scrum Teams in turn have the satisfaction of seeing their hard work being accepted by the customer and other stakeholders.

The chief goals of self-organizing teams are as follows:

- Understand the Project Vision and why the project delivers value to the organization
- Estimate User Stories during the *Approve, Estimate, and Commit User Stories* process and assign tasks to themselves during the *Create Sprint Backlog* process
- Create tasks independently during the *Create Tasks* process
- Apply and leverage their expertise from being a cross-functional team to work on the tasks during the *Create Deliverables* process
- Deliver tangible results which are accepted by the customer and other stakeholders during the *Demonstrate and Validate Sprint* process
- Resolve individual problems together by addressing them during Daily Standup Meetings
- Clarify any discrepancies or doubts and be open to learning new things
- Upgrade knowledge and skill on a continuous basis through regular interactions within the team
- Maintain stability of team members throughout the duration of the project by not changing members, unless unavoidable

Figure 2-5 illustrates the goals of a self-organizing team.

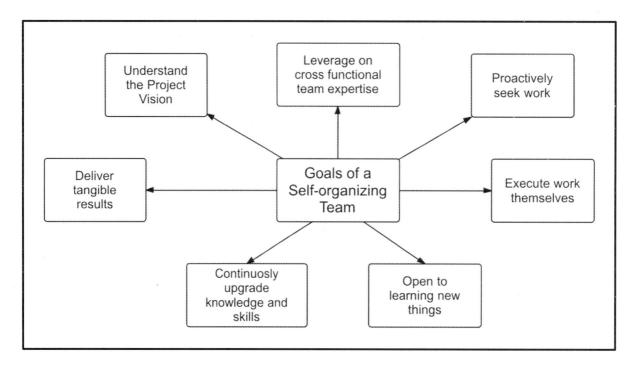

Figure 2-5: Goals of a Self-Organizing Team

2.5   Collaboration

Collaboration in Scrum refers to the Scrum Core Team working together and interfacing with the stakeholders to create and validate the deliverables of the project to meet the goals outlined in the Project Vision. It is important to note the difference between cooperation and collaboration here. Cooperation occurs when the work product consists of the sum of the work efforts of various people on a team. Collaboration occurs when a team works together to play off each other's inputs to produce something greater.

The core dimensions of collaborative work are as follows:

- *Awareness*—Individuals working together need to be aware of each other's work.
- *Articulation*—Collaborating individuals must partition work into units, divide the units among team members, and then after the work is done, reintegrate it.
- *Appropriation*—Adapting technology to one's own situation; the technology may be used in a manner completely different than expected by the designers.

2.5.1   Benefits of Collaboration in Scrum Projects

The Agile Manifesto (Fowler & Highsmith, 2001) stresses "customer collaboration over contract negotiation." Thus, the Scrum framework adopts an approach in which the Scrum Core Team members (Product Owner, Scrum Master, and Scrum Team), collaborate with each other and the stakeholders to create the deliverables that provide greatest possible value to the customer. This collaboration occurs throughout the project.

Collaboration ensures that the following project benefits are realized:

1. The need for changes due to poorly clarified requirements is minimized. For example, during the *Create Project Vision, Develop Epic(s)*, and *Create Prioritized Product Backlog* processes, the Product Owner collaborates with stakeholders to create the Project Vision, Epic(s), and Prioritized Product Backlog, respectively. This will ensure that there is clarity among Scrum Core Team members on the work that is required to complete the project. The Scrum Team collaborates continuously with the Product Owner and stakeholders through a transparent Prioritized Product Backlog to create the project deliverables. The processes *Conduct Daily Standup, Groom Prioritized Product Backlog,* and *Retrospect Sprint* provide scope to the Scrum Core Team members to discuss what has been done and collaborate on what needs to be done. Thus the number of Change Requests from the customer and rework is minimized.

2. Risks are identified and dealt with efficiently. For example, risks to the project are identified and assessed in the *Develop Epic(s), Create Deliverables,* and *Conduct Daily Standup* processes by the Scrum Core Team members. The Scrum meeting tools such as the Daily Standup Meeting, Sprint Planning Meeting, Prioritized Product Backlog Review Meeting, and so on provide opportunities to

the team to not only identify and assess risks, but also to implement risk responses to high-priority risks.

3. True potential of the team is realized. For example, the *Conduct Daily Standup* process provides scope for the Scrum Team to collaborate and understand the strengths and weaknesses of its members. If a team member has missed a task deadline, the Scrum Team members align themselves collaboratively to complete the task and meet the targets agreed to for completing the Sprint.

4. Continuous improvement is ensured through lessons learned. For example, the Scrum Team uses the *Retrospect Sprint* process to identify what went well and what did not go well in the previous Sprint. This provides an opportunity to the Scrum Master to work with the team to rework and improve the team for the next scheduled Sprint. This will also ensure that collaboration is even more effective in the next Sprint.

Figure 2-6 illustrates the benefits of collaboration in Scrum projects.

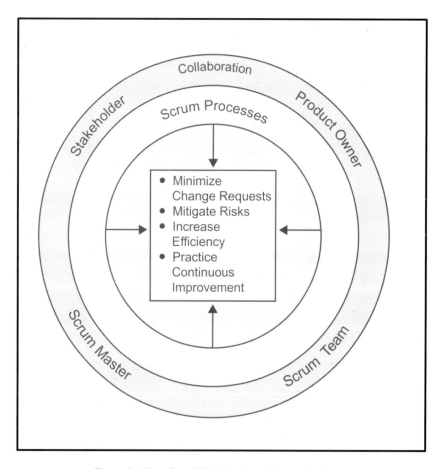

Figure 2-6: Benefits of Collaboration in Scrum Projects

2.5.2   Importance of Colocation in Collaboration

For many of the Scrum practices, high-bandwidth communication is required. To enable this, it is preferred that team members are colocated. Colocation allows both formal and informal interaction between team members. This provides the advantage of having team members always at hand for coordination, problem-solving, and learning. Some of the benefits of colocation are the following:

- Questions get answered quickly.
- Problems are fixed on the spot.
- Less friction occurs between interactions.
- Trust is gained and awarded much more quickly.

Collaboration tools that can be used for colocated or distributed teams are as follows:

1. **Colocated Teams** (i.e., teams working in the same office)—In Scrum, it is preferable to have colocated teams. If colocated, preferred modes of communication include face-to-face interactions, Decision Rooms or War Rooms, Scrumboards, wall displays, shared tables, and so on.

2. **Distributed Teams** (i.e., teams working in different physical locations)—Although colocated teams are preferred, at times the Scrum Team may be distributed due to outsourcing, offshoring, different physical locations, work-from-home options, etc. Some tools that could be used for effective collaboration with distributed teams include video conferencing, instant messaging, chats, social media, shared screens, and software tools which simulate the functionality of Scrumboards, wall displays, and so on.

2.6   Value-based Prioritization

The Scrum framework is driven by the goal of delivering maximum business value in a minimum time span. One of the most effective tools for delivering the greatest value in the shortest amount of time is prioritization.

Prioritization can be defined as determination of the order and separation of what must be done now, from what needs to be done later. The concept of prioritization is not new to project management. The traditional Waterfall model of project management proposes using multiple task prioritization tools. From the Project Manager's point of view, prioritization is integral because certain tasks must be accomplished first to expedite the development process and achieve the project goals. Some of the traditional techniques of task prioritization include setting deadlines for delegated tasks and using prioritization matrices.

Scrum, however, uses Value-based Prioritization as one of the core principles that drives the structure and functionality of the entire Scrum framework—it helps projects benefit through adaptability and iterative development of the product or service. More significantly, Scrum aims at delivering a valuable product or service to the customer on an early and continuous basis.

Prioritization is done by the Product Owner when he or she prioritizes User Stories in the Prioritized Product Backlog. The Prioritized Product Backlog contains a list of all the requirements needed to bring the project to fruition.

Once the Product Owner has received the business requirements from the customer and written these down in the form of workable User Stories, he or she works with the customer and sponsor to understand which business requirements provide maximum business value. The Product Owner must understand what the customer wants and values in order to arrange the Prioritized Product Backlog Items (User Stories) by relative importance. Sometimes, a customer may mandate all User Stories to be of high priority. While this might be true, even a list of high-priority User Stories needs to be prioritized within the list itself. Prioritizing a backlog involves determining the criticality of each User Story. High-value requirements are identified and moved to the top of the Prioritized Product Backlog. The processes in which the principle of Value-based Prioritization is put into practice are *Create Prioritized Product Backlog* and *Groom Prioritized Product Backlog*.

Simultaneously, the Product Owner must work with the Scrum Team to understand the project risks and uncertainty as they may have negative consequences associated with them. This should be taken into account while prioritizing User Stories on a value-based approach (refer to the Risk chapter for more information). The Scrum Team also alerts the Product Owner of any dependencies that arise out of implementation. These dependencies must be taken into account during prioritization. Prioritization may be based on a subjective estimate of the projected business value or profitability, or it can be based on results and analysis of the market using tools including, but not limited to, customer interviews, surveys, and financial models and analytical techniques.

The Product Owner has to translate the inputs and needs of the project stakeholders to create the Prioritized Product Backlog. Hence, while prioritizing the User Stories in the Prioritized Product Backlog, the following three factors are considered (see Figure 2-7):

1. Value
2. Risk or uncertainty
3. Dependencies

Thus prioritization results in deliverables that satisfies the requirements of the customer with the objective of delivering the maximum business value in the least amount of time.

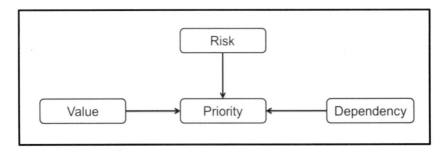

Figure 2-7: Value-based Prioritization

2.7 Time-boxing

Scrum treats time as one of the most important constraints in managing a project. To address the constraint of time, Scrum introduces a concept called 'Time-boxing' which proposes fixing a certain amount of time for each process and activity in a Scrum project. This ensures that Scrum Team members do not take up too much or too little work for a particular period of time and do not expend their time and energy on work for which they have little clarity.

Some of the advantages of Time-boxing are as follows:

- Efficient development process
- Less overheads
- High velocity for teams

Time-boxing can be utilized in many Scrum processes, for example, in the *Conduct Daily Standup* process, the duration of the Daily Standup Meeting is Time-boxed. At times, Time-boxing may be used to avoid excessive improvement of an item (i.e., gold-plating).

Time-boxing is a critical practice in Scrum and should be applied with care. Arbitrary Time-boxing can lead to de-motivation of the team and may have the consequence of creating an apprehensive environment, so it should be used appropriately.

2.7.1   Scrum Time-boxes

- **Sprint**—A Sprint is a Time-boxed iteration of one to six weeks in duration during which the Scrum Master guides, facilitates, and shields the Scrum Team from both internal and external impediments during the *Create Deliverables* process. This aids in avoiding vision creep that could affect the Sprint goal. During this time, the team works to convert the requirements in the Prioritized Product Backlog into shippable product functionalities. To get maximum benefits from a Scrum project, it is always recommended to keep the Sprint Time-boxed to 4 weeks, unless there are projects with very stable requirements, where Sprints can extend up to 6 weeks.

- **Daily Standup Meeting**—The Daily Standup Meeting is a short daily meeting, Time-boxed to 15 minutes. The team members get together to report the progress of the project by answering the following three questions:

  1. What did I complete yesterday?
  2. What will I complete today?
  3. What impediments or obstacles (if any) am I currently facing?

  This meeting is carried out by the team as part of the *Conduct Daily Standup* process.

- **Sprint Planning Meeting**—This meeting is conducted prior to the Sprint as part of the *Create Sprint Backlog* process. It is Time-boxed to eight hours for a one-month Sprint. The Sprint Planning Meeting is divided into two parts:

  1. Objective Definition—During the first half of the meeting, the Product Owner explains the highest priority User Stories or requirements in the Prioritized Product Backlog to the Scrum Team. The Scrum Team in collaboration with the Product Owner then defines the Sprint goal.

  2. Task Estimation—During the second half of the meeting, the Scrum Team decides "how" to complete the selected Prioritized Product Backlog Items to fulfill the Sprint goal.

  At times, the Task Planning Meetings (conducted during the *Create Tasks* process) and the Task Estimation Meetings (conducted during *Estimate Tasks* process) are also referred to as Sprint Planning Meetings.

- **Sprint Review Meeting**—The Sprint Review Meeting is Time-boxed to four hours for a one-month Sprint. During the Sprint Review Meeting that is conducted in the *Demonstrate and Validate Sprint* process, the Scrum Team presents the deliverables of the current Sprint to the Product Owner. The Product Owner reviews the product (or product increment) against the agreed Acceptance Criteria and either accepts or rejects the completed User Stories.

- **Retrospect Sprint Meeting**—The Retrospect Sprint Meeting is Time-boxed to 4 hours for a one-month Sprint and conducted as part of the *Retrospect Sprint* process. During this meeting, the Scrum Team gets together to review and reflect on the previous Sprint in terms of the processes followed, tools employed, collaboration and communication mechanisms, and other aspects relevant to the project. The team discusses what went well during the previous Sprint and what did not go well, the goal being to learn and make improvements in the Sprints to follow. Some improvement opportunities or best practices from this meeting could also be updated as part of the Scrum Guidance Body documents.

Figure 2-8 illustrates the Time-boxed durations for Scrum-related meetings.

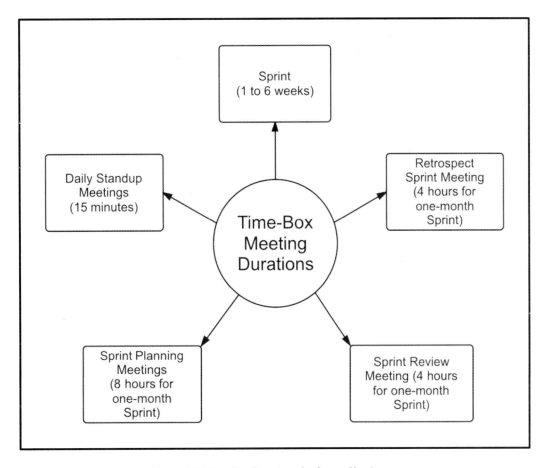

Figure 2-8: Time-Box Durations for Scrum Meetings

2.8   Iterative Development

The Scrum framework is driven by the goal of delivering maximum business value in a minimum time span. To achieve this practically, Scrum believes in Iterative Development of Deliverables.

In most complex projects, the customer may not be able to define very concrete requirements or is not confident of what the end product may look like. The iterative model is more flexible in ensuring that any change requested by the customer can be included as part of the project. User Stories may have to be written constantly throughout the duration of the project. In the initial stages of writing, most User Stories are high-level functionalities. These User Stories are known as Epic(s). Epic(s) are usually too large for teams to complete in a single Sprint. Therefore, they are broken down into smaller User Stories.

Each complex aspect of the project is broken down through progressive elaboration during the *Groom Prioritized Product Backlog* process. The *Create User Stories* and the *Estimate, Approve, and Commit User Stories* processes are used to add new requirements to the Prioritized Product Backlog. The Product Owner's task is to ensure increased ROI by focusing on value and its continuous delivery with each Sprint. The Product Owner should have a very good understanding of the project's business justification and the value the project is supposed to deliver as he drafts the Prioritized Product Backlog and thereby decides what deliverables and hence values are delivered in each Sprint. Then the *Create Tasks, Estimate Tasks,* and *Create Sprint Backlog* processes produce the Sprint Backlog which the team uses to create the deliverables.

In each Sprint, the *Create Deliverables* process is used to develop the Sprint's outputs. The Scrum Master has to ensure that the Scrum processes are followed and facilitates the team to work in the most productive manner possible. The Scrum Team self-organizes and aims to create the Sprint Deliverables from the User Stories in the Sprint Backlog. In large projects, various cross-functional teams work in parallel across Sprints, delivering potentially shippable solutions at the end of each Sprint. After the Sprint is complete, The Product Owner accepts or rejects the deliverables based on the Acceptance Criteria in the *Demonstrate and Validate Sprint* process.

As illustrated in Figure 2-9, Scrum projects are completed in an iterative manner delivering value throughout the lifecycle of the project.

2

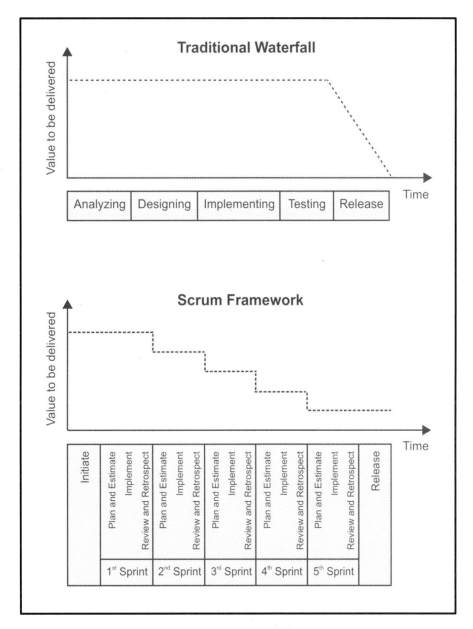

Figure 2-9: Scrum vs. Traditional Waterfall

The benefit of iterative development is that it allows for course correction as all the people involved get better understanding of what needs to be delivered as part of the project and incorporate these learning in an iterative manner. Thus the time and effort required to reach the final end point is greatly reduced and the team produces deliverables that are better suited to the final business environment.

2.9 Scrum vs. Traditional Project Management

The emphasis in traditional Project Management is to conduct detailed upfront planning for the project with emphasis on fixing the scope, cost, and schedule and managing those parameters. Traditional project management may at times lead to a situation where the plan has succeeded yet the customer is not satisfied.

The Scrum Framework is founded on the belief that the knowledge workers of today can offer much more than just their technical expertise, and that trying to fully map out and plan for an ever-changing environment is not efficient. Therefore, Scrum encourages data-based, iterative decision making. In Scrum, the primary focus is on delivering products that satisfy customer requirements in small iterative shippable increments.

To deliver the greatest amount of value in the shortest amount of time, Scrum promotes prioritization and Time-boxing over fixing the scope, cost and schedule of a project. An important feature of Scrum is self-organization, which allows the individuals who are actually doing the work to estimate and take ownership of tasks.

3. ORGANIZATION

3.1 Introduction

In this section, we will be discussing the various facets of a Scrum project organization as well as core and non-core roles and how to form high performance Scrum Teams.

Organization, as defined in *A Guide to the Scrum Body of Knowledge (SBOK™ Guide)*, is applicable to the following:

- Portfolios, programs, and/or projects in *any* industry
- Products, services, or any other results to be delivered to stakeholders
- Projects of any size or complexity

The term "product" in the *SBOK™ Guide* may refer to a product, service, or other deliverable. Scrum can be applied effectively to any project in any industry—from small projects or teams with as few as six team members to large, complex projects with up to several hundred team members.

This chapter is divided into the following sections:

3.2 Roles Guide—This section identifies which section or subsection is important for a Product Owner, Scrum Master, and Scrum Team.

3.3 Scrum Project Roles—This section covers all the key core and non-core roles associated with a Scrum project.

3.4 Product Owner—This section highlights the key responsibilities of the Product Owner in relation to a Scrum project.

3.5 Scrum Master—This section focuses on the key responsibilities of the Scrum Master in the context of a Scrum project.

3.6 Scrum Team—This section emphasizes the key responsibilities of the Scrum Team in the context of a Scrum project.

3.7 Scrum in Projects, Programs, and Portfolios—This section focuses on how Scrum framework can be tailored and used in the different contexts of programs and portfolios. It also highlights the specific responsibilities of the Scrum Team members in relation to communication, integration, and working with the corporate and program management teams.

3.8 Responsibilities—This section describes the responsibilities relevant to the Organization theme, for everyone working on a project, based on their roles.

3.9 Scrum vs. Traditional Project Management—This section explains the key differences and advantages of the Scrum model in relation to the traditional Waterfall model of project management.

3.10 Popular HR Theories and their Relevance to Scrum—This section contains some of the most popular HR theories useful for all the members in the Scrum Core Team.

3.2   Roles Guide

1. Product Owner—It is imperative for Product Owners to read the entire chapter.

2. Scrum Master—The Scrum Master should also be familiar with this entire chapter with primary focus on sections 3.3, 3.5, 3.6, 3.8 and 3.10.4.

3. Scrum Team— The Scrum Team should mainly focus on sections 3.3, 3.6, and 3.8.

3.3   Scrum Project Roles

Understanding defined roles and responsibilities is very important for ensuring the successful implementation of Scrum projects.

Scrum roles fall into two broad categories:

1. **Core Roles**—Core roles are those roles which are mandatorily required for producing the product of the project, are committed to the project, and ultimately are responsible for the success of each Sprint of the project and of the project as a whole.

2. **Non-core Roles**—Non-core roles are those roles which are not mandatorily required for the Scrum project, and may include team members who are interested in the project, have no formal role on the project team, may interface with the team, but may not be responsible for the success of the project. The non-core roles should also be taken into account in any Scrum project.

3.3.1   Core Roles

There are three core roles in Scrum that are ultimately responsible for meeting the project objectives. The core roles are the Product Owner, Scrum Master, and Scrum Team. Together they are referred to as the Scrum Core Team. It is important to note that, of these three roles, no role has authority over the others.

1. **Product Owner**

   The Product Owner is the person responsible for maximizing business value for the project. He or she is responsible for articulating customer requirements and maintaining business justification for the project. The Product Owner represents the *Voice of the Customer*.

   Corresponding to a Product Owner role in a project, there could be a Program Product Owner for a program or a Portfolio Product Owner for a portfolio.

2. **Scrum Master**

   The Scrum Master is a facilitator who ensures that the Scrum Team is provided with an environment conducive to completing the product's development successfully. The Scrum Master guides, facilitates, and teaches Scrum practices to everyone involved in the project; clears impediments for the team; and, ensures that Scrum processes are being followed.

   Note that the Scrum Master role is very different from the role played by the Project Manager in a traditional Waterfall model of project management, in which the Project Manager works as a manager or leader for the project. The Scrum Master only works as a facilitator and he or she is at the same hierarchical level as anyone else in the Scrum Team—any person from the Scrum Team who learns how to facilitate Scrum projects can become the Scrum Master for a project or for a Sprint.

   Corresponding to a Scrum Master role in a project, there could be a Program Scrum Master for a program or a Portfolio Scrum Master for a portfolio.

3. **Scrum Team**

   The Scrum Team is a group or team of people who are responsible for understanding the business requirements specified by the Product Owner, estimating User Stories, and final creation of the project Deliverables.

   Figure 3-1 presents an overview of the Core Scrum Team roles.

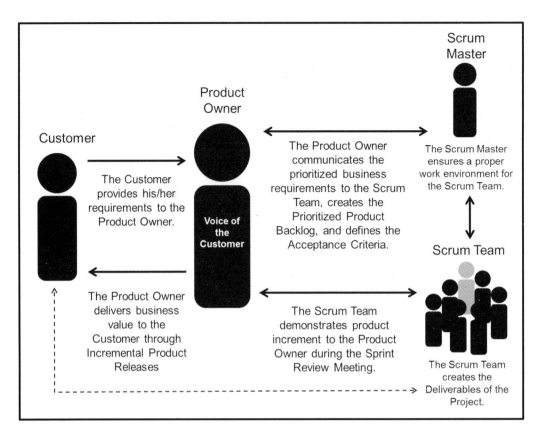

Figure 3-1: Scrum Roles—Overview

3.3.2 Non-core Roles

The non-core roles are those roles which are not mandatorily required for the Scrum project and may not be continuously or directly involved in the Scrum process. However, knowing non-core roles is important as they could play a significant part in some Scrum projects.

Non-core roles can include the following:

1. Stakeholder(s)

Stakeholder(s) is a collective term that include customers, users, and sponsors, who frequently interface with the Product Owner, Scrum Master and Scrum Team to provide them with inputs and facilitate creation of the project's product, service, or other result. Stakeholder(s) influence the project throughout the project's development. Stakeholders may also have a role to play during the *Develop Epic(s), Create Prioritized Product Backlog, Conduct Release Planning, Retrospect Sprint*, and other important processes in Scrum.

- **Customer**

  The customer is the individual or the organization that acquires the project's product, service, or other result. For any organization, depending on the project, there can be both internal customers (i.e., within the same organization) or external customers (i.e., outside of the organization).

- **Users**

    Users are the individual or the organization that directly uses the project's product, service, or other result. Like customers, for any organization, there can be both internal and external users. Also, in some industries customers and users may be the same.

- **Sponsor**

    The sponsor is the individual or the organization that provides resources and support for the project. The sponsor is also the stakeholder to whom everyone is accountable in the end.

At times, the same person or organization can play multiple stakeholder roles; for example, the sponsor and the customer may be the same.

2. **Vendors**

    Vendors include external individuals or organizations that provide products and services that are not within the core competencies of the project organization.

3. **Scrum Guidance Body**

    The Scrum Guidance Body (SGB) is an optional role. It generally consists of a group of documents and/or a group of experts who are typically involved with defining objectives related to quality, government regulations, security, and other key organizational parameters. These objectives guide the work carried out by the Product Owner, Scrum Master, and Scrum Team. The Scrum Guidance Body also helps capture the best practices that should be used across all Scrum projects in the organization.

    The Scrum Guidance Body does not make decisions related to the project. Instead it acts as a consulting or guidance structure for all the hierarchy levels in the project organization—the portfolio, program, and project. Scrum Teams have the option of asking the Scrum Guidance Body for advice as required.

3.4 Product Owner

The Product Owner represents the interests of the stakeholder community to the Scrum Team. The Product Owner is responsible for ensuring clear communication of product or service functionality requirements to the Scrum Team, defining Acceptance Criteria, and ensuring those criteria are met. In other words, the Product Owner is responsible for ensuring that the Scrum Team delivers value. The Product Owner must always maintain a dual view. He or she must understand and support the needs and interests of all stakeholders, while also understanding the needs and workings of the Scrum Team. Because the Product

Owner must understand the needs and priorities of the stakeholders, including customers and users, this role is commonly referred to as the Voice of the Customer.

Table 3-1 summarizes the Product Owner's responsibilities in the various Scrum processes.

Process	Product Owner Responsibilities
8.1 Create Project Vision	• Defines the Project Vision • Helps create the Project Charter and Project Budget
8.2 Identify Scrum Master and Stakeholder(s)	• Helps finalize Scrum Master for the project • Identifies Stakeholder(s)
8.3 Form Scrum Team	• Helps determine Scrum Team members • Helps develop a Collaboration Plan • Helps develop the Team Building Plan with Scrum Master(s)
8.4 Develop Epic(s)	• Creates Epic(s) and Personas
8.5 Create Prioritized Product Backlog	• Prioritizes Prioritized Product Backlog Items • Defines Done Criteria
8.6 Conduct Release Planning	• Creates Release Planning Schedule • Helps determine Length of Sprint
9.1 Create User Stories	• Helps create User Stories • Defines Acceptance Criteria for every User Story
9.2 Approve, Estimate and Commit User Stories	• Approves User Stories • Facilitates Scrum Team and commit User Stories
9.3 Create Tasks	• Explains User Stories to the Scrum Team while creating the Task List
9.4 Estimate Tasks	• Provides guidance and clarification to the Scrum Team in estimating effort for tasks
9.5 Create Sprint Backlog	• Clarifies requirements to the Scrum Team while creating the Sprint Backlog
10.1 Create Deliverables	• Clarifies business requirements to the Scrum Team
10.3 Groom Prioritized Product Backlog	• Grooms the Prioritized Product Backlog
11.2 Demonstrate and Validate Sprints	• Accepts/Rejects Deliverables • Provides necessary feedback to Scrum Master and Scrum Teams • Updates Release Plan and Prioritized Product Backlog
12.1 Ship Deliverables	• Helps deploy Product Releases and coordinates this with the customer
12.2 Retrospect Project	• Participates in Retrospective Sprint Meetings

Table 3-1: Responsibilities of the Product Owner in Scrum Processes

The other responsibilities of a Product Owner are:

- Determining the project's initial overall requirements and kicking off project activities; this may involve interaction with the Program Product Owner and the Portfolio Product Owner to ensure that the project aligns with direction provided by senior management.
- Representing user(s) of the product or service with a thorough understanding of the user community
- Securing the initial and ongoing financial resources for the project.
- Focusing on value creation and overall Return on Investment (ROI).
- Assessing the viability and ensuring the delivery of the product or service.

3.4.1　Voice of the Customer (VOC)

As the representative of the customer, the Product Owner is said to be the Voice of the Customer as he ensures that the explicit and implicit needs of the customer are translated into User Stories in the Prioritized Product Backlog and later on used to create project Deliverables for the customer.

3.4.2　Chief Product Owner

In the case of large projects with numerous Scrum Teams, having a Chief Product Owner may be a necessity. This role is responsible for coordinating the work of multiple Product Owners. The Chief Product Owner prepares and maintains the overall Prioritized Product Backlog for the large project, using it to coordinate work through the Product Owners of the Scrum Teams. The Product Owners, in turn, manage their respective parts of the Prioritized Product Backlog.

The Chief Product Owner also interfaces with the Program Product Owner to ensure alignment of the large project with the program goals and objectives.

3.5　Scrum Master

The Scrum Master is the "servant leader" of the Scrum Team who moderates and facilitates team interactions as team coach and motivator. The Scrum Master is responsible for ensuring that the team has a productive work environment by guarding the team from external influences, removing any obstacles, and enforcing Scrum principles, aspects, and processes.

Table 3-2 summarizes the Scrum Master's responsibilities in the various Scrum processes.

Processes	Scrum Master Responsibilities
8.2 Identify Scrum Master and Stakeholder(s)	• Helps identify Stakeholder(s) for the project
8.3 Form Scrum Team	• Facilitates selection of the Scrum Team • Facilitates creation of the Collaboration Plan and the Team Building Plan • Ensures back-up resources are available for smooth project functioning
8.4 Develop Epic(s)	• Facilitates creation of Epic(s) and Personas
8.5 Create Prioritized Product Backlog	• Helps Product Owner in creation of the Prioritized Product Backlog and in definition of the Done Criteria
8.6 Conduct Release Planning	• Coordinates creation of Release Planning Schedule • Determines Length of Sprint
9.1 Create User Stories	• Assists the Scrum Team in creating User Stories and their Acceptance Criteria
9.2 Approve, Estimate and Commit User Stories	• Facilitates meetings of the Scrum Team to estimate and Create User Stories
9.3 Create Tasks	• Facilitates the Scrum Team in creating the Task List for the next Sprint
9.4 Estimate Tasks	• Assists the Scrum Team in estimating the effort required to complete the tasks agreed to for the Sprint
9.5 Create Sprint Backlog	• Assists the Scrum Team in developing the Sprint Backlog and the Sprint Burndown Chart
10.1 Create Deliverables	• Supports the Scrum Team in creating the Deliverables agreed to for the Sprint • Helps update the Scrumboard and the Impediment Log
10.2 Conduct Daily Standup	• Ensures that the Scrumboard and the Impediment Log remain updated
10.3 Groom Prioritized Product Backlog	• Facilitates Prioritized Product Backlog Review Meetings
11.1 Convene Scrum of Scrums	• Ensures that issues affecting the Scrum Team are discussed and resolved
11.2 Demonstrate and Validate Sprints	• Facilitates presentation of completed Deliverables by the Scrum Team for the Product Owner's approval
11.3 Retrospect Sprint	• Ensures that ideal project environment exists for the Scrum Team in the succeeding Sprints
12.2 Retrospect Project	• Represents the Scrum Core Team to provide lessons from the current project, if necessary

Table 3-2: Responsibilities of the Scrum Master in Scrum Processes

3.5.1   Chief Scrum Master

Large projects require multiple Scrum Teams to work in parallel. Information gathered from one team may need to be appropriately communicated to other teams. The Chief Scrum Master is responsible for this activity.

Coordination across various Scrum Teams working on a project is typically done through the Scrum of Scrums (SoS) Meeting (see section 3.7.2.1). This is analogous to the Daily Standup Meeting and is facilitated by the Chief Scrum Master. The Chief Scrum Master is typically the individual responsible for addressing impediments that impact more than one Scrum Team.

Figure 3-2 provides questions that are asked during a Scrum of Scrums (SoS) Meeting.

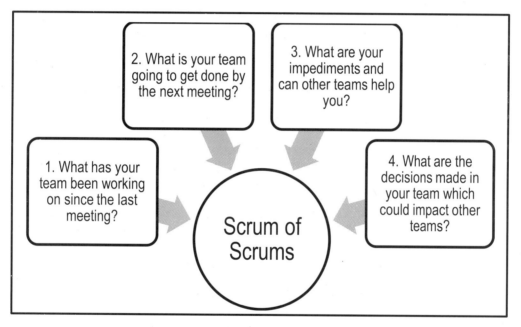

Figure 3-2: Questions asked during a Scrum of Scrums Meeting

Typically, any inter-team issues are addressed by the interested parties in a session immediately following the Scrum of Scrums Meeting. The Chief Scrum Master facilitates this session.

3.6   Scrum Team

The Scrum Team is sometimes referred to as the Development Team since they are responsible for developing the product, service, or other result. It consists of a group of individuals who work on the User Stories in the Sprint Backlog to create the Deliverables for the project.

Table 3-3 summarizes the Scrum Team's responsibilities in the various Scrum processes.

Processes	Scrum Team Responsibilities
8.3 Form Scrum Team	• Provides inputs for creation of the Collaboration Plan and the Team Building Plan
8.4 Develop Epic(s)	• Ensures a clear understanding of Epic(s) and Personas
8.5 Prioritized Product Backlog	• Understands the User Stories in the Prioritized Product Backlog
8.6 Conduct Release Planning	• Agrees with other Scrum Core Team members on the Length of Sprint • Seeks clarification on new products or changes in the existing products, if any, in the refined Prioritized Product Backlog
9.1 Create User Stories	• Provides inputs to the Product Owner on creation of User Stories
9.2 Approve, Estimate and Commit User Stories	• Estimates User Stories approved by the Product Owner • Commits User Stories to be done in a Sprint
9.3 Create Tasks	• Develops Task List based on agreed User Stories and dependencies
9.4 Estimate Tasks	• Estimates effort for tasks identified and if necessary, updates the Task List
9.5 Create Sprint Backlog	• Develops the Sprint Backlog and the Sprint Burndown Chart
10.1 Create Deliverables	• Creates Deliverables • Identifies risks and implements risk mitigation actions, if any • Updates Impediment Log and dependencies
10.2 Conduct Daily Standup	• Updates Burndown Chart, Scrumboard, and Impediment Log • Discusses issues faced by individual members and seeks solutions to motivate the team • Identifies risks, if any • Submits Change Requests, if required
10.3 Groom Prioritized Product Backlog	• Participates in Prioritized Product Backlog Review Meetings
11.1 Convene Scrum of Scrums	• Provides inputs to Scrum Master for Scrum of Scrums (SoS) Meetings
11.2 Demonstrate and Validate Sprints	• Demonstrates completed deliverables to the Product Owner for approval
11.3 Retrospect Sprint	• Identifies improvement opportunities, if any, from the current Sprint and agrees on any actionable improvements for the next Sprint
12.2 Retrospect Project	• Participates in the Retrospect Project Meeting

Table 3-3: Responsibilities of the Scrum Team in Scrum Processes

3.6.1   Personnel Selection

Figure 3-3 lists the desirable traits for the core Scrum roles.

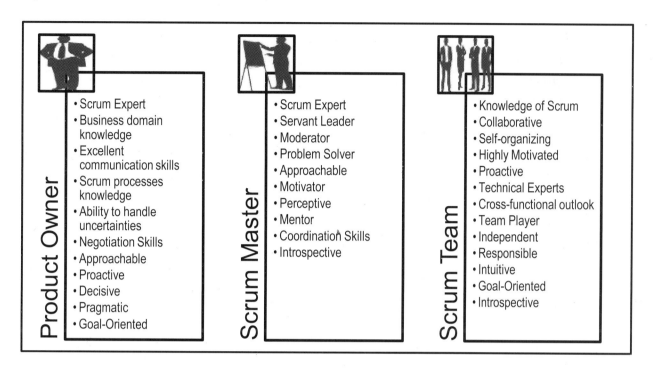

Product Owner
- Scrum Expert
- Business domain knowledge
- Excellent communication skills
- Scrum processes knowledge
- Ability to handle uncertainties
- Negotiation Skills
- Approachable
- Proactive
- Decisive
- Pragmatic
- Goal-Oriented

Scrum Master
- Scrum Expert
- Servant Leader
- Moderator
- Problem Solver
- Approachable
- Motivator
- Perceptive
- Mentor
- Coordination Skills
- Introspective

Scrum Team
- Knowledge of Scrum
- Collaborative
- Self-organizing
- Highly Motivated
- Proactive
- Technical Experts
- Cross-functional outlook
- Team Player
- Independent
- Responsible
- Intuitive
- Goal-Oriented
- Introspective

Figure 3-3: Desirable Traits for the Core Scrum Roles

3.6.2   Scrum Team Size

It is important for the Scrum Team to possess all the essential skills required to carry out the work of the project. It is also necessary to have a high level of collaboration to maximize productivity, so that minimal coordination is required to get things done.

The optimum size for a Scrum Team is six to ten members—large enough to ensure adequate skill sets, but small enough to collaborate easily. A key benefit of a six to ten member team is that communication and management are typically simple and require minimal effort. However, there may also be drawbacks. One major drawback is that smaller teams are more significantly impacted by the loss of a team member than larger teams, even for a short period of time. To address this problem, it may be possible for team members to have expert knowledge and skills outside their own specific role. However, this may be difficult and depends on the type of project, industry, and size of the organization. It is also recommended to have back-up persons to replace any person who may have to leave the Scrum Team.

3.7 Scrum in Projects, Programs, and Portfolios

3.7.1 Definition of Project, Program, and Portfolio

- **Project**—A project is a collaborative enterprise to either create new products or services or to deliver results as defined in the Project Vision Statement. Projects are usually impacted by constraints of time, cost, scope, quality, people and organizational capabilities. The objective of the project team is to create Deliverables as defined in Prioritized Product Backlog.

- **Program**—A program is a group of related projects, with the objective to deliver business outcomes as defined in the Program Vision Statement. The Prioritized Program Backlog incorporates the Prioritized Product Backlogs for all the projects in the program.

- **Portfolio**—A portfolio is a group of related programs, with the objective to deliver business outcomes as defined in the Portfolio Vision Statement. The Prioritized Portfolio Backlog incorporates the Prioritized Program Backlogs for all the programs in the portfolio.

The following are examples of projects, programs, and portfolios from different industries and sectors:

Example 1: Construction Company

- Project—Construction of a house
- Program—Construction of a housing complex
- Portfolio—All the housing projects of the company

Example 2: Aerospace Organization

- Project—Building the launch vehicle
- Program—Successful launch of a satellite
- Portfolio—All the active satellite programs

Example 3: Information Technology (IT) Company

- Project—Development of the shopping cart module
- Program—Development of a fully functional e-commerce website
- Portfolio—All the websites developed by the company so far

3.7.2   Scrum in Projects

Since Scrum favors small teams, one may think that this method can only be used on small projects, but this is not the case. Scrum can also be used effectively on large-scale projects. When more than ten people are required to carry out the work, multiple Scrum Teams may be formed. The project team consists of multiple Scrum Teams working together to create Deliverables and Product Releases, so as to achieve outcomes desired for the overall project.

Since a project can have multiple Scrum Teams working in parallel, coordination between different teams becomes important. The Scrum Teams usually communicate and coordinate with each other in a variety of ways, but the most common approach is known as a Scrum of Scrums (SoS) Meeting. Members representing each Scrum Team come together to discuss progress, issues and to coordinate activities between teams. These meetings are similar in format to the Daily Standup Meetings; however, the frequency of the Scrum of Scrums could be at predetermined intervals or coordinated as required by the different Scrum Teams.

3.7.2.1   Scrum of Scrums (SoS) Meeting

A Scrum of Scrums Meeting is an important element when scaling Scrum to large projects. Typically, there is one representative in the meeting from each Scrum Team—usually the Scrum Master—but it is also common for anyone from the Scrum Team to attend the meeting if required. This meeting is usually facilitated by the Chief Scrum Master and is intended to focus on areas of coordination and integration between the different Scrum Teams. This meeting is conducted at predetermined intervals or when required by the Scrum Teams.

In organizations that have several Scrum Teams working on portions of a project simultaneously, the SoS Meeting can be scaled up another level to what is referred to as a Scrum of Scrum of Scrums Meeting. In this situation, an SoS Meeting is held to coordinate each group of Scrum Teams working on portions of a related project and then a Scrum of Scrum of Scrums Meeting may be held to coordinate and integrate projects at a higher level. Teams have to carefully evaluate the benefits of having Scrum of Scrum of Scrums meetings, as the third layer adds a significant amount of logistical complexity.

Figure 3-4 illustrates the concept of the Scrum of Scrums (SoS) and the Scrum of Scrum of Scrums Meetings.

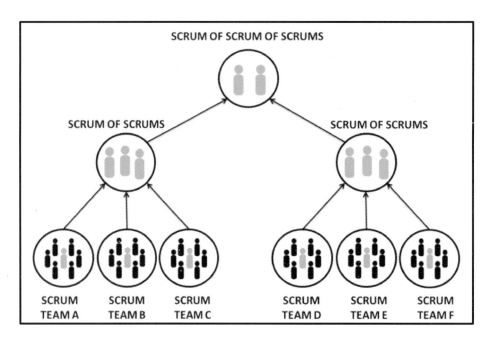

Figure 3-4: Scrum of Scrums (SoS) Meeting

In this example, there are six Scrum Teams working simultaneously. Scrum Teams A, B, and C are working on portions of a related project while Scrum Teams D, E, and F are working on portions of another related project. A Scrum of Scrums Meeting is held to coordinate the interdependencies between the related projects. A Scrum of Scrums of Scrums Meeting may then be conducted to coordinate and manage dependencies across all projects.

3.7.3　Scrum in Portfolios and Programs

3.7.3.1　Portfolios

In portfolios, important roles to manage Scrum portfolios are:

1. **Portfolio Product Owner**—Defines the strategic objectives and priorities for the portfolio.

2. **Portfolio Scrum Master**—Solves problems, removes impediments, facilitates, and conducts meetings for the portfolio.

These roles are similar to those of the Product Owner and Scrum Master except they meet the needs of their portfolio or company rather than those of a single Scrum Team.

3.7.3.2　Programs

In programs, important roles to manage Scrum programs are:

1. **Program Product Owner**—Defines the strategic objectives and priorities for the program.

2. **Program Scrum Master**—Solves problems, removes impediments, facilitates, and conducts meetings for the program.

These roles are similar to those of the Product Owner and Scrum Master except they meet the needs of their program or business unit rather than those of a single Scrum Team.

Figure 3-5 illustrates how Scrum can be used across the organization for portfolios, programs or projects.

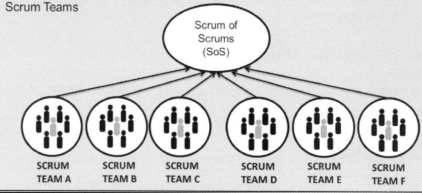

Scrum Guidance Body

- Optional

- Could be just a set of documents and/or group of experts

- Define objectives related to quality, government regulation, security and other key parameters

- Used by Scrum Teams when needed for their work

Portfolio
- Manage all programs and projects
- Work to be done is contained in a Portfolio Backlog
- Conduct Prioritized Portfolio Backlog meeting at four to twelve month intervals

Program
- Manage related projects
- Work to be done is contained in a Program Backlog
- Conduct Prioritized Program Backlog meeting at two to six months intervals

Projects
- Individual projects managed by respective Scrum Teams
- A project may have one or more Scrum Teams
- Work to be done is contained in a Product Backlog
- Work accomplished in Sprints of one to six weeks
- Conduct Scrum of Scrums (SoS) meetings to coordinate and communicate amongst Scrum Teams

Scrum of Scrums (SoS)

SCRUM TEAM A   SCRUM TEAM B   SCRUM TEAM C   SCRUM TEAM D   SCRUM TEAM E   SCRUM TEAM F

Figure 3-5: Scrum Across the Organization for Projects, Programs, and Portfolios

3.7.3.3 Working with Portfolio and Program Teams

When applying Scrum to manage projects within the context of a program or portfolio, it is strongly recommended that the general principles of Scrum presented in this publication are adhered to. It is understood though, that in order to accommodate the overall program or portfolio activities and interdependencies, minor adjustments to the set of tools, as well as the organizational structure may be required. If the Scrum Guidance Body exists, it may be responsible to scrutinize the organization at different levels to understand and define appropriate application of Scrum, and to act as a consulting body for everyone working on a project, program, or portfolio.

Portfolios and programs have separate teams with different sets of objectives. Program management teams aim to deliver capabilities and realize certain goals that contribute toward the achievement of specific program objectives. In contrast, the portfolio team has to balance the objectives of various programs to achieve the strategic objectives of the organization as a whole.

3.7.3.4 Managing Communication with Portfolio and Program Teams

The problems and issues faced when using Scrum within a program or portfolio primarily involve coordination across numerous teams. This can lead to failure if not carefully managed. Tools used for communication need to be scaled to match the requirements of the many teams involved in a program or portfolio. Each Scrum Team must address not only internal communications, but also external communications with other teams and the relevant stakeholders of the program or portfolio.

3.7.4 Maintaining Stakeholder Involvement

Scrum requires complete support from the project stakeholders. The responsibility for keeping stakeholders engaged lies with the Product Owner. The following are actions recommended for maintaining stakeholder engagement and support:

- Ensure effective collaboration and stakeholder involvement in the project
- Continually assess business impact
- Maintain regular communication with stakeholders
- Manage stakeholders' expectations

One key stakeholder is the sponsor—the individual who provides the funding and other resources for a project. Sponsors want to understand the financial bottom line related to a product or service and are typically more concerned with final outcomes rather than with individual tasks.

It is important that the sponsors who are funding the project have clarity on the following issues:

- Benefits of implementing Scrum
- Target deadlines and estimated costs of Scrum projects
- Overall risks involved in Scrum projects and the steps to mitigate them
- Expected release dates and final Deliverables

3.8 Summary of Responsibilities

Role	Responsibilities
Scrum Guidance Body	• Establishes overall guidelines and metrics for developing role descriptions for Scrum Team members • Acts as a consultant to projects across organization at different levels • Understands and defines appropriate levels of grouping, roles, and meetings for Scrum projects
Portfolio Product Owner	• Defines the strategic objectives and priorities for portfolios
Portfolio Scrum Master	• Solves problems and coordinates meetings for portfolios
Program Product Owner	• Defines the strategic objectives and priorities for programs
Program Scrum Master	• Solves problems and coordinates meetings for programs
Stakeholder(s)	• Is a collective term that includes customers, users, and sponsors • Frequently interfaces with the Product Owner, Scrum Master, and Scrum Team to provide them inputs and facilitates creation of the Deliverables of the project.
Product Owner	• Creates the project's initial overall requirements and gets the project rolling • Appoints appropriate people to the Scrum Master and Scrum Team roles • Provides the initial and ongoing financial resources for the project • Determines Product Vision • Assesses the viability and ensures delivery of the product or service • Ensures transparency and clarity of Prioritized Product Backlog Items • Decides minimum marketable release content • Provides Acceptance Criteria for the User Stories to be developed in a Sprint • Inspects deliverables • Decides Sprint duration
Scrum Master	• Ensures that Scrum processes are correctly followed by all team members including the Product Owner • Ensures that development of the product or service is progressing smoothly and the Scrum Team members have all the necessary tools to get the work done • Oversees Release Planning Meeting and schedules other meetings
Scrum Team	• Takes collective responsibility and ensures that the project deliverables are created per requirements • Assures Product Owner and Scrum Master that the allocated work is being performed according to plan

Table 3-4: Summary of Responsibilities Relevant to Organization

3.9   Scrum vs. Traditional Project Management

Organization structure and definition of roles and associated responsibilities are some of the areas where Scrum differs in a major way from traditional project management methods.

In traditional project management methods, the organization structure is hierarchical and authority for all aspects of the project is delegated from higher level to lower (e.g., project sponsor delegates authority to project manager and the project manager delegates authority to team members). Traditional project management methods emphasize on individual accountability for project responsibilities rather than group ownership or accountability. Any deviation from the delegated authority is looked at as a sign of issues and may be escalated to the higher level in the organization hierarchy. It is usually the project manager who is responsible for successful completion of the project and he or she takes decisions on various aspects of the project, including initiating, planning, estimating, executing, monitoring and controlling, and closing.

The emphasis in Scrum is on self-organization and self-motivation where the team assumes greater responsibility in making a project successful. This also ensures that there is team buy-in and shared ownership. This, in turn, results in team motivation leading to an optimization of team efficiencies. The Product Owner, Scrum Master, and the Scrum Team work very closely with relevant Stakeholder(s) for refining requirements as they go through the *Develop Epic(s), Create Prioritized Product Backlog,* and *Create User Stories* processes. This ensures that there is no scope for isolated planning in Scrum. Team experience and expertise in product development are used to assess the inputs needed to plan, estimate and execute project work. Collaboration among Scrum Core Team members ensures that the project is carried out in an innovative and creative environment that is conducive to growth and team harmony.

3

3.10 Popular HR Theories and their Relevance to Scrum

3.10.1 Tuckman's Model of Group Dynamics

The Scrum approach and method may initially seem quite different and difficult for a new Scrum Team. A new Scrum Team, like any other new team, generally evolves through a four-stage process during its first Scrum project. This process is known as Tuckman's Model of group dynamics (Tuckman, 1965). The main idea is that the four stages—Forming, Storming, Norming and Performing—are imperative for a team to develop by mitigating problems and challenges, finding solutions, planning work, and delivering results.

The four stages of the model are the following:

1. **Forming**—This is often experienced as a fun stage because everything is new and the team has not yet encountered any difficulties with the project.
2. **Storming**—During this stage, the team tries to accomplish the work; however, power struggles may occur, and there is often chaos or confusion among team members.
3. **Norming**—This is when the team begins to mature, sort out their internal differences, and find solutions to work together. It is considered a period of adjustment.
4. **Performing**—During this stage, the team becomes its most cohesive, and it operates at its highest level in terms of performance. The members have evolved into an efficient team of peer professionals who are consistently productive.

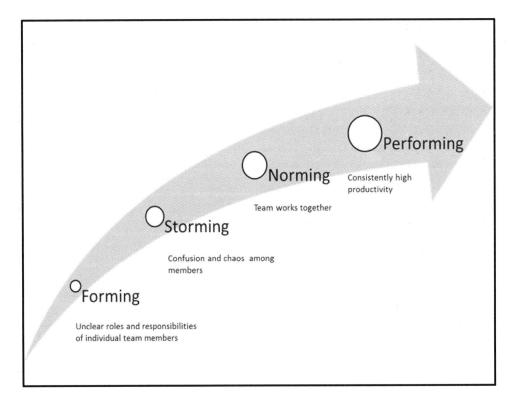

Figure 3-6: Tuckman's Stages of Group Development

3.10.2   Conflict Management

Organizations applying the Scrum framework encourage an open environment and dialogue among employees. Conflicts among Scrum Team members are generally resolved independently, with little or no involvement from management or others outside the Scrum Team.

Conflict can be healthy when it promotes team discussions and encourages debates, as this usually results in benefits for the project and the respective team members. It is therefore important that the resolution of conflicts be encouraged, promoting an open environment where team members feel welcome to express their opinions and concerns with each other and about the project, and ultimately agree on what is to be delivered and how the work in each Sprint will be performed.

Conflict management techniques are used by team members to manage any conflicts that arise during a Scrum project. Sources of conflict evolve primarily due to schedules, priorities, resources, reporting hierarchy, technical issues, procedures, personality, and costs.

3.10.3   Conflict Management Techniques

Usually there are four approaches to managing conflict in an organization applying Scrum processes:

1. Win-Win
2. Lose-Win
3. Lose-Lose
4. Win-Lose

3.10.3.1   Win-Win

It is usually best for team members to face problems directly with a cooperative attitude and an open dialogue to work through any disagreements to reach consensus. This approach is called *Win-Win*. Organizations implementing Scrum should promote an environment where employees feel comfortable to openly discuss and confront problems or issues and work through them to reach Win-Win outcomes.

3.10.3.2   Lose-Win

Some team members may at times feel that their contributions are not being recognized or valued by others, or that they are not being treated equally. This may lead them to withdraw from contributing effectively to the project and agree to whatever they are being told to do, even if they are in disagreement. This approach is called Lose-Win. This situation may happen if there are members in the team (including managers) who use an authoritative or directive style of issuing orders and/or do not treat all team members equally. This approach is not a desired conflict management technique for Scrum projects, since active contribution of every member of the team is mandatory for successful completion of each Sprint. The Scrum Master should encourage the involvement of any team members who appear to be withdrawing from conflict situations. For example, it is important for all team members to speak and contribute at each Daily Standup Meeting so that any issues or impediments can be made known and managed effectively.

3.10.3.3 Lose-Lose

In conflict situations, team members may attempt to bargain or search for solutions that bring only a partial degree or temporary measure of satisfaction to the parties in a dispute. This situation could happen in Scrum Teams where team members try to negotiate for suboptimal solutions to a problem. This approach typically involves some "give and take" to satisfy every team member—instead of trying to solve the actual problem. This generally results in an overall *Lose-Lose* outcome for the individuals involved and consequently the project. The Scrum Team should be careful to ensure that team members do not get into a Lose-Lose mentality. Scrum Daily Standup and other Scrum meetings are conducted to ensure that actual problems get solved through mutual discussions.

3.10.3.4 Win-Lose

At times, a Scrum Master or another influential team member may believe he or she is a de facto leader or manager and try to exert their viewpoint at the expense of the viewpoints of others. This conflict management technique is often characterized by competitiveness and typically results in a *Win-Lose* outcome. This approach is not recommended when working on Scrum projects, because Scrum Teams are by nature self-organized and empowered, with no one person having true authority over another team member. Although the Scrum Team may include persons with different levels of experience and expertise, every member is treated equally and no person has the authority to be the primary decision maker.

3.10.4   Leadership Styles

Leadership styles vary depending on the organization, the situation, and even the specific individuals and objectives of the Scrum project. Some common leadership styles are as follows:

- **Servant Leadership**—Servant leaders employ listening, empathy, commitment, and insight while sharing power and authority with team members. Servant leaders are stewards who achieve results by focusing on the needs of the team. This style is the embodiment of the Scrum Master role.

- **Delegating**—Delegating leaders are involved in the majority of decision making; however, they delegate some planning and decision-making responsibilities to team members, particularly if they are competent to handle the assigned tasks. This leadership style is appropriate in situations where the leader is in tune with specific project details, and when time is limited.

- **Autocratic**—Autocratic leaders make decisions on their own, allowing team members little, if any, involvement or discussion before a decision is made. This leadership style should only be used on rare occasions.

- **Directing**— Directing leaders instruct team members which tasks are required, when they should be performed and how they should be performed.

- **Laissez Faire**—With this leadership style, the team is left largely unsupervised, so the leader does not interfere with their daily work activities. Often this style leads to a state of anarchy.

- **Coaching/Supportive**—Coaching and supportive leaders issue instructions and then support and monitor team members through listening, assisting, encouraging, and presenting a positive outlook during times of uncertainty.

- **Task-Oriented**—Task-oriented leaders enforce task completion and adherence to deadlines.

- **Assertive**—Assertive leaders confront issues and display confidence to establish authority with respect.

3.10.4.1   Servant Leadership

The preferred leadership style for Scrum projects is Servant Leadership. This term was first described by Robert K. Greenleaf in an essay entitled *The Servant as Leader*. Below is an excerpt where he explains the concept:

> The servant-leader *is* servant first...It begins with the natural feeling that one wants to serve, to serve *first*. Then conscious choice brings one to aspire to lead. That person is sharply different from one who is *leader* first, perhaps because of the need to assuage an unusual power drive or to acquire material possessions...The leader-first and the servant-first are two extreme types. Between them there are shadings and blends that are part of the infinite variety of human nature....

> The difference manifests itself in the care taken by the servant-first to make sure that other people's highest priority needs are being served. The best test, and difficult to administer, is: Do those served grow as persons? Do they, *while being served*, become healthier, wiser, freer, more

autonomous, more likely themselves to become servants? *And*, what is the effect on the least privileged in society? Will they benefit or at least not be further deprived? (Greenleaf 1970, 6)

Elaborating on the writings of Greenleaf, Larry Spears identifies ten traits that every effective servant-leader should possess:

1. **Listening**—Servant leaders are expected to listen intently and receptively to what is being said, or not said. They are able to get in touch with their inner voice to understand and reflect on their own feelings.

2. **Empathy**—Good servant leaders accept and recognize individuals for their special and unique skills and abilities. They assume workers have good intentions and accept them as individuals, even when there are behavioral or performance issues.

3. **Healing**—The motivation and potential to heal oneself and one's relationship with others is a strong trait of servant leaders. Servant leaders recognize and take the opportunity to help their colleagues who are experiencing emotional pain.

4. **Awareness**—Awareness and particularly self-awareness is a trait of servant leaders. This allows them to better understand and integrate issues such as those related to ethics, power, and values.

5. **Persuasion**—Servant leaders use persuasion, rather than their positional authority to gain group consensus and make decisions. Rather than forcing compliance and coercion as is typical in some authoritarian management styles, servant leaders practice persuasion.

6. **Conceptualization**—The ability to view and analyze problems (in an organization) from a broader conceptual and visionary perspective, rather than focusing on merely the immediate short-term goals, is a unique skill of good servant leaders.

7. **Foresight**—Their intuitive minds allow servant leaders to use and apply past lessons and present realities to foresee the outcome of current situations and decisions.

8. **Stewardship**—Stewardship demands a commitment to serving others. Servant leaders prefer persuasion over control to ensure that they gain the trust of others in the organization.

9. **Commitment to the growth of others**—Servant leaders have a deep commitment to the growth of people within their organization. They take on the responsibility of nurturing the personal, professional, and spiritual growth of others (e.g., providing access to resources for personal and professional development, encouraging workers to participate in decision making).

10. **Building community**—Servant leaders are interested in building communities within a working environment, particularly given the shift in societies away from smaller communities to large institutions shaping and controlling human lives.

Scrum believes that all leaders of Scrum projects (including the Scrum Master and Product Owner) should be servant-leaders who have the above traits.

3.10.5 Maslow's Hierarchy of Needs Theory

Maslow (1943) presented a need hierarchy which recognizes that different people are at different levels in their needs. Usually people start out looking for physiological needs and then progressively move up the needs hierarchy.

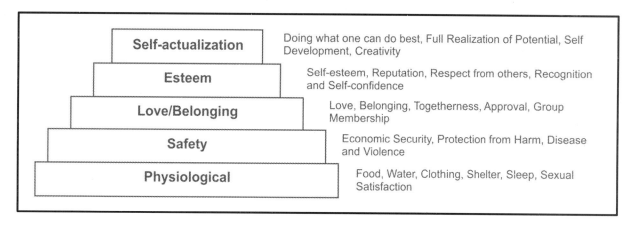

Figure 3-7: Maslow's Hierarchy of Needs Theory

To be successful, a Scrum Team needs both core and non-core team members who have reached the esteem or self-actualization levels. The concept of self-organizing teams, which is a key principle in Scrum, requires team members to be self-motivated, and to participate and contribute fully towards meeting the project goals.

As a leader, the Scrum Master needs to understand where each person on the team is relative to the pyramid. This understanding will help to determine the best approach in motivating each individual.

Additionally, everyone fluctuates up and down the levels in the needs hierarchy throughout life due to their own motivation and efforts to move up the hierarchy or sometimes due to factors beyond their control that may push them down. The Scrum Master's goal is to work with individuals on the team to build their skills and knowledge and help them move up the needs hierarchy. This support results in a team that consists of individuals who are motivated and strong contributors to the project and to the organization as a whole.

3.10.6   Theory X and Theory Y

Douglas McGregor (1960) proposed two management theories:

- **Theory X**—Theory X leaders assume employees are inherently unmotivated and will avoid work if possible, warranting an authoritarian style of management.

- **Theory Y**—Theory Y leaders, on the other hand, assume employees are self-motivated and seek to accept greater responsibility. Theory Y involves a more participative management style.

Scrum projects are not likely to be successful with organizations that have Theory X leaders in the roles of Scrum Master or Product Owner. All leaders in Scrum projects should subscribe to Theory Y, whereby they view individuals as important assets and work towards developing their team members' skills and empowering their team members while expressing appreciation for the work the team has completed to accomplish the project objectives.

4. BUSINESS JUSTIFICATION

4.1 Introduction

The purpose of this chapter is to understand the concept and purpose of Business Justification as it relates to Scrum projects. It is important for an organization to perform a proper business justification and create a viable Project Vision Statement prior to starting any project. This helps key decision makers understand the business need for a change or for a new product or service and the justification for moving forward with a project. It also helps the Product Owner to create a Prioritized Product Backlog along with the business expectations of Senior Management & Stakeholder(s).

Business Justification, as defined in *A Guide to the Scrum Body of Knowledge (SBOK™ Guide)*, is applicable to the following:

- Portfolios, programs, and/or projects in *any* industry
- Products, services, or any other results to be delivered to stakeholders
- Projects of any size or complexity

The term "product" in the *SBOK™ Guide* may refer to a product, service, or other deliverables. Scrum can be applied effectively to any project in any industry—from small projects or teams with as few as six team members to large, complex projects with up to several hundred team members.

This chapter is divided into the following sections:

4.2 Roles Guide—This section provides guidance on which sections are relevant for each of the core Scrum roles: Product Owner, Scrum Master, and Scrum Team.

4.3 Value-driven Delivery—This section describes the concept of business value and its importance in any project. It also provides information regarding the responsibilities of the various individuals including the Product Owner, involved in achieving business value.

4.4 Importance of Business Justification—This section details the importance of business justification, the factors that determine it, and how it is maintained and verified throughout the project.

4.5 Business Justification Techniques—This section describes in detail how business justification is assessed and verified using various tools.

4.6 Continuous Value Justification—This section details the importance of continuous value justification and expands on how it is achieved.

4.7 Confirm Benefits Realization—This section describes how benefits are realized throughout the project.

4.8 Summary of Responsibilities—This section defines the responsibilities relevant to business justification for project team members based on their roles.

4.9 Scrum vs. Traditional Project Management—This section highlights the business benefits of the Scrum method over traditional project management models.

4.2 Roles Guide

1. Product Owner—Business justification is primarily conducted by the Product Owner; therefore, this entire chapter is most applicable to this role.

2. Scrum Master—The Scrum Master should be familiar with this entire chapter, with primary focus on sections 4.3, 4.4, 4.6, 4.7 and 4.8.

3. Scrum Team—The Scrum Team should focus primarily on sections 4.3, 4.7 and 4.8.

4.3 Value-driven Delivery

A project is a collaborative enterprise to either create new products or services or to deliver results as defined in the Project Vision Statement. Projects are usually impacted by constraints of time, cost, scope, quality, people, and organizational capabilities. Usually, the results generated by projects are expected to create some form of business or service value.

Since value is a primary reason for any organization to move forward with a project, Value-driven Delivery must be the main focus. Delivering value is ingrained in the Scrum framework. Scrum facilitates delivery of value very early on in the project and continues to do so throughout the project lifecycle.

One of the key characteristics of any project is the uncertainty of results or outcomes. It is impossible to guarantee project success at completion, irrespective of the size or complexity of a project. Considering this uncertainty of achieving success, it is therefore important to start delivering results as early in the project as possible. This early delivery of results, and thereby value, provides an opportunity for reinvestment and proves the worth of the project to interested stakeholders.

In order to provide Value-driven Delivery, it is important to:

1. Understand what adds value to customers and users and to prioritize the high value requirements on the top of the Prioritized Product Backlog.

2. Decrease uncertainty and constantly address risks that can potentially decrease value if they materialize. Also work closely with project stakeholders showing them product increments at the end of each Sprint, enabling effective management of changes.

3. *Create Deliverables* based on the priorities determined by producing potentially shippable product increments during each Sprint so that customers start realizing value early on in the project.

The concept of Value-driven Delivery in Scrum makes Scrum framework very attractive for business stakeholders and senior management. This concept is very different when compared with traditional project management models where:

1. Requirements are not prioritized by business value.
2. Changing requirements after project initiation is difficult and can only be done through a time consuming change management process.
3. Value is realized only at the end of the project when the final product or service is delivered.

Figure 4-1 contrasts Value-driven Delivery in Scrum versus Traditional projects.

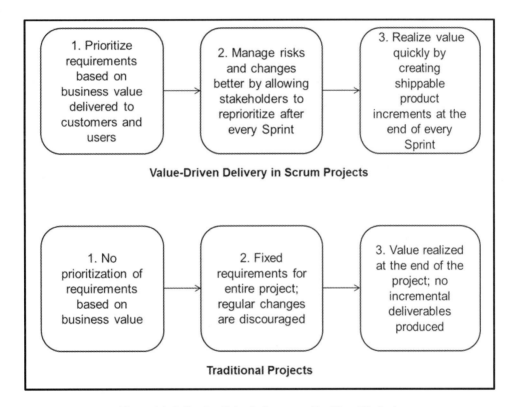

Figure 4-1: Delivering Value in Scrum vs. Traditional Projects

4.3.1 Responsibilities of the Product Owner in Business Justification

The responsibility of prioritizing and delivering business value in an organization for projects lies primarily with the Product Owner. For programs and portfolios, the responsibility lies with the Program Product Owner and Portfolio Product Owner, respectively. Their role is to act as effective representatives of the customer and/or sponsor. The guidelines for evaluating and measuring business value may typically be set forth by a Scrum Guidance Body.

Figure 4-2 illustrates the business justification responsibilities in a hierarchical order.

Portfolio Product Owner	• Delivers value for portfolios • Creates business justification for portfolios • Provides value guidance for programs • Approves business justification for programs
Program Product Owner	• Delivers value for programs • Creates business justification for programs • Provides value guidance for projects • Approves business justification for projects
Product Owner	• Delivers value for projects • Creates business justification for projects • Confirms benefit realization to stakeholders

Figure 4-2: Hierarchy for Business Justification Responsibilities

4.3.2 Responsibilities of Other Scrum Roles in Business Justification

It is important to note that although the Product Owner is primarily responsible for business justification, other persons working in Scrum projects also contribute significantly as follows:

1. The **sponsor** provides funding for the project and constantly monitors the project to confirm realization of benefits.

2. **Customers** and **users** are involved in defining the prioritized list of requirements and User Stories in the Prioritized Product Backlog, reviewing Deliverables after every Sprint or release, and confirming that benefits are realized.

3. The **Scrum Guidance Body** may provide guidelines and recommendations related to business justification techniques and confirming benefits realization and so forth. Such guidelines and recommendations may then be referred to by Scrum Core Teams and Stakeholder(s).

4. The **Scrum Master** facilitates creation of the project's deliverables; manages risks, changes, and impediments during *Conduct Daily Standup*, *Retrospect Sprint*, and other Scrum processes. The Scrum Master coordinates with the Scrum Team to create the deliverables and with the Product Owner and other stakeholders to ensure that benefits from the project are realized.

5. The **Scrum Team** works on creating the deliverables of the project and contributes to realizing business value for all stakeholders and the project. The Scrum Team is also involved in the *Develop Epic(s)*; *Create Prioritized Product Backlog*; *Create User Stories*; *Approve, Estimate, and Commit User Stories*; and associated processes where the business requirements are defined and prioritized. The Scrum Team also helps in identifying risks and submits Change Requests for improvements in Sprint Retrospect Meetings and other meetings.

4.4 Importance of Business Justification

Business justification demonstrates the reasons for undertaking a project. It answers the question "Why is this project needed?" Business justification drives all decision making related to a project. So, it is important to assess the viability and achievability of a project not only before committing to significant expenditures or investment at initial stages of the project but also to verify the business justification for continuance throughout the project's lifecycle. A project should be terminated if it is found to be unviable; the decision should be escalated to the relevant stakeholders and to senior management. The business justification for a project must be assessed at the beginning of the project, at pre-defined intervals throughout the project, and at any time when major issues or risks that threaten the project viability arise.

4.4.1 Factors Used to Determine Business Justification

There are numerous factors a Product Owner must consider to determine the business justification for a project. The following are some of the most important factors:

1. **Project Reasoning**

   Project reasoning includes all factors which necessitate the project, whether positive or negative, chosen or not (e.g., inadequate capacity to meet existing and forecasted demand, decrease in customer satisfaction, low profit, legal requirement, etc.).

2. **Business Needs**

   Business needs are those business outcomes that the project is expected to fulfill, as documented in the Project Vision Statement.

3. **Project Benefits**

Project benefits include all measurable improvements in a product, service, or result which could be provided through successful completion of a project.

4. **Opportunity Cost**

Opportunity cost covers the next best business option or project that was discarded in favor of the current project.

5. **Major Risks**

Risks include any uncertain or unplanned events that may affect the viability and potential success of the project.

6. **Project Timescales**

Timescales reflect the length or duration of a project and the time over which its benefits will be realized.

7. **Project Costs**

Project costs are investment and other development costs for a project.

4.4.2 Business Justification and the Project Lifecycle

Business justification is first assessed prior to a project being initiated and is continuously verified throughout the project lifecycle. The following steps capture how business justification is determined:

1. **Assess and Present a Business Case**

Business justification for a project is typically analyzed and confirmed by the Product Owner. It is documented and presented in the form of a project Business Case prior to Initiate phase and involves considering the various factors specified in section 4.4.1. Once documented, the Product Owner should create a Project Vision Statement and obtain approval of the Project Vision Statement from the key decision-makers in the organization. Generally, this consists of executives and/or some form of a project or program management board.

2. **Continuous Value Justification**

Once the decision makers approve the Project Vision Statement, it is then baselined and forms the business justification. The business justification is validated throughout project execution, typically at predefined intervals or milestones, such as during portfolio, program, and Prioritized Product

Backlog Review Meetings and when major issues and risks that threaten project viability are identified. This could happen in several Scrum processes including *Conduct Daily Standup* and *Groom Prioritized Product Backlog*. Throughout the project, the Product Owner should keep the business justification in the Project Vision Statement updated with relevant project information to enable the key decision makers to continue making informed decisions.

3. Confirm Benefits Realization

The Product Owner confirms the achievement of organizational benefits throughout the project, as well as upon completion of the User Stories in the Prioritized Product Backlog. Benefits from Scrum projects are realized during *Demonstrate and Validate Sprint*, *Retrospect Sprint*, *Ship Deliverables* and *Retrospect Project* processes.

Figure 4-3 summarizes the steps to determine business justification.

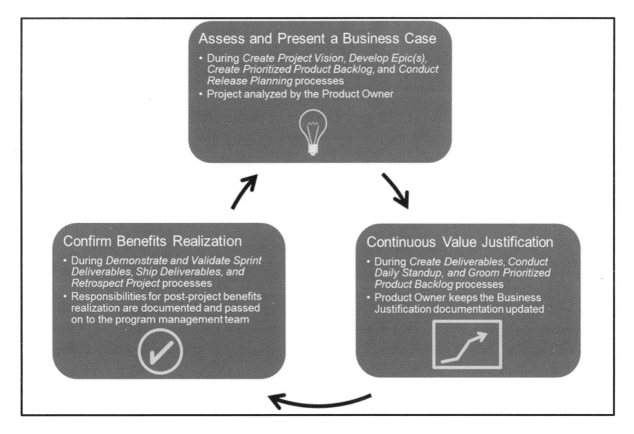

Figure 4-3: Business Justification and the Project Lifecycle

4.5   Business Justification Techniques

The following sections deal with some of the tools used to assess and evaluate business justification, as well as some other aspects associated with project justification and project selection. It is not necessary, or even recommended to use every available technique for every project. Some techniques are not appropriate depending on the specific project, and techniques may be used to assess projects individually or to compare the expected value of multiple projects.

The Scrum Guidance Body (SGB), which can be a panel of experts or a set of documents on organizational standards and procedures, defines the guidelines and metrics that will be used to assess business value. Each respective Product Owner, however, is responsible for performing the activities that verify and track business value for his or her respective projects, programs, or portfolios.

4.5.1   Estimation of Project Value

The value to be provided by business projects can be estimated using various methods such as Return on Investment (ROI), Net Present Value (NPV), and Internal Rate of Return (IRR).

1. **Return on Investment (ROI)**

   Return on Investment (ROI) when used for project justification, assesses the expected net income to be gained from a project. It is calculated by deducting the expected costs or investment of a project from its expected revenue and then dividing this (net profit) by the expected costs in order to get a return rate. Other factors such as inflation and interest rates on borrowed money may be factored into ROI calculations.

   ROI formula:

   $$ROI = (Project\ Revenue - Project\ Cost) / Project\ Cost$$

   Example: The ROI for a project that will cost $125,000 to develop, with expected financial benefits estimated at $300,000 is calculated as follows:

   ROI = ($300,000 - $125,000) / $125,000 = 1.4

   Therefore, the ROI is 1.4 times the investment (or 140%).

   Frequent product or service increments, is a key foundation of Scrum that allows earlier verification of ROI. This aids in assessing the justification of continuous value.

2. Net Present Value (NPV)

Net Present Value (NPV) is a method used to determine the current net value of a future financial benefit, given an assumed inflation or interest rate. In other words, NPV is the total expected income or revenue from a project, minus the total expected cost of the project, taking into account the time-value of money.

> *Example:* Which of the following two projects is better to select if NPV is used as the selection criterion?
>
> - Project A has a NPV of $1,500 and will be completed in 5 years.
> - Project B has a NPV of $1,000 and will be completed in 1 year.
>
> *Solution:* Project A, since its NPV is higher; the fact that Project B has a shorter duration than Project A is not considered here, because time is already accounted for in the NPV calculations (i.e., due to the fact that it is the current, not future value that is being considered in the calculation).

3. Internal Rate of Return (IRR)

Internal Rate of Return (IRR) is a discount rate on an investment in which the present value of cash inflows is made equal to the present value of cash outflows for assessing a project's rate of return. When comparing projects, one with a higher IRR is typically better.

Though IRR is not used to justify projects as often as some other techniques, such as NPV, it is an important concept to know.

> *Example:* Based on IRR, which project is most desirable?
>
> - Project A, which has an IRR of 15% and will be completed in 5 years.
> - Project B, which has an IRR of 10% and will be completed in 1 year.
>
> *Solution:* Project A, since its IRR is higher; the fact that Project B has a shorter duration than Project A is not considered here because time is already taken into account in the IRR calculations (i.e., as with NPV, it is the current, not future value that is used to determine the IRR).

4.5.2   Planning for Value

After justifying and confirming the value of a project, the Product Owner should consider the organizational policies, procedures, templates, and general standards dictated by the Scrum Guidance Body (or similar organizational project board or office) when planning a project; at the same time maximizing Value-driven Delivery. The onus for determining *how* the value is created falls on the stakeholders (sponsor, customers, and/or users), while the Scrum Team concentrates on *what* is to be developed. Some common tools recommended by a Scrum Guidance Body might include the following:

1. Value Stream Mapping

Value Stream Mapping uses flowcharts, to illustrate the flow of information needed to complete a process. This technique may be used to streamline a process by helping to determine non-value-added elements.

2. Customer Value-based Prioritization

Customer Value-based Prioritization places primary importance on the customer and strives to implement User Stories with the highest value first. Such high value User Stories are identified and moved to the top of the Prioritized Product Backlog.

A team can use a variety of prioritization schemes to determine high-value features.

a. Simple Schemes

Simple schemes involve labeling items as Priority "1", "2", "3" or "High", "Medium" and "Low" and so on. Although this is a simple and straightforward approach, it can become problematic because there is often a tendency to label everything as Priority "1" or "High". Even "High," "Medium," and "Low" prioritization schemes can encounter similar difficulties.

b. MoSCoW Prioritization

The MoSCoW prioritization scheme derives its name from the first letters of the phrases "Must have," "Should have," "Could have," and "Won't have". This prioritization method is generally more effective than simple schemes. The labels are in decreasing order of priority with "Must have" features being those without which the product will have no value and "Won't have" features being those that, although they would be nice to have, are not necessary to be included.

c. Monopoly Money

This technique involves giving the customer "monopoly money" or "false money" equal to the amount of the project budget and asking them to distribute it among the User Stories under consideration. In this way, the customer prioritizes based on what they are willing to pay for each User Story.

d. 100-Point Method

The 100-Point Method was developed by Dean Leffingwell and Don Widrig (2003). It involves giving the customer 100 points they can use to vote for the features that they feel are most important.

e. Kano Analysis

The Kano analysis was developed by Noriaki Kano (1984) and involves classifying features or requirements into four categories based on customer preferences:

1. *Exciters/Delighters:* Features that are new, or of high value to the customer

2. *Satisfiers:* Features that offer value to the customer

3. *Dissatisfiers:* Features which, if not present, are likely to cause a customer to dislike the product, but do not affect the level of satisfaction if they are present

4. *Indifferent:* Features that will not affect the customer in any way and should be eliminated

Figure 4-4 depicts an illustration of Kano Analysis.

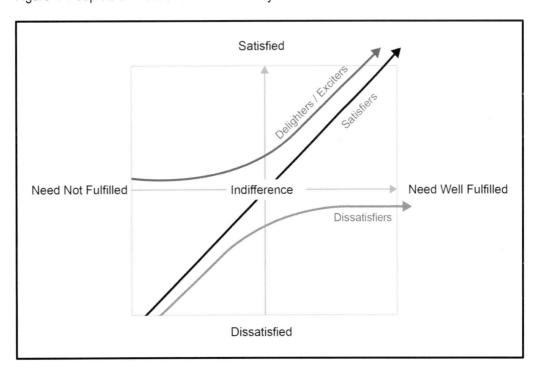

Figure 4-4: Kano Analysis

Interestingly, features usually move down the classification list over time; customers will come to expect features (e.g., cameras on phones) and these features will move from being exciters/delighters to satisfiers and eventually to dissatisfiers.

4.5.3 Relative Prioritization Ranking

A simple listing of User Stories in order of priority is an effective method for determining the desired User Stories for each iteration or release of the product or service. The purpose is to create a simple, single list with the goal of prioritizing features, rather than being distracted by multiple prioritization schemes.

This simple list also provides a basis for incorporating changes and identified risks when necessary. Each change or identified risk can be inserted in the list based on its priority relative to the other User Stories in the list. Typically, new changes will be included at the expense of features that have been assigned a lower priority.

Defining the Minimum Marketable Features (MMF) is extremely important during this process, so that the first release or iteration happens as early as possible, leading to increased ROI. Normally, these User Stories would rank highest in priority.

4.5.4 Story Mapping

This is a technique to provide a visual outline of the product and its key components. Story Mapping, first formulated by Jeff Patton (2005), is commonly used to illustrate product roadmaps.

Story maps depict the sequence of product development iterations and map out which features will be included in the first, second, third, and subsequent releases.

4.6 Continuous Value Justification

Business value should be assessed regularly to determine whether the justification or viability of executing the project continues to exist. Frequent assessment of investment in the project relative to business value being created qualifies the continued viability of a project. The expected requirements from the project may change frequently, which can impact both project investment and value creation. A key aspect of Scrum is its ability to quickly adjust to chaos created by a rapidly changing business model. In projects with ambiguous user requirements and significant potential for frequent changes, Scrum provides considerable advantages over other development models.

Monitoring the rate of delivering value is an important requirement for Scrum projects. Periodically tracking and reporting the creation of value assists in assessing project status and provides important information to the customer and other stakeholders.

4.6.1   Earned Value Analysis

Although commonly used, tools such as bar charts and Gantt Charts have limitations in tracking and reporting progress when it comes to project performance. Earned Value Analysis (EVA) is used for this purpose.

EVA analyzes actual project performance against planned performance at a given point in time. For tracking techniques to be effective, the initial baseline project plan needs to be accurate. EVA often uses graphs and other visuals (e.g., S-curve), as a way to depict project status information.

Earned Value Analysis measures current variances in the project's schedule and cost performance and forecasts the final cost based on the determined current performance. EVA is typically done at the end of each Sprint after the User Stories in Sprint Backlog are completed.

Table 4-1 summarizes the formulas used in Earned Value Analysis.

Term Definition	Acronym	Formula
Planned Value	PV	
Earned Value	EV	
Actual Cost	AC	
Budget at Completion	BAC	
Schedule Variance	SV	EV - PV
Cost Variance	CV	EV - AC
Schedule Performance Index	SPI	EV / PV
Cost Performance Index	CPI	EV / AC
Percent Complete	% Complete	(EV / BAC) x 100

Estimate at Completion
   1.   Estimating assumptions not valid
   2.   Current Variances are atypical
   3.   Current Variances are typical
	EAC	1. AC + ETC
		2. AC + BAC - EV
		3. BAC / CPI

Estimate to Complete	ETC	EAC - AC
Variance at Completion	VAC	BAC - EAC

Table 4-1: Earned Value Formulas

Example: A website with 4,000 web pages needs to be developed—we assume that every web page takes the same time to complete, and that each web page is a unique User Story of equal priority in the Prioritized Product Backlog. The estimated cost of completing the project is $400,000 and the time limit for the project is 12 months. After 6 months, $300,000 has been spent and the work completed is 1,000 web pages.

What have we been provided with?
- Budget at Completion (BAC) = $400,000 (Cost Baseline for the project)
- Planned Value (PV) = $200,000 (since we planned to complete 2,000 web pages)
- Earned Value (EV) = $100,000 (value of 1,000 web pages that are complete)
- Actual Cost (AC) = $300,000 (what has been spent so far)

S-curve for the data:

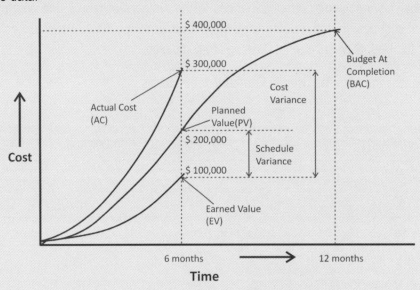

Formulas:
- Schedule Variance (SV) = EV - PV = $100,000 - $200,000 = - $100,000
- Cost Variance (CV) = EV - AC = $100,000 - $300,000 = - $200,000
  - The negative variances in our project indicate that we are behind schedule and over budget.
- Schedule Performance Index (SPI) = EV / PV = $100,000 / $200,000 = 0.5
  - SPI < 1 indicates that the work completed so far is only 50% of what we planned to have completed at 6 months.
- Cost Performance Index (CPI) = EV / AC = $100,000 / $300,000 = 0.33
  - CPI < 1 indicates that we are only getting 33% of work done for the amount of money being spent.
- Percent Complete = EV / BAC x 100 = $100,000 / $400,000 x 100 = 25%
  - So, 25% of the work on the project is complete at this point in time.

4.6.2 Cumulative Flow Diagram (CFD)

A Cumulative Flow Diagram (CFD) is a useful tool for reporting and tracking project performance. It provides a simple, visual representation of project progress at a particular point in time. It is usually used to provide a higher level status of the overall project and not daily updates for individual Sprints.

Figure 4-5 is an example of a CFD for a large project. It shows how many User Stories are yet to be created, in process of being created, and have been created. As customer requirements change, there is a change in the Cumulative User Stories which have to be delivered. Change points 1 and 2 are where the Product Owner removed existing user Stories in the Risk Adjusted Prioritized Product Backlog and Change points 3 and 4 are where the Product Owner added new User Stories in the Risk Adjusted Prioritized Product Backlog

This type of diagram can be a great tool for identifying roadblocks and bottlenecks within processes. For example, if the diagram shows one band becoming narrower while the previous band is becoming wider over time, there may be a bottleneck and changes may be needed to increase efficiency and/or improve project performance.

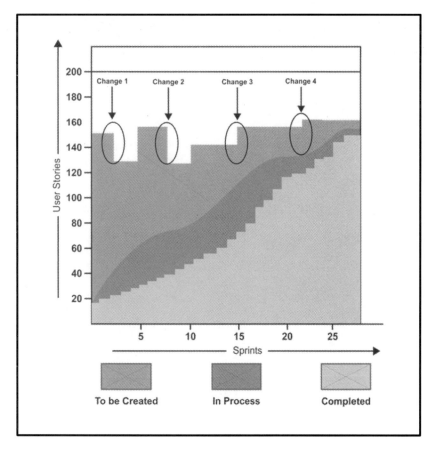

Figure 4-5: Sample Cumulative Flow Diagram (CFD)

4.7 Confirm Benefits Realization

Throughout a project, it is important to verify whether benefits are being realized. Whether the products of a Scrum project are tangible or intangible, appropriate verification techniques are required to confirm that the team is creating the deliverables that will achieve the benefits and value defined at the beginning of the project.

4.7.1 Prototypes, Simulations, and Demonstrations

Demonstrating prototypes to customers and simulating their functionalities are commonly used techniques for confirming value.

Often, after using the features or having them demonstrated, customers can more clearly determine whether the features are adequate and suitable for their needs. They might realize a need for additional features, or may decide to modify previously defined feature requirements. In product development, this customer experience has come to be known as IKIWISI (I'll Know It When I See It).

Through demonstrations or access to early iterations, customers can also evaluate to what degree the team has successfully interpreted their requirements and met their expectations.

4.8 Summary of Responsibilities

Role	Responsibilities
Scrum Guidance Body	• Establishes overall guidelines and metrics for evaluating value • Acts in a consulting capacity and provides guidance for projects, programs, and portfolios as required
Portfolio Product Owner	• Ensures value delivery for portfolios • Creates the business justification for portfolios • Provides value guidance for programs within portfolios • Approves the business justification of programs within a portfolio
Portfolio Scrum Master	• Ensures the desired outcomes of the portfolio are achieved • Performs Continuous Value Justification for portfolios
Program Product Owner	• Ensures value delivery for programs • Creates the business justification for programs • Provides value guidance for projects within a program • Approves the business justification of projects within a program
Program Scrum Master	• Ensures the desired outcomes of the program are communicated and understood • Performs Continuous Value Justification for programs
Stakeholder(s)	• Helps prioritize User Stories and requirements in the Prioritized Product Backlog • Communicates with Scrum Team and confirms realization of value at the end of every Sprint, Release, and the project
Product Owner	• Ensures value delivery for projects • Maintains the business justification for projects • Confirms and communicates project benefits to stakeholders
Scrum Master	• Ensures the desired outcomes of the project are communicated to and understood by the Scrum Team • Performs Continuous Value Justification for projects
Scrum Team	• Ensures that project deliverables are completed in accordance with agreed Acceptance Criteria • Performs Continuous Value Justification for projects

Table 4-2: Summary of Responsibilities Relevant to Business Justification

4.9   Scrum vs. Traditional Project Management

Traditional projects emphasize on extensive upfront planning and adherence to the project plan created by the project manager. Usually, changes are managed through a formal change management system and value is created at the end of the project when the final product is delivered.

In Scrum projects, extensive long-term planning is not done prior to project execution. Planning is done in an iterative manner before each Sprint. This allows quick and effective response to change, which results in lower costs and ultimately increased profitability and Return on Investment (ROI). Moreover, Value-Driven Delivery (section 4.3) is a key benefit of the Scrum framework and provides significantly better prioritization and quicker realization of business value. Because of the iterative nature of Scrum development, there is always at least one release of the product with Minimum Marketable Features (MMF) available. Even if a project is terminated, there are usually some benefits or value created prior to termination.

5. QUALITY

5.1   Introduction

The purpose of this chapter is to define quality as it relates to projects and to present the Scrum approach to achieve the required levels of quality.

Quality, as defined in *A Guide to the Scrum Body of Knowledge (SBOK™ Guide)*, is applicable to the following:

- Portfolios, programs, and/or projects in *any* industry
- Products, services, or any other results to be delivered to stakeholders
- Projects of any size or complexity

The term "product" in the *SBOK™ Guide* may refer to a product, service, or other deliverable. Scrum can be applied effectively to any project in any industry—from small projects or teams with as few as six team members to large, complex projects with up to several hundred team members.

This chapter is divided into the following sections:

5.2 Roles Guide—This section provides guidance on which sections are relevant for each Scrum role: Product Owner, Scrum Master, and Scrum Team.

5.3 Quality Defined—This section provides the Scrum definition of quality, with a clear distinction from scope, and describes the relationship between quality and business value.

5.4 Acceptance Criteria and the Prioritized Product Backlog—This section emphasizes the importance of Acceptance Criteria, the Prioritized Product Backlog, and their relationship. It also explains the Scrum definition of Done.

5.5 Quality Management in Scrum—This section provides details on quality planning, quality control, and quality assurance in the context of Scrum.

5.6 Summary of Responsibilities—This section describes the responsibilities relevant to quality for each person or role in a project.

5.7 Scrum vs. Traditional Project Management—This section highlights the benefits of quality management in Scrum method over traditional project management models.

5.2   Roles Guide

1.   Product Owner—It is important for anyone assuming the role of Product Owner in Scrum projects to read this complete chapter.

2.   Scrum Master—The Scrum Master should also be familiar with this entire chapter with primary focus on sections 5.3, 5.4, 5.5.3, and 5.6.

3.   Scrum Team—The Scrum Team should mainly focus on sections 5.3, 5.4, and 5.6.

5.3   Quality Defined

There are numerous ways to define quality.

In Scrum, quality is defined as the ability of the completed product or deliverables to meet the Acceptance Criteria and achieve the business value expected by the customer.

To ensure that a project meets quality requirements, Scrum adopts an approach of continuous improvement whereby the team learns from experience and stakeholder engagement to constantly keep the Prioritized Product Backlog updated with any changes in requirements. The Prioritized Product Backlog is simply never complete until the closure or termination of the project. Any changes to the requirements reflect changes in the internal and external business environment and allow the team to continually work and adapt to achieve those requirements. Since Scrum requires work to be completed in increments during Sprints, this means that errors or defects get noticed earlier through repetitive quality testing, rather than when the final product or service is near completion. Moreover, important quality-related tasks (e.g., development, testing, and documentation) are completed as part of the same Sprint by the same team—this ensures that quality is inherent in any Done deliverable created as part of a Sprint. Thus, continuous improvement with repetitive testing optimizes the probability of achieving the expected quality levels in a Scrum project. Constant discussions between the Scrum Core Team and stakeholders (including customers and users) with actual increments of the product being delivered at the end of every Sprint, ensures that the gap between customer expectations from the project and actual deliverables produced is constantly reduced.

5.3.1 Quality and Scope

Scope and quality requirements for a project are determined by taking into consideration various factors such as the following:

- The business need the project will fulfill
- The capability and willingness of the organization to meet the identified business need
- The current and future needs of the target audience

The scope of a project is the total sum of all the product increments and the work required for developing the final product. Quality is the ability of the deliverables to meet the quality requirements for the product and satisfy customer needs. In Scrum, the scope and quality of the project are captured in the Prioritized Product Backlog, and the scope for each Sprint is determined by refining the large Prioritized Product Backlog Items (PBIs) into a set of small but detailed User Stories that can be planned, developed, and verified within a Sprint.

The Prioritized Product Backlog is continuously groomed by the Product Owner. The Product Owner ensures that any User Stories that the Scrum Team is expected to do in a Sprint are refined prior to the start of the Sprint. In general, the most valuable requirements in solving the customers' problems or meeting their needs are prioritized as high and the remaining are given a lower priority. Less important User Stories are developed in subsequent Sprints or can be left out altogether according to the customer's requirements. During Sprint execution, the Product Owner, customer, and the Scrum Team can discuss the list of features of the product to comply with the changing needs of the customers.

5.3.2 Quality and Business Value

Quality and business value are closely linked. Therefore, it is critical to understand the quality and scope of a project in order to correctly map the outcomes and benefits the project and its product must achieve in order to deliver business value. To determine the business value of a product, it is important to understand the business need that drives the requirements of the product. Thus, business need determines the product required, and the product, in turn provides the expected business value.

Quality is a complex variable. An increase in scope without increasing time or resources tends to reduce quality. Similarly, a reduction in time or resources without decreasing scope also generally results in a decrease in quality. Scrum believes in maintaining a "sustainable pace" of work, which helps improve quality over a period of time.

The Scrum Guidance Body may define minimum quality requirements and standards required for all projects in the organization. The standards must be adhered to by all Scrum Teams in the company.

5.4   Acceptance Criteria and the Prioritized Product Backlog

The Prioritized Product Backlog is a single requirements document that defines the project scope by providing a prioritized list of features of the product or service to be delivered by the project. The required features are described in the form of User Stories. User Stories are specific requirements outlined by various stakeholders as they pertain to the proposed product or service. Each User Story will have associated User Story Acceptance Criteria (also referred to as "Acceptance Criteria"), which are the objective components by which a User Story's functionality is judged. Acceptance Criteria are developed by the Product Owner according to his or her expert understanding of the customer's requirements. The Product Owner then communicates the User Stories in the Prioritized Product Backlog to the Scrum Team members and their agreement is sought. Acceptance Criteria should explicitly outline the conditions that User Stories must satisfy. Clearly defined Acceptance Criteria are crucial for timely and effective delivery of the functionality defined in the User Stories, which ultimately determines the success of the project.

At the end of each Sprint, the Product Owner uses these criteria to verify the completed deliverables; and can either accept or reject individual deliverables and their associated User Stories. If deliverables are accepted by the Product Owner, then the User Story is considered Done. A clear definition of Done is critical because it helps clarify requirements and allows the team to adhere to quality norms. It also helps the team think from the user's perspective when working with User Stories.

User Stories corresponding to rejected deliverables are added back to the Updated Prioritized Product Backlog during the *Groom Prioritized Product Backlog* process, to be completed in future Sprints. The rejection of a few individual deliverables and their corresponding User Stories is not a rejection of the final product or product increment. The product or product increment could be potentially shippable even if a few User Stories are rejected.

Figure 5-1 illustrates the concept of Acceptance Criteria along with product increment flow.

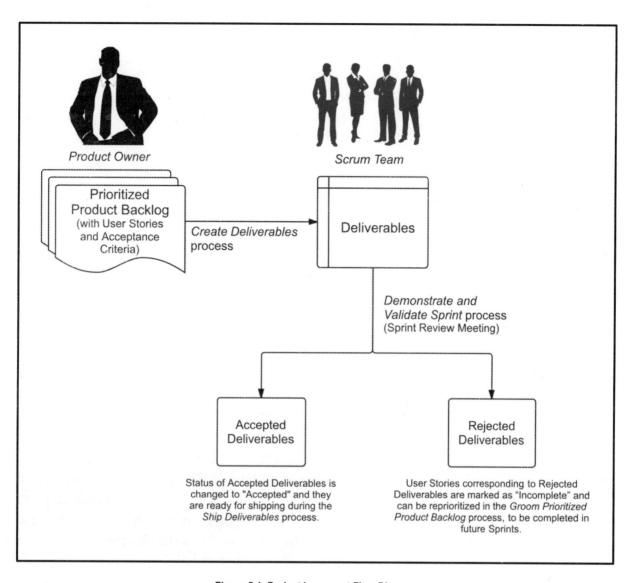

Figure 5-1: Project Increment Flow Diagram

5.4.1 Writing Acceptance Criteria

Acceptance Criteria are unique to each User Story and are not a substitute for a requirements list.

Example:

Persona: Janine is a married 36 year old working professional with a family of three children. She is a busy, successful woman who balances her professional and personal life. She is comfortable with technology and is an early adopter of innovative services and products. She is always connected to the internet through multiple devices and regularly shops on e-commerce portals.

User Story: "As an online grocery shopper Janine, I should be able to save and view my draft order from any of my devices so that I can complete the order process at my convenience."

Acceptance Criteria:

- Every in-progress order must be saved every 5 seconds to the logged in user account as a draft order
- New draft orders must show up as notifications on any devices the user logs in

---

It is important for a Product Owner to note that User Stories that fulfill most, but not all, Acceptance Criteria cannot be accepted as Done. Scrum projects operate in Time-boxed Sprints, with a dedicated Sprint Backlog for each Sprint. Often, the last bit of work might be the most complicated part of a User Story and might take longer than expected. If incomplete User Stories were given partial credit for being Done and carried over to the next Sprint, then the progress of the subsequent Sprint could be disrupted. Therefore, the Done status is black and white. A User Story can only be either Done or not Done.

5.4.2 Minimum Acceptance Criteria

A higher level business unit may announce mandatory minimum Acceptance Criteria, which then become part of the Acceptance Criteria for any User Story for that business unit. Any functionality defined by the business unit must satisfy these minimum Acceptance Criteria, if it is to be accepted by the respective Product Owner. The introduction of this Acceptance Criteria may lead to a cascading set of Acceptance Criteria for the portfolio, program, and project (see Figure 5-2). The overall quality standards, guidelines, and templates for an entire portfolio are set by the Portfolio Product Owner while the minimum Acceptance Criteria for programs are set by the Program Product Owner. Thus the Acceptance Criteria for a User Story in a project will implicitly include all the minimum Acceptance Criteria from the higher levels, as applicable.

Portfolio Product Owner	• Sets the minimum Acceptance Criteria for the entire portfolio • Reviews portfolio deliverables
Program Product Owner	• Sets the minimum Acceptance Criteria for the entire program, which includes the Acceptance Criteria from the portfolio • Reviews program deliverables
Product Owner	• Sets the minimum Acceptance Criteria for the project, which includes the Acceptance Criteria from the program • Reviews project deliverables

Figure 5-2: Cascading Acceptance Criteria

Once the minimum Acceptance Criteria are defined, such criteria may then be documented in the Scrum Guidance Body documents and referred to by Scrum Teams as required.

5.4.3 Definition of Done

There is one key difference between "Done Criteria" and "Acceptance Criteria". While Acceptance Criteria are unique for individual User Stories, Done Criteria are a set of rules that are applicable to all User Stories in a given Sprint. General Done Criteria could include any of the following:

- Reviewed by other team members
- Completed unit testing of the User Story
- Completion of quality assurance tests
- Completion of all documentation related to the User Story
- All issues are fixed
- Successful demonstration to stakeholders and/or business representatives

As with the Acceptance Criteria, all conditions of the Done Criteria must be satisfied for the User Story to be considered Done.

The Scrum Team should use a checklist of the general Done Criteria to ensure a task is finished and the result meets the Definition of Done (DoD). A clear Definition of Done is critical because it helps remove ambiguity and allows the team to adhere to required quality norms. The definition of Done is typically determined and documented by the Scrum Guidance Body.

The required records and data to comply with the project's documentation requirements can be generated as the team proceeds through Sprints and Releases.

The inclusion of activities such as holding review meetings and writing design documents can help ensure compliance with internal and external quality standards. The basic principles of Scrum such as short iterations, incremental building, customer involvement, adaptation to changing requirements, and constantly adjusting scope, time, and cost within the project will still apply.

5.4.4 Acceptance or Rejection of Prioritized Product Backlog Items

Toward the end of any iteration, the respective business unit and stakeholders participate in a Sprint Review Meeting in which the product increment is demonstrated to the Product Owner, sponsor, customer, and users. While feedback from all the stakeholders is gathered, only the Product Owner has the power to accept or reject a particular User Story as Done, according to the agreed upon Acceptance Criteria. Thus, the role of Acceptance Criteria in maintaining quality is critical and needs to be clearly understood by the team. It is the responsibility of the Scrum Master to ensure that the Acceptance Criteria for a User Story are not changed by the Product Owner in the middle of a Sprint. Partially completed User Stories are rejected as not Done and moved back into the Prioritized Product Backlog.

5.5 Quality Management in Scrum

The customer is the most important stakeholder for any project. Therefore, it is important to understand the customer's needs and requirements. The Voice of the Customer (VOC) can be referred to as the explicit and implicit requirements of the customer, which must be understood prior to the designing of a product or service. Generally, in a Scrum environment, the Product Owner's focus is on business requirements and objectives, which together represent the Voice of the Customer. The Product Owner can benefit greatly from the guidance available from the Scrum Guidance Body (either through quality documents or standards, or from quality experts). These specialists should work with the Product Owner and the customer to ensure the appropriate level of detail and information in the User Stories, since User Stories are the basis for the success of any Scrum project.

It should be noted that external stakeholders are not directly involved at the Scrum Team level and, instead, interact primarily with the Product Owner. For any Scrum project, the customer may be either of the following:

- Internal (that is, within the same organization)
- External (that is, outside the organization)

Quality management in Scrum enables customers to become aware of any problems in the project early and helps them recognize if a project is going to work for them or not. In Scrum, quality is about customer satisfaction and a working product, not necessarily meeting arbitrary metrics. This distinction becomes very important from the customer's point of view because they are the ones investing time and money in the project.

Quality management in Scrum is facilitated through three interrelated activities:

1. Quality planning
2. Quality control
3. Quality assurance

5.5.1   Quality Planning

One of the guiding principles of Scrum is to develop the functionality of the highest priority to the customer first. Less important features are developed in subsequent Sprints or can be left out altogether according to the customer's requirements. This approach gives the Scrum Team the required time to focus on the quality of essential functionality. A key benefit of quality planning is the reduction of technical debt. Technical debt— also referred to as design debt or code debt—refers to the work that teams prioritize lower, omit, or do not complete as they work toward creating the primary deliverables associated with the project's product. Technical debt accrues and must be paid in the future.

Some causes of technical debt can include the following:

- Quick-fix and building deliverables that do not comply with standards for quality, security, long-term architecture goals, etc.
- Inadequate or incomplete testing
- Improper or incomplete documentation
- Lack of coordination among different team members, or if different Scrum Teams start working in isolation, with less focus on final integration of components required to make a project or program successful
- Poor sharing of business knowledge and process knowledge among the stakeholders and project teams
- Too much focus on short-term project goals instead of the long-term objectives of the company. This oversight can result in poor-quality Working Deliverables that incur significant maintenance and upgrade costs.

In Scrum projects, any technical debt is not carried over beyond a Sprint, because there should be clearly defined Acceptance and Done Criteria. The functionality must satisfy these criteria to be considered Done. As the Prioritized Product Backlog is groomed and User Stories are prioritized, the team creates Working Deliverables regularly, preventing the accumulation of significant technical debt. The Scrum Guidance Body may also include documentation and definition of processes which help in decreasing technical debt.

To maintain a minimal amount of technical debt, it is important to define the product required from a Sprint and the project along with the Acceptance Criteria, any development methods to be followed, and the key responsibilities of Scrum Team members in regards to quality. Defining Acceptance Criteria is an important part of quality planning and it allows for effective quality control to be carried out during the project.

Technical debt is a very big challenge with some traditional project management techniques where development, testing, documentation, etc. are done sequentially and often-times by different persons, with no one person being responsible for any particular Working Deliverable. As a result, technical debt accrues, leading to significantly higher maintenance, integration, and product release costs in the final stages of a project's release. Also, the cost of changes is very high in such circumstances as problems surface in later stages of the project. Scrum framework prevents the issues related to technical debt by ensuring that Done deliverables with Acceptance Criteria are defined as part of the Sprint Backlog and key tasks including

5

development, testing, and documentation are done as part of the same Sprint and by the same Scrum Team.

5.5.1.1 Continuous Integration and Sustainable Pace

Maintaining a sustainable pace is one of the most important tenets of Scrum. Sustainable pace translates to increased employee satisfaction, stability, and increased estimation accuracy, all of which ultimately leads to increased customer satisfaction. To develop a truly high quality product and maintain a healthy work environment, it is important to carry out integration-type activities regularly, rather than delaying the integration work until the end in such circumstances. To provide value at frequent intervals, the team should continuously develop, test, and integrate the functionalities of each Prioritized Product Backlog Item (PBI) in every Sprint with the use of techniques, such as continuous integration and automated product testing. It is also important, from the team's point of view, to ensure that the effort expended in the current Sprint is similar to the effort spent in the preceding Sprint in order to sustain an even pace throughout the project Sprints. This helps the team avoid phases of intense periods of work, ensuring they are always able to put forth the level of effort required to accomplish the work that needs to be done.

5.5.2 Quality Control and Quality Assurance

Quality control refers to the execution of the planned quality activities by the Scrum Team in the process of creating deliverables that are potentially shippable. It also includes learning from each set of completed activities in order to achieve continuous improvement. Within the cross-functional team, it is important to have the skills necessary to perform quality control activities. During the Sprint Retrospect Meeting, team members discuss lessons learned. These lessons act as inputs into continuous improvement and contribute to the improvement of ongoing quality control.

Quality is required not only in products, but also in processes. Quality assurance refers to the evaluation of processes and standards that govern quality management in a project to ensure that they continue to be relevant. Quality assurance activities are carried out as part of the work. In fact, quality assurance is a significant factor of the definition of Done. The deliverable isn't complete if appropriate quality assurance has not been conducted. Often, quality assurance is demonstrated during the Sprint Review Meeting.

Product Owners for respective projects, programs, and portfolios can monitor and evaluate quality assurance activities to ensure each team continues to agree and comply with the quality standards that have been set. End-to-end quality assurance may be addressed during final testing of the product, a Release, or a Sprint. A comparison of the number of issues encountered versus the number of User Stories completed can be done. The product components that have defects can be incorporated as Prioritized Product Backlog Items (PBIs), which can be worked upon by either the team or by one person at certain times during the Sprint, depending on the number of defects.

At times, the Scrum Guidance Body can define the processes and documents that can be referred to by Scrum Teams when doing their projects to ensure that uniform quality norms are followed by all projects within the company.

5.5.3   Plan-Do-Check-Act (PDCA) Cycle

The Plan-Do-Check-Act Cycle—also known as the Deming or Shewhart Cycle—was developed by Dr. W. Edwards Deming, considered the father of modern quality control and Dr. Walter A. Shewhart. The following are some important points of Deming's philosophy:

- Management guidelines define quality. When management is able to provide a conducive environment and is able to motivate its employees to improve quality on a continuous basis, each employee will be able to make a contribution toward a superior quality product. Deming's "Theory of Profound Knowledge" advocates what management should do in order to create an environment in which each employee can make significant contributions to quality improvement.

Deming modified Plan-Do-Check-Act to Plan-Do-Study-Act (PDSA) because he felt the term 'Study' emphasized analysis rather than simply inspection, as implied by the term 'Check.'

Both Scrum and the Deming/Shewhart/PDCA Cycle are iterative methods that focus on continuous improvement. Figure 5-3 illustrates the stages of the PDCA Cycle and their correlation with various Scrum processes.

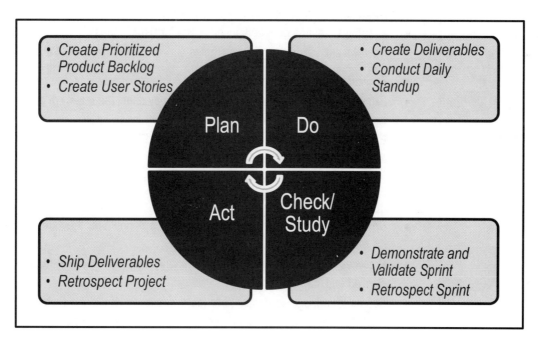

Figure 5-3: PDCA Cycle in Scrum

5.6   Summary of Responsibilities

Role	Responsibilities
Scrum Guidance Body	• Provides definition of Done • Provides framework and guidance for developing Acceptance Criteria • Defines the range of tools that can be used by the Scrum Team to develop and verify the product
Portfolio Product Owner	• Sets minimum Acceptance Criteria for the entire portfolio • Reviews portfolio Deliverables
Portfolio Scrum Master	• Ensures that a sustainable pace is maintained in which the focus is on quality of features rather than strictly on velocity
Program Product Owner	• Sets the minimum Acceptance Criteria for the entire program • Reviews program Deliverables
Program Scrum Master	• Ensures that a sustainable pace is maintained in which the focus is on quality of features rather than strictly on velocity
Stakeholder(s)	• Reviews and accepts the Deliverables and final product
Product Owner	• States the business requirements for the product and defines requirements clearly in the Prioritized Product Backlog • Assesses viability and ensures that Deliverables meet the quality requirements • Sets the minimum Acceptance Criteria for the entire project, including the Acceptance Criteria of the respective program • Facilitates creation of Acceptance Criteria for User Stories • Reviews and validates the Deliverables during *Demonstrate and Validate Sprint*
Scrum Master	• Facilitates a 'team first' mentality when it comes to quality • Eliminates environmental obstructions that may affect the quality of deliverables and processes • Ensures that a sustainable pace is maintained in which the focus is on quality of features rather than strictly on velocity • Ensures that Scrum processes are correctly followed by all team members, including the Product Owner
Scrum Team	• Develops and maintains all Deliverables during Sprints until they are handed over to the end users • Practices and encourages good communication so that the requirements are clarified and fully understood • Shares knowledge to ensure that team members familiarize themselves with the whole feature set and therefore benefit from the experience of others • Makes appropriate changes to Deliverables swiftly

Table 5-1: Summary of Responsibilities Relevant to Quality

5.7   Scrum vs. Traditional Project Management

Although there are similarities in Scrum and traditional project management methods with regard to definition of 'quality' (i.e., the ability of the product to meet the agreed Acceptance Criteria and achieve the business value expected by the customer), differences exist in terms of how the approaches address the implementation and achievement of the required quality levels.

In traditional project management methods, the users clarify their expectations; the project manager defines those expectations in measurable terms and gains agreement from the users. After detailed planning, the project team develops the product over an agreed period of time. If any of the agreed criteria are to be changed, changes can happen only through a formal change management system where impact of changes is estimated and the Project Manager gets approval from all relevant stakeholders.

In Scrum, however, the Product Owner collaborates with the Scrum Team and defines the Acceptance Criteria for the User Stories related to the product to be delivered. The Scrum Team then develops the product in a series of short iterations called Sprints. The Product Owner can make changes to the requirements to keep pace with the user needs and these changes can be addressed by the Scrum Team either by terminating the current Sprint or including the adjusted requirements in the next Sprint as each Sprint is of very short duration (i.e., one to six weeks).

One of the major advantages of Scrum is the emphasis on creating potentially shippable deliverables at the end of each Sprint cycle, instead of at the end of the entire project. So, the Product Owner and customers constantly inspect, approve, and accept Deliverables after each Sprint. Also, even if a Scrum project is terminated early, there is some value created prior to termination through the Deliverables created in individual Sprints.

5

6. CHANGE

6.1 Introduction

Every project, regardless of its method or framework is exposed to change. It is imperative that project team members understand that the Scrum development processes are designed to embrace change. Organizations should try to maximize the benefits that arise from change and minimize any negative impacts through diligent change management processes in accordance with the principles of Scrum.

Change, as defined in *A Guide to the Scrum Body of Knowledge* (SBOK™ Guide), is applicable to the following:

- Portfolios, programs, and/or projects in *any* industry
- Products, services, or any other results to be delivered to stakeholders
- Projects of any size or complexity

The term "product" in the *SBOK™ Guide* may refer to a product, service, or other deliverable. Scrum can be applied effectively to any project in any industry—from small projects or teams with as few as six team members to large, complex projects with up to several hundred team members.

This chapter is divided into the following sections:

6.2 Roles Guide—This section provides guidance on which sections are relevant for each of the primary Scrum roles: Product Owner, Scrum Master, and Scrum Team.

6.3 Overview—This section defines the concept of change, specifically within the context of Scrum processes. It also addresses how Change Requests are handled in Scrum processes.

6.4 Change in Scrum—This section details the importance of effectively managing change in a Scrum project. It also addresses how flexibility and stability can be achieved through appropriate handling of the Change Requests that arise throughout a project.

6.5 Integrating Change—This section details how Change Requests are assessed and approved (or rejected) when applying the Scrum framework.

6.6 Change to Programs and Portfolios—This section describes the impact of changes to programs and portfolios.

6.7 Summary of Responsibilities—This section defines the change management responsibilities of project team members.

6.8 Scrum vs. Traditional Project Management—This section discusses the benefits of managing change using Scrum methods over the methods used in traditional project management models.

6.2   Roles Guide

1. Product Owner—The responsibility of initiating change in a project lies primarily with the Product Owner; therefore, this entire chapter is applicable to this role.

2. Scrum Master—The Scrum Master should also be familiar with this entire chapter with primary focus on sections 6.3, 6.4, 6.5, and 6.7.

3. Scrum Team—The Scrum Team should mainly focus on sections 6.3, 6.4.2, 6.5 and 6.7.

6.3   Overview

Change is inevitable in all projects. In today's hypercompetitive world where technology, market conditions, and business patterns are continuously shifting, change is the only constant.

A primary principle of Scrum is its acknowledgement that a) stakeholders (e.g., customers, users, and sponsors) do change their minds about what they want and need throughout a project (sometimes referred to as 'requirements churn') and b) that it is very difficult, if not impossible, for stakeholders to define all requirements during project initiation.

Scrum development projects welcome change by using small development cycles that incorporate customer feedback on the project's deliverables after each Sprint. This enables the customer to regularly interact with the Scrum Team members, view product increments as they are ready, and change requirements earlier on in the development cycle. Also, the portfolio or program management teams can respond to Change Requests pertaining to Scrum projects applicable at their level.

Scrum embodies a key principle from the Agile Manifesto (Fowler and Highsmith, 2001): "Responding to change over following a plan." Scrum is practiced on the basis of embracing change and turning it into a competitive advantage. Therefore, it is more important to be flexible than to follow a strict, predefined plan. This means it is essential to approach project management in an adaptive manner that enables change throughout rapid product development or service development cycles.

Being adaptive to change is a key advantage of the Scrum framework. Although Scrum works well for all projects in all industries, it can be very effective when the product or other project requirements are not fully understood or cannot be well defined up front, when the product's market is volatile, and/or when the focus is on making the team flexible enough to incorporate changing requirements. Scrum is especially useful for complex projects with a lot of uncertainty. Long-term planning and forecasting is typically ineffective for such projects and they involve high quantities of risk. Scrum guides the team through *transparency*, *inspection*, and *adaptation* to the most valuable business outcomes.

6.3.1   Unapproved and Approved Change Requests

Request for changes are usually submitted as Change Requests. Change Requests remain unapproved until they get formally approved. The Scrum Guidance Body usually defines a process for approving and managing changes throughout the organization. In the absence of a formal process, it is recommended that small changes that do not have significant impact on the project be directly approved by the Product Owner. The tolerance for such small changes could be defined at an organizational level or by the sponsor for a particular project. In most projects, 90% of Change Requests could be classified as small changes that should be approved by the Product Owner. So, the Product Owner plays a very important role in managing changes in a Scrum Project.

Changes that are beyond the tolerance level of the Product Owner may need approval from relevant stakeholders working with the Product Owner.

At times, if a requested change could have a substantial impact on the project or organization, approval from senior management (e.g., Executive Sponsor, Portfolio Product Owner, Program Product Owner, or Chief Product Owner) may be required.

Change Requests for the project are discussed and approved during the *Develop Epic(s), Create Prioritized Product Backlog,* and *Groom Prioritized Product Backlog* processes. *Approved Change Requests* are then prioritized along with other product requirements and their respective User Stories and then incorporated into the Prioritized Product Backlog.

Figure 6-1 summarizes the change approval process and Figure 6-2 explains how Prioritized Product Backlog is updated with approved changes.

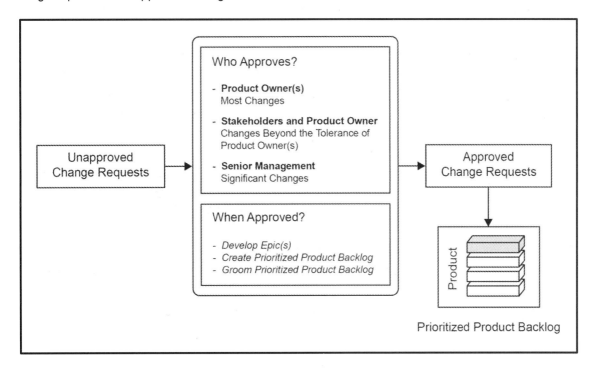

Figure 6-1: Sample Change Approval Process

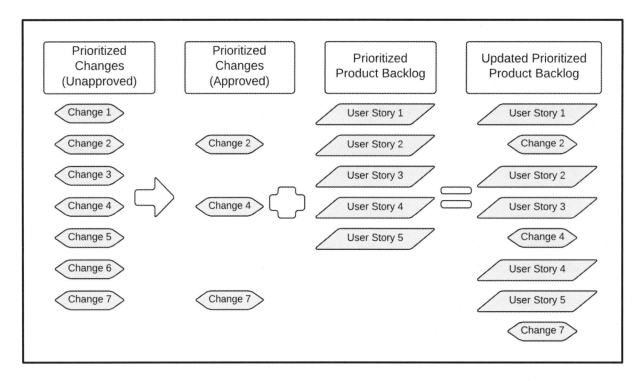

Figure 6-2: Updating Prioritized Product Backlog with Approved Changes

6.4   Change in Scrum

6.4.1   Balancing Flexibility and Stability

Scrum helps organizations become more flexible and open to change. However, it is important to understand that although the Scrum framework emphasizes flexibility, it is also important to maintain stability throughout the change process. In the same way that extreme rigidity is ineffective, extreme flexibility is also unproductive. The key is to find the right balance between flexibility and stability because stability is needed in order to get work done. Therefore, Scrum uses iterative delivery and its other characteristics and principles to achieve this balance. Scrum maintains flexibility in that Change Requests can be created and approved at any time during the project; however, they get prioritized when the Prioritized Product Backlog is created or updated. At the same time, Scrum ensures that stability is maintained by keeping the Sprint Backlog fixed and by not allowing interference with the Scrum Team during a Sprint.

In Scrum, all requirements related to an ongoing Sprint are frozen during the Sprint. No change is introduced until the Sprint ends, unless a change is deemed to be significant enough to stop the Sprint. In the case of an urgent change, the Sprint is terminated and the team meets to plan a new Sprint. This is how Scrum accepts changes without creating the problem of changing release dates.

6.4.2   Achieving Flexibility

Scrum facilitates flexibility through *transparency*, *inspection*, and *adaptation* to ultimately achieve the most valuable business outcomes. Scrum provides an adaptive mechanism for project management in which a change in requirements can be accommodated without significantly impacting overall project progress. It is necessary to adapt to emerging business realities as part of the development cycle. Flexibility in Scrum is achieved through five key characteristics (see Figure 6-3): iterative product development, Time-boxing, cross-functional teams, customer value-based prioritization, and continuous integration.

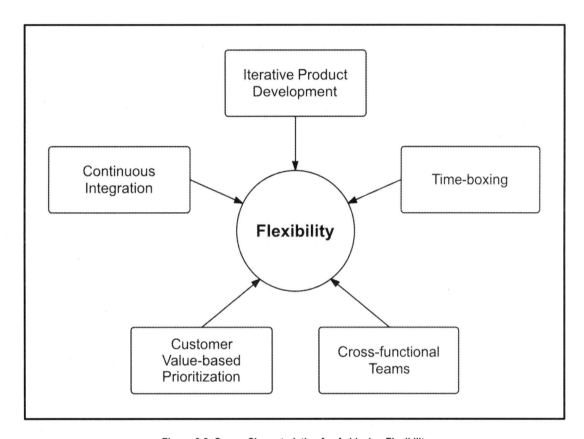

Figure 6-3: Scrum Characteristics for Achieving Flexibility

6.4.2.1 Flexibility through Iterative Product Development

Scrum follows an iterative and incremental approach to product and service development, making it possible to incorporate change at any step in the development process. As the product is developed, a Change Request for the project can come from multiple sources as follows:

1. **Stakeholders**

   Project stakeholders—particularly sponsors, customers, and users—may submit Change Requests at any time throughout the project. Change Requests could be due to change in market conditions, organizational direction, legal or regulatory issues, or various other reasons. Moreover, stakeholders may submit Change Requests as they are reviewing the deliverables during the *Demonstrate and Validate Sprint*, *Retrospect Sprint*, or *Retrospect Project* processes. All Change Requests get added to the Project Prioritized Product Backlog (also referred to as Prioritized Product Backlog or Product Backlog) once approved. Figure 6-4 demonstrates some of the reasons that stakeholders initiate the Change Request process.

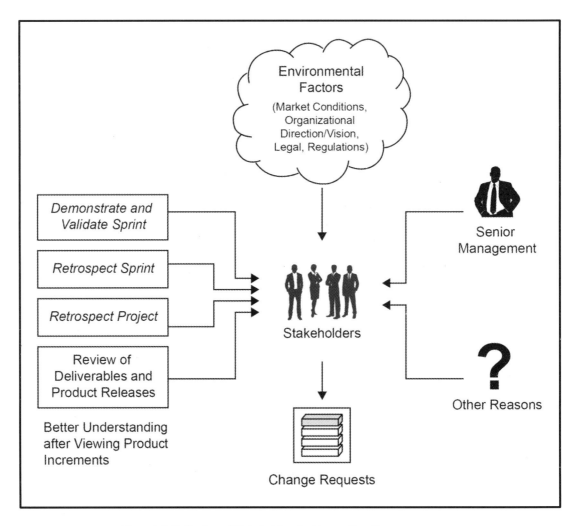

Figure 6-4: Motivation of Stakeholders for Requesting Changes

2. Scrum Core Team

The Scrum Core Team (i.e., the Product Owner, Scrum Master, and Scrum Team) are involved in creating the product deliverables. Ongoing interaction between the Scrum Core Team members in a Scrum Team and others, such as other Scrum Teams in the project, and internal and external project stakeholders, may motivate Scrum Core Team members to suggest changes or improvements to the product, service, or some other part of the project. Usually such changes—like any others—are captured in Change Requests, and the Product Owner makes a final decision about which suggested changes from the Scrum Team and Scrum Master should be considered as formal Change Requests.

There may at times be challenges with creating certain Deliverables, which may result in Change Requests. For example, the team may decide on a new feature to be added or modified to improve product performance. In most Scrum projects, recommendations for changes from the Scrum Core Team happen as Scrum Teams work to *Create Deliverables*, or when they participate in *Conduct Daily Standup Meeting* or *Retrospect Sprint Meetings*. Figure 6-5 demonstrates some of the reasons that the Scrum Core Team may initiate Change Requests.

6

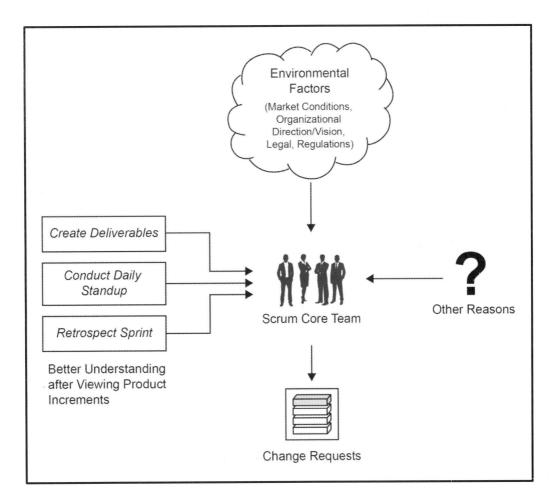

Figure 6-5: Motivation of Scrum Core Team for Requesting Changes

3. **Senior Management**

Senior management—including portfolio and program management—can recommend changes that affect the project. This can be because of changes in the strategic direction of the company, competitive landscape, funding-related issues, and so forth. Note that such changes get added to the Prioritized Product Backlog and need to go through the usual change management process. If any of these changes are urgent, any impacted Sprint may need to be terminated (see section 6.6 for details).

4. **Scrum Guidance Body**

The Scrum Guidance Body may submit Change Requests that affect all projects due to any of the following examples:

- Change in government regulations (e.g., privacy, security standards, or new legislation)
- Corporate directives for quality, security, or other organizational initiatives that need to be implemented across the company
- Benchmarks or best practices to meet a certain standard
- Lessons learned from previous projects, which could be implemented by other Scrum Teams

The hallmark of Scrum is that it is change tolerant and adaptive. Scrum does not promote determining and firmly setting plans way in advance because it operates on the premise that project development is extremely prone to change and risk. The result is a high degree of flexibility and tolerance for change. The project is planned, executed, and managed incrementally, so it is typically easy to incorporate changes throughout.

6.4.2.2   Flexibility through Time-boxing

Time-boxing refers to setting short periods of time for work to be done. If the work undertaken remains incomplete at the end of the Time-box, it is moved into a subsequent Time-box. Examples of Time-boxing include limiting the Daily Standup Meetings to 15 minutes and setting Sprint durations to be one to six weeks. Time-boxes provide the structure needed for Scrum projects, which have an element of uncertainty, are dynamic in nature, and are prone to frequent changes. Time-boxes aid in gauging the progress of the project and allow the team to easily identify when they may need to modify a process or approach.

Time-boxed Sprints contribute greatly toward meeting deadlines and achieving high levels of productivity. Sprints promote order and consistency in a volatile work environment. They provide a platform to gauge results and obtain feedback in a short span of time. Sprints also allow for frequent assessment of progress and the methods used to manage the project, including effective change management. Errors or problems can be identified early and can be rectified quickly.

By using Time-boxing in Sprints, the team frequently revisits the process of estimating the work to be done, so the projection of time and effort required becomes more accurate with each subsequent Sprint as the project progresses. These iterative cycles also motivate team members to achieve projected targets and incremental goals toward reaching the larger objective.

6.4.2.3   Flexibility through Cross-functional and Self-organized Teams

The cross-functional and self-organized structures of the Scrum Team allow team members to be extremely focused on the desired Sprint results. The team has a defined set of objectives during each Sprint and the flexibility to account for a change in objectives prior to beginning the next Sprint.

The use of cross-functional teams also ensures that all of the skills and knowledge required to carry out the work of the project exists within the team itself. This provides an efficient working model that result in the creation of deliverables that are potentially shippable and ready for demonstration to the Product Owner and/or other stakeholders.

Self-organization ensures that Scrum Team members determine on their own, *how* to do the work of the project without a senior manager micromanaging their tasks.

Having cross-functional and self-organized teams allows the group to adapt and effectively manage the ongoing work and any minor issues or changes without having to obtain support or expertise from members outside the team, and in the process, create deliverables that are ready to be shipped if necessary.

6.4.2.4   Flexibility through Customer Value-based Prioritization

The prioritization of requirements and work in a Scrum project is always determined based on the value provided to the customer. First, at the start of a project, the initial requirements are prioritized based on the value each requirement will provide—this is documented in the Prioritized Product Backlog. Then, when a request is made for a new requirement or a change to an existing one, it is evaluated during the *Groom Prioritized Product Backlog* process. If the change is deemed to provide more value than other existing requirements, it will be added and prioritized accordingly in the updated Prioritized Product Backlog. So, the Prioritized Product Backlog provides scope for incorporating changes and adding new requirements when necessary.

It is important to note that new requirements and changes added to the Prioritized Product Backlog may lower the priority of other existing User Stories in the Backlog: so, such lower prioritized User Stories may be implemented later depending on their new prioritization. Because customers are very closely involved with the prioritization of requirements and their corresponding User Stories in the Prioritized Product Backlog, this practice ensures that the requirements that customers deem as "high value" get completed sooner and that the project starts delivering significant value much earlier on.

6.4.2.5   Flexibility through Continuous Integration

Using continuous integration techniques, Scrum Team members can incorporate new and modified features into the deliverables whenever possible. This mitigates the risk of multiple team members making changes to redundant components (e.g., obsolete code in software products, old designs for manufacturing parts). This ensures that only the latest feature or version is being worked on and avoids compatibility issues.

6.5   Integrating Change

Depending on the industry and type of project, the priority of features and requirements for a project may remain fixed for significant durations of time, or they may change frequently. If project requirements are generally stable, there are typically only minor changes made to the Prioritized Product Backlog throughout development, and Scrum Teams can work sequentially completing requirements that will provide maximum customer value as prioritized in the Prioritized Product Backlog. The length of the Sprint is usually longer, 4 to 6 weeks, in such stable environments.

If project requirements change throughout the project, for example due to changed business requirements, the same method continues to be effective. Before beginning a Sprint—during the *Create Prioritized Product Backlog* or *Groom Prioritized Product Backlog* processes—the highest priority requirements in the Prioritized Product Backlog are typically selected to be completed in that Sprint. Because changes have been accounted for in the Prioritized Product Backlog, the team only needs to determine how many tasks they can accomplish in the Sprint based on time and resources provided. Change management is executed in the ongoing processes of prioritizing and adding tasks to the Prioritized Product Backlog.

6.5.1   Changes to a Sprint

If there is a Change Request that may have significant impact on a Sprint in progress, the Product Owner, after consultation with relevant stakeholders, decides whether the change can wait until the next Sprint or represents an urgent situation which may require ending the current Sprint and starting a new one.

Scrum framework clearly specifies that the scope of a Sprint cannot be changed once the Sprint begins. If the required change is so important that the results of the Sprint would be worthless without it, then the Sprint should be terminated. If not, then the change is incorporated into a later Sprint (as shown in Figure 6-6).

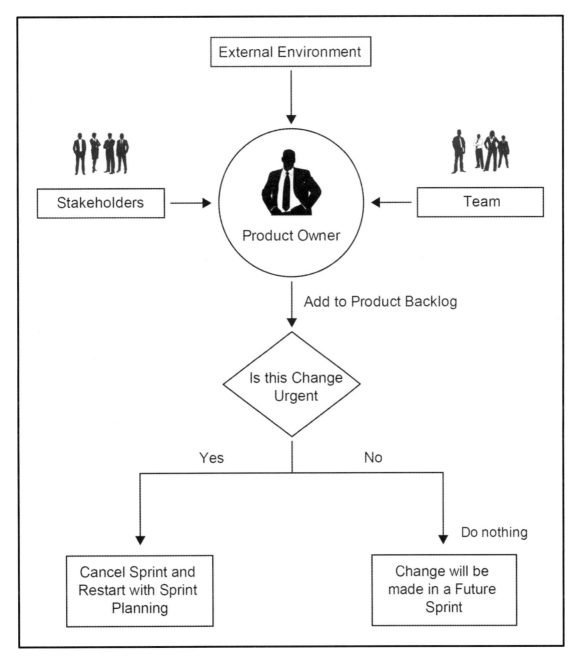

Figure 6-6: Integrating Change in Scrum

There is only one exception to this rule about not changing the scope of a Sprint once a Sprint begins. If the Scrum Team determines it has heavily overestimated the effort during the Sprint and has spare capacity to implement additional User Stories, the team can ask the Product Owner which additional User Stories should be included in the current Sprint.

By locking down the scope of every Sprint, the team is able to efficiently optimize and manage their work and effort. An additional benefit is that the team does not have to worry about managing changes once they start working on a Sprint. This is a big advantage of the Scrum framework as compared with traditional project management.

In traditional project management, changes can be requested and approved anytime during the project's lifecycle. This often creates confusion for project team members, decreases team motivation due to discontinuity, and results in a lack of focus and the team feeling that "nothing ever gets done." On the other hand, in Scrum projects, changes are not allowed once a Sprint starts. This ensures that in every Sprint, the team completes deliverables and tasks are Done. Furthermore, the business recognizes tangible benefits from potentially shippable Deliverables at the end of each Sprint.

Moreover, since the Product Owner and Stakeholders are aware that changes are not allowed once a Sprint begins and a Sprint lasts between 1 and 6 weeks, they define and prioritize requirements during the appropriate processes of *Create Epic(s)*, *Create Prioritized Product Backlog*, and *Groom Prioritized Product Backlog*.

6.5.1.1   Impact of Expected Change on the Length of Sprint

Because changes are not allowed during a Sprint, the impact and frequency of expected changes may have an impact on the decision related to the length of the Sprint when it is determined during the *Conduct Release Planning* process.

If project requirements are generally stable and major changes are not expected in the near future, the Length of a Sprint may be set to be longer, 4 to 6 weeks. This provides stability to the Scrum Team members to work on the Prioritized Product Backlog requirements for lengthy periods of time without having to go through the *Create User Stories*, *Approve, Estimate, and Commit User Stories*, *Create Tasks*, *Estimate Task*, and other related processes that are conducted for every Sprint.

However, if project requirements are not very well defined or if significant changes are expected in the immediate future, the Length of Sprint may be relatively shorter, 1 to 3 weeks. This provides stability to the Scrum Team members to work on shorter Sprints and deliver results, which can be evaluated by the Product Owner and stakeholders at the end of the Sprint. This also provides enough flexibility for them to clarify requirements and make changes to the Prioritized Product Backlog at the end of each Sprint.

To get maximum benefits from a Scrum project, it is always recommended to keep the Sprint Time-boxed to 4 weeks, unless there are projects with very stable requirements, where Sprints can extend up to 6 weeks.

Figure 6-7 depicts the impact of expected change on the Length of Sprint.

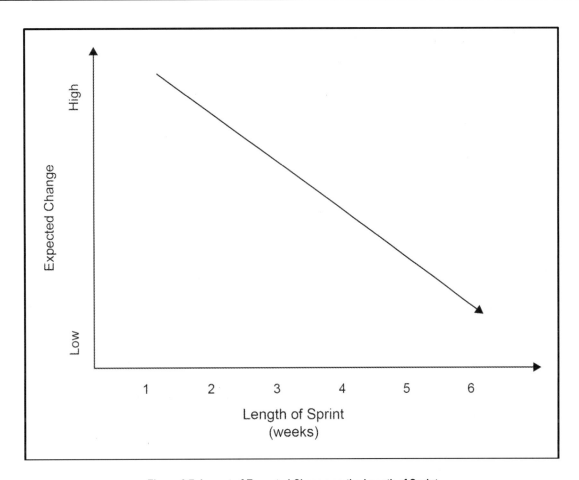

Figure 6-7: Impact of Expected Change on the Length of Sprint

However, it is important to note that expected change is not the only factor used to determine the Length of Sprint. Other factors that also need to be considered include:

- Actual time to get work done (if the project or corporate environment needs a specific time to get tasks done, that could determine the Length of Sprint)
- Planned date for a release (the Length of Sprint should take into consideration the release dates for the overall product or service)
- Any other factor as determined by the Product Owner or Scrum Master, that need to be considered while determining the Length of Sprint

It is important to note that changing the Length of Sprint should not be decided lightly or periodically (e.g. it is not advisable to have the sprint length as 3 weeks this sprint, 2 weeks the next, 4 weeks for the third sprint etc.) Length of Sprint should preferably be consistent. One of the greatest impacts of changing the Length of Sprint is that it causes a reset on all tracking at the project level. Previous velocities may become useless for forecasting and planning of future Sprints. Without an accurate velocity (which is a primary metric in any scrum project), the Scrum Team cannot be measured for effectiveness or adequately choose the number of User Stories to take on when planning for the next sprint. So, once the Length of Sprint is decided, it should preferably be kept constant over the duration of the project or through multiple Sprint cycles.

6.5.1.2 Managing Changes through Prioritized Product Backlog Grooming

A typical Prioritized Product Backlog will contain all User Stories, their time estimates (including any revised estimates), and the status of higher priority requirements. Any new or revised User Stories resulting from changes to business requirements, customer requests, external market conditions, and/or lessons learned from previous Sprints are also incorporated.

One of the Product Owner's key responsibilities is grooming the Prioritized Product Backlog to ensure the prioritized requirements in the Prioritized Product Backlog to be included in the next two to three Sprints are refined into suitable User Stories. It is recommended that the Product Owner should spend a significant amount of the time in each Sprint for Prioritized Product Backlog grooming. The Product Owner is responsible for adding and revising Prioritized Product Backlog Items in response to any changes and is responsible for providing more detailed User Stories that will be used for the next Sprint.

Grooming helps ensure that refining of requirements and their User Stories is done well in advance of the Sprint Planning Meeting so that the team has a well-analyzed and clearly defined set of stories that can be easily broken down into tasks and subsequently estimated. Based on lessons learned from the current Sprint, there may be changes to requirements, or there may be reprioritization that can be easily incorporated into subsequent Sprints. Grooming supports and enhances the flexibility of the Scrum model by incorporating the latest business and technical insights into future Sprints.

A Product Backlog Review Meeting (also referred to as a Prioritized Product Backlog Grooming Session) is a formal meeting during the *Groom Prioritized Product Backlog* process, which helps the Scrum Team review and gain consensus about the Prioritized Product Backlog. However, other than the Prioritized Product Backlog Review Meeting, Prioritized Product Backlog grooming should happen throughout the project and can include situations in which the Product Owner writes new User Stories or reprioritizes User Stories in the existing Prioritized Product Backlog, Scrum Team members or Stakeholders give their suggestions about new User Stories to the Product Owner, and so forth.

It is important to note that any item in the Prioritized Product Backlog is always open for re-estimation until the Sprint Backlog is finalized in the *Create Sprint Backlog* process. After that, changes can continue to be made until immediately prior to the Sprint Planning Meeting, if required.

6.5.1.2.1 Effective Product Backlog Review Meeting (or Prioritized Product Backlog Grooming Session)

The Product Owner takes the lead in a Product Backlog Review Meeting which is conducted during the *Groom Prioritized Product Backlog* process. It is important that the Product Owner sets the objectives and ideally develop an agenda before the Product Backlog Review Meeting begins. Without these, the session will be unstructured and may prove unproductive. It is also important to limit the number of stakeholders participating in the meeting. Having too many participants tends to decrease the overall efficiency of the meeting. The Product Owner should invite only those stakeholders whose feedback is required for the grooming session. All Scrum Team members should be included because their input is valuable to the work being done and any issues encountered. If the grooming session results in any reprioritization of or change in the Prioritized Product Backlog, it is important that the team is in agreement with those changes.

An effective grooming session should result in clearly defined Prioritized Product Backlog Items (PBIs) so that the Scrum Team clearly understands what the customer's requirements are. This also helps the team become familiar with all User Stories in case one or more of them needs to be included in a Sprint on short notice. Acceptance and Done Criteria may also be discussed during grooming sessions.

Scrum does not Time-box grooming exercises. Prioritized Product Backlog grooming is a continuous activity for the Product Owner.

6.5.1.3   Managing Changes During Demonstrate and Validate Sprint

Although the Product Owner has the final say on Prioritized Product Backlog Items and whether to accept or reject any User Stories (corresponding to Approved Change Requests) presented during the *Demonstrate and Validate Sprint* process, it is the Scrum Master's responsibility to ensure that the requirements and Acceptance Criteria are not altered during the Sprint Review Meeting for the User Stories completed in the current Sprint. This prevents the rejection of completed User Stories based on the fact that they do not meet newly changed requirements. If any requirements need to be changed, any corresponding PBI needs to be revised to accommodate the modified requirements in a future Sprint.

6.6   Change in Portfolios and Programs

Any change that arises in either the programs or portfolios may have a cascading effect on all dependent projects and Sprints. Therefore, it is advisable to minimize changes at these higher levels. If a change is required and all stakeholders are in agreement to make the change at these levels, the following should be kept in mind.

6.6.1   In Portfolio

1. It is not recommended to make changes in between two Portfolio Backlog Meetings.
2. If the change is minor, the Portfolio Product Owner should secure approval from the relevant stakeholders (e.g., sponsor, customer, and end user) and then add the requirements to the Portfolio Backlog. Product Owners of the program and project will consider those requirements for inclusion in future Sprints.
3. If the change is major, the portfolio efforts along with associated programs, projects, and Sprints need to stop, and a Portfolio Backlog Meeting should be conducted to determine next steps.

4. Portfolio Prioritized Product Backlog Meetings (also referred to as Portfolio Backlog Meetings), should be conducted at 4 - 12-month intervals. The frequency and impact of changes to a portfolio largely determine the time duration between two Portfolio Backlog Meetings. If there are several expected changes in portfolio, it is preferable to conduct Portfolio Backlog Meetings at more regular intervals (e.g., 4 - 6 months); but if there are fewer expected changes and if requirements are stable, the duration between two Portfolio Backlog Meetings could be increased (e.g., 9 to 12 months).

6.6.2   In Program

1. It is not recommended to make changes in between two Program Backlog Meetings.
2. If the change is minor, the Program Product Owner should secure approval from the relevant stakeholders (e.g., sponsor, customer, and end user) and the Portfolio Product Owner and then add the requirements to the Program Backlog. Product Owners for the project will consider those requirements for inclusion in future Sprints.
3. If the change is major, the program efforts along with associated projects and Sprints need to stop, and a Prioritized Product Backlog Meeting should be conducted to determine next steps.
4. Program Prioritized Product Backlog Meetings (also referred to as Program Backlog Meetings), should preferably be conducted at 2- to 6-month intervals. The frequency and impact of changes to a program largely determine the time duration between two Program Backlog Meetings. If there are several expected changes in program, it is preferable to conduct Program Backlog Meetings at more regular intervals (e.g., 2 to 3 months); but if there are fewer expected changes and if requirements are stable, the duration between two Program Backlog Meetings could be increased (e.g., 5 to 6 months).

Figure 6-8 demonstrates how changes can be managed within the Scrum flow for both portfolios and programs.

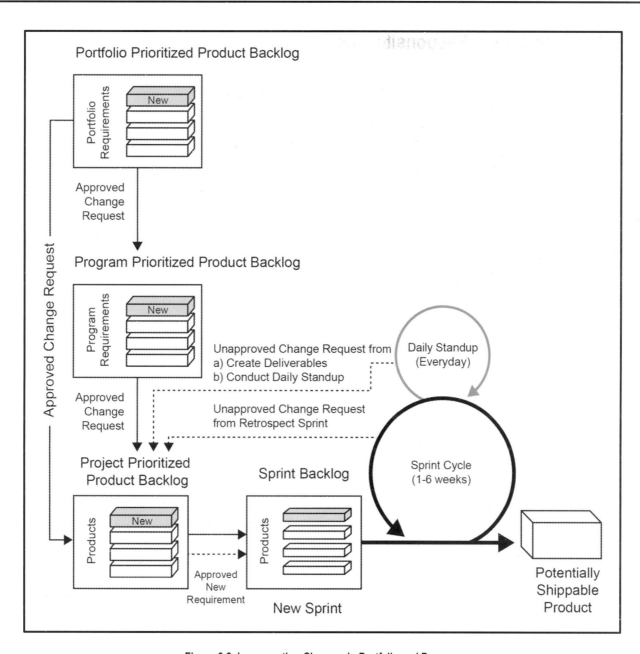

Figure 6-8: Incorporating Changes in Portfolio and Program

6.7   Summary of Responsibilities

Role	Responsibilities
Scrum Guidance Body	• Provides overall guidance for the change management procedures to be followed throughout the project
Portfolio Product Owner	• Provides Change Requests for portfolios • Approves products that are amended, removed, or added according to portfolio requirements
Portfolio Scrum Master	• Facilitates identification, assessment, and management of Change Requests for portfolios
Program Product Owner	• Provides request for change for programs • Approves products that are amended, removed, or added according to program requirements
Program Scrum Master	• Facilitates identification, assessment, and management of Change Requests for programs
Stakeholder(s)	• Provides request for changes • Involved with approving and prioritizing Change Requests
Product Owner	• Provides requests for changes in a project • Assesses the impact of requests for change raised for the portfolio, program, or project • Prioritizes User Stories in the project's Prioritized Product Backlog • Assesses the impact of problems on project objectives identified by the Scrum Team • Provides clear communication to stakeholders on reprioritized Product Backlog Items
Scrum Master	• Facilitates identification, assessment, and escalation of problems and Change Requests by the Scrum Team
Scrum Team	• Suggests improvements or changes during the *Create Deliverables* and *Conduct Daily Standup* processes

Table 6-1: Summary of Responsibilities Relevant to Change

6.8   Scrum vs. Traditional Project Management

Change management in traditionally managed projects is closely related to Configuration Management. All changes are considered based on their magnitude of variation from a baseline value. The Project Manager is given tolerances within which he or she can manage the day-to-day activities and decisions of the project. When a Change Request exceeds the defined tolerances, the Project Manager must escalate the proposed change to higher levels of management and await their decision before implementing the change. The Project Manager first logs the request for change in an Issue Log or Change Log and then escalates the change to higher authorities. These might include the sponsor of the project, as well as other relevant stakeholders and decision makers. At some point, an impact assessment will be conducted. Based on the estimated impact of the change, a decision will be made regarding whether the change should be implemented or not. The Project Manager may also propose possible solutions to any problems posed by the change. If a decision is made by the higher authorities to proceed with making the change, the Project Manager is responsible for ensuring that the change is implemented correctly.

Change in Scrum works very differently as compared with Traditional Project Management. The Scrum framework is highly tuned toward managing changes effectively and efficiently. Whenever the Product Owner or the Scrum Team recognizes a problem or defect or identifies a Prioritized Product Backlog Item that needs to be amended, replaced, or added, the change is made to the Prioritized Product Backlog. Similarly, senior management, the Product Owner, or Stakeholder(s) can add Change Requests to the Prioritized Product Backlog. The Product Owner and Stakeholder(s) approve Change Requests and reprioritize the Backlog accordingly. Whenever there is a problem or new requirement that needs to be addressed immediately and mandates a change affecting the current Sprint, the Product Owner terminates the Sprint, with approval from relevant stakeholders. Once terminated, the Sprint will be re-planned and restarted to incorporate the new requirements.

However, if the problem or change is not major and does not warrant a change within the current Sprint, the change will be added to the Prioritized Product Backlog and incorporated into the planning for a subsequent Sprint. This gives stakeholders the ability to respond to changes in the external environment, while still maintaining a certain degree of control over the ongoing activities within the project. Also, at the end of each Sprint, Done deliverables are demonstrated by the Scrum Team. These deliverables are potentially shippable and can be reviewed by the Product Owner and other stakeholders.

6

7. RISK

7.1 Introduction

The purpose of this chapter is to define risk, discuss the management of risks in a Scrum environment, and consider the tools that facilitate the management of risks. To ensure business viability, reduce the probability of project failure, and make more informed business decisions, it is important that risks are effectively managed through a well-organized and methodical approach.

In a Scrum environment, risks are generally minimized, largely due to the work being done in Sprints whereby a continuous series of Deliverables is produced in very short cycles, Deliverables are compared to expectations, and the Product Owner is actively engaged in the project. However, even in the simplest of projects, things can go wrong, so it is important to have a strategy to identify and address risks.

Risk, as defined in *A Guide to the Scrum Body of Knowledge* (*SBOK™ Guide*), is applicable to the following:

- Portfolios, programs, and/or projects in *any* industry
- Products, services, or any other results to be delivered to stakeholders
- Projects of any size or complexity

The term "product" in the *SBOK™ Guide* may refer to a product, service, or other deliverable. Scrum can be applied effectively to any project in any industry—from small projects or teams with as few as six team members to large, complex projects with up to several hundred team members.

This chapter is divided into the following sections:

7.2 Roles Guide—This section provides guidance on which sections are relevant for each Scrum role: Product Owner, Scrum Master, and Scrum Team.

7.3 What is Risk?—This section defines risk and explains how it can affect the objectives of a project and contribute to the success or failure of a project.

7.4 Risk Management Procedure—This section presents key techniques of risk management and elaborates on developing strategies to identify, assess, and manage risks.

7.5 Minimizing Risks through Scrum—This section explains the key aspects of Scrum that make it an ideal management framework for effectively handling risks at various levels—portfolio, program, and project.

7.6 Summary of Responsibilities—This section describes the responsibilities for each person or role on a project relative to risk management.

7.7 Scrum vs. Traditional Project Management—This section discusses the benefits of managing risk using Scrum methods over the methods used in traditional project management models.

7

7.2   Roles Guide

1. Product Owner—The major responsibilities of handling risks in a project lie with the Product Owner; therefore, the entire chapter is most applicable to this role.

2. Scrum Master—The Scrum Master should be familiar with this entire chapter with primary focus on sections 7.3, 7.4, and 7.7.

3. Scrum Team—The Scrum Team should focus primarily on sections 7.3 and 7.7.

7.3   What is Risk?

Risk is defined as an uncertain event that can affect the objectives of a project and may contribute to its success or failure. Risks with a potential for positive impact on the project are called opportunities, whereas threats are risks that could negatively impact a project. Managing risk must be done proactively, and it is an iterative process that should begin at project inception and continue throughout the life of the project. The process of managing risk should follow some standardized steps to ensure that risks are identified, evaluated, and a proper course of action is determined and acted upon accordingly.

Risks should be identified, assessed, and responded to based primarily on two factors: the probability of an occurrence and the probable impact in the event of the occurrence. Risks with high probability and high impact rating should be addressed before those with a lower rating. In general, once a risk is identified, it is important to understand the basic aspects of the risk with regard to the possible causes, the area of uncertainty, and the potential effects if the risk occurs.

7.3.1   Difference between Risks and Issues

Risks are the uncertainties related to a project that could significantly alter the outcome of the project in a positive or negative way. Since risks are future uncertainties, they have no current impact on the project, but could have a potential impact on the future. The following are some examples of risks:

*   Even after extensive training, the customer service representatives might not be ready to take orders on the go-live date.
*   The painting crew might be delayed due to heavy rain, which could negatively impact the project schedule.

Issues are generally well-defined certainties that are currently happening on the project: so there is no need for conducting a probability assessment as we would for a risk. Issues must be dealt with. Some examples of issues include the following:

- Funding is not approved.
- Requirements are unclear.

Risks, if not addressed in time, may become issues. The goal of risk management is to be prepared, with plans in place to deal with any risks that may occur.

7.3.2   Risk Attitude

Stakeholders include all people or organizations impacted by the project as well as those that have the ability to impact the project. It is important to understand the risk attitude of the stakeholders. Risk attitude is influenced by the following three factors:

1. Risk appetite: refers to how much uncertainty the stakeholder or organization is willing to take on.
2. Risk tolerance: indicates the degree, amount, or volume of risk stakeholders will withstand.
3. Risk threshold: refers to the level at which a risk is acceptable to the stakeholder organization. A risk will fall above or below the risk threshold. If it is below, then the stakeholder or organization is more likely to accept the risk.

Essentially, the risk attitude of the stakeholders determines how much risk the stakeholders consider acceptable and hence when they will decide to take actions to mitigate potential adverse impacts of risks. Therefore, it is important to understand the tolerance levels of the stakeholders in relation to various factors including cost, quality, scope, and schedule.

Utility Function is a model used for measuring stakeholder risk preference or attitude toward risk. It defines the stakeholders' level or willingness to accept risk. The three categories of Utility Function are the following:

1. Risk averse: Stakeholder is unwilling to accept a risk no matter what the anticipated benefit or opportunity.
2. Risk neutral: Stakeholder is neither risk averse nor risk seeking and any given decision is not affected by the level of uncertainty of the outcomes. When two possible scenarios carry the same level of benefit, the risk neutral stakeholder will not be concerned if one scenario is riskier than the other.
3. Risk seeking: Stakeholder is willing to accept risk even if it delivers a marginal increase in return or benefit to the project.

7.4   Risk Management Procedure

Risk Management consists of five steps:

1. Risk identification: Using various techniques to identify all potential risks.
2. Risk assessment: Evaluating and estimating the identified risks.
3. Risk prioritization: Prioritizing risk to be included in the Prioritized Product Backlog.
4. Risk mitigation: Developing an appropriate strategy to deal with the risk.
5. Risk communication: Communicating the findings from the first four steps to the appropriate stakeholders and determining their perception regarding the uncertain events.

7.4.1   Risk Identification

The Scrum Team members should attempt to identify all risks that could potentially impact the project. Only by looking at the project from different perspectives, using a variety of techniques, can they do this job thoroughly. Risk Identification is done throughout the project and Identified Risks become inputs to several Scrum processes including *Create Prioritized Product Backlog, Groom Prioritized Product Backlog,* and *Demonstrate and Validate Sprint.*

The following techniques are commonly used to identify risks.

7.4.1.1   Risk Identification Techniques

1. **Review Lessons Learned from Retrospect Sprint or Retrospect Project Processes**

   Learning from similar projects and earlier Sprints in the same project and exploring the uncertainties that affected those projects and Sprints can be a useful way to identify risks.

2. **Risk Checklists**

   Risk checklists can include key points to be considered when identifying risks, common risks encountered in the Scrum project, or even categories of risks that should be addressed by the team. Checklists are a valuable tool to help ensure comprehensive risk identification.

3. **Risk Prompt Lists**

   Risk prompt lists are used in stimulating thoughts regarding the source from which risks may originate. Risk prompt lists for various industries and project types are available publicly.

4. **Brainstorming**

Sessions where relevant stakeholders and members in the Scrum Core Team openly share ideas through discussions and knowledge sharing sessions, which are normally conducted by a facilitator.

5. **Risk Breakdown Structure (RBS)**

One of the key tools used in identifying risks is a risk breakdown structure. In this structure, risks are grouped based on their categories or commonalities. For example, risks may be categorized as financial, technical, or safety related. This allows the team to better plan for and address each risk.

7.4.1.2 Risk-Based Spike

A concept that can be useful in identifying risks is that of a risk-based spike. A spike is an experiment that involves research or prototyping to better understand potential risks. In a spike, an intense two to three day exercise is conducted (preferably at the beginning of a project before the *Develop Epic(s)* or *Create Prioritized Product Backlog* processes) to help the team determine the uncertainties that could affect the project. Risk-based spikes are useful when the Scrum Team is working with and getting accustomed to new technologies or tools, or when User Stories are lengthy. They also help in estimating time and effort more accurately.

7.4.2 Risk Assessment

The assessment of risk helps in understanding the potential impact of a risk, how likely it is to occur, and when the risk could materialize. The overall effect on business value should be estimated; if that impact is significant enough to outweigh the business justification, a decision must be made whether to continue the project.

The assessment of risks is done with regard to probability, proximity, and impact. Probability of risks refers to the likelihood of the risks occurring, whereas proximity refers to when the risk might occur. Impact refers to the probable effect of the risks on the project or the organization.

To estimate the probability of a risks, various techniques may be used, including Probability Trees, Pareto Analysis, and a Probability and Impact Matrix.

In addition to probability, risk assessment also evaluates the potential net effect of risks on the project or organization. These effects can be estimated using techniques such as Risk Models and Expected Monetary Value.

7.4.2.1   Risk Assessment Techniques

1.   Risk Meeting

Risks could be easily prioritized by the Product Owner by calling a meeting of the Scrum Core Team and optionally inviting relevant Stakeholders to the meeting. The team could meet and prioritize different risks based on their subjective assessment of the impact of the risks on project objectives.

2.   Probability Trees

Potential events are represented in a tree with a branch extended for each possible outcome of a risk event. The probability of each possible outcome is indicated on the appropriate branch and then multiplied by its assessed impact to get an expected value for each outcome possibility. The outcome values are then summed together to calculate the overall expected impact of a risk to a project (see Figure 7-1).

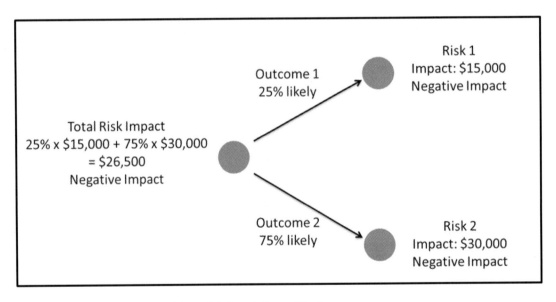

Figure 7-1: Sample Probability Tree

3. Pareto Analysis

This technique of assessing risk involves ranking risks by magnitude which helps the Scrum Team address the risks in the order of their potential impact on the project. For example, in Figure 7-2, Risk 1 has the highest impact and should preferably be addressed first.

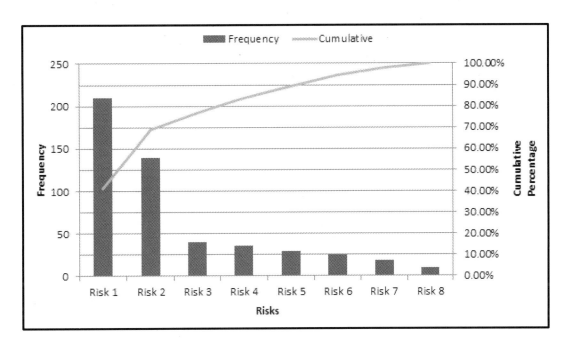

Figure 7-2: Sample Pareto Chart

4. Probability Impact Grid

Each risk is assessed for its probability of occurrence and for its potential impact on project objectives. Generally, a numerical rating is assigned for both probability and impact independently. The two values are then multiplied to derive a risk severity score (or PI value), which can be used to prioritize risks.

For example, the risk severity score for a risk with a Probability of 50% and an Impact rating of .6 would be calculated as follows:

$$0.5(Probability) \times 0.6(Impact) = 0.3$$

The rating schemes used are determined within the organization or for the project. Often a decimal scale is used, from zero to one, where a 0.5 probability rating would indicate 50% likelihood. Other options include a scale of one to ten, or High (3), Medium (2), and Low (1).

Figure 7-3 depicts the use of the decimal scale. Each risk is rated on its probability of occurrence and impact on an objective scale.

Probability and Impact Matrix

Probability	Threats			Opportunities		
0.90	0.09	0.27	0.72	0.72	0.27	0.09
0.75	0.075	0.225	0.60	0.60	0.225	0.075
0.50	0.05	0.15	0.40	0.40	0.15	0.05
0.30	0.03	0.09	0.24	0.24	0.09	0.03
0.10	0.01	0.03	0.08	0.08	0.03	0.01
	Low 0.1	Medium 0.3	High 0.8	High 0.8	Medium 0.3	Low 0.1

Impact

☐ Low PI value   ▨ Moderate PI value   ▩ High PI value

Figure 7-3: Sample Probability and Impact Matrix

The method of assigning probability and impact values to risks varies depending on the project and number of risks being evaluated, as well as existing organizational processes and procedures. However, by applying the simple P x I formula, risk severity can be calculated on a numerical or categorical scale.

5. Expected Monetary Value (EMV)

The monetary value of the risk is based on its Expected Monetary Value (EMV). EMV is calculated by multiplying the monetary impact by the risk's probability, as approximated by the customer.

Expected Monetary Value = Risk impact (in dollars) x Risk probability (as percentage)

For example, a risk with an estimated negative impact of $1,000 and a 50% probability of occurring would result in an EMV as follows:

EMV = $1,000 x 0.50 = $500

7.4.3   Risk Prioritization

Scrum allows for quick identification and assessment of risks. Identified Risks are taken into account when creating a Prioritized Product Backlog during the *Create Prioritized Product Backlog* process, or when we update the Prioritized Product Backlog during the *Groom Prioritized Product Backlog* process—so a Prioritized Product Backlog could also be referred to as a Risk Adjusted Prioritized Product Backlog.

The risks could be identified and assessed based on any of the Risk Identification and Risk Assessment techniques mentioned earlier.

In the *Create Prioritized Product Backlog* or *Groom Prioritized Product Backlog* processes, the prioritized User Stories from the existing Prioritized Product Backlog and the prioritized list of risks are then combined to create an updated Prioritized Product Backlog which includes the Identified Risks:

Steps for updating a Prioritized Product Backlog with Identified Risks:

1. Create a list of prioritized risks. (e.g., the risks can be prioritized by value using Expected Monetary Value technique).

2. Select those Identified Risks that can be mitigated; and for which the team decides to take specific risk action during the Sprint to mitigate such risks.

3. Create a list of User Stories in the Prioritized Product Backlog, which are prioritized by value (e.g., the value of each User Story may be evaluated based on its expected Return on Investment).

4. Combine lists in step 2 and step 3 and prioritize them by value to arrive at the Updated Prioritized Product Backlog.

Figure 7-4 illustrates the risk prioritization process.

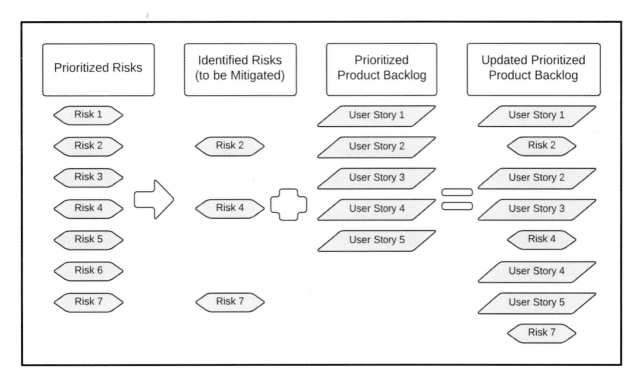

Figure 7-4: Process for Risk Prioritization

7.4.4   Risk Mitigation

The response to each risk will depend on the probability and impact of the risk. However, the iterative nature of Scrum with its rapid turnaround time and feedback cycles allows for early detection of failures; therefore, practically speaking, it has a natural mitigation feature built in.

Risk can be mitigated by implementing a number of responses. In most situations, responses are proactive or reactive. In the case of a risk, a plan B may be formulated, which can be used as a fall-back in case the risk materializes—such a plan B is a reactive response. Sometimes risks are accepted and are an example of a risk response which is neither proactive nor reactive. Risks are accepted because of various reasons, as in a situation where the probability or impact of the risk is too low for a response. Acceptance can also be the case in a situation where the apprehension of secondary risks may deter the product owner from taking any action. The effort made by the Product Owner to reduce the probability or impact—or both—of the risk is an example of a proactive response to mitigating risks.

Once Identified Risks are included as part of the Prioritized Product Backlog (see Figure 7-4), several risks get mitigated during the *Create Deliverables* process when the Tasks related to User Stories defined in the Prioritized Product Backlog process get completed.

In Scrum, the ownership of risk is clearly on the Product Owner for managing risks related to business aspects and on the Scrum Team for implementing risk responses during the course of a Sprint. The Scrum Guidance Body can be approached for advice on the way risk responses are implemented and whether the actions align with the guidelines of the organization as a whole. The Scrum Master keeps a close eye on the potential risks that could affect the project and keeps the Product Owner and Scrum Team informed.

7.4.5   Risk Communication

Because stakeholders have an interest in the project, it is important to communicate with them regarding risks. Information provided to stakeholders related to risk should include potential impact and the plans for responding to each risk. This communication is on-going and should occur in parallel with the four sequential steps discussed thus far—risk identification, assessment, prioritization and mitigation. The Scrum Team may also discuss specific risks related to their Tasks with the Scrum Master during Daily Standup Meetings. The Product Owner is responsible for the prioritization of risks and for communicating the prioritized list to the Scrum Team.

An important tool which can be used for communicating information related to risks is the Risk Burndown Chart.

7.4.5.1   Risk Burndown Chart

Risk management is integral to ensuring value creation; therefore, risk management activities are performed throughout the project lifecycle and not just during project initiation.

Each risk could be assessed using different Risk Assessment tools. However, the preferred tool for assessing risks to create a Risk Burndown Chart is Expected Monetary Value (EMV) as described in section 7.4.2.1.

The information gathered during risk assessment may be used to create a Risk Burndown Chart. This depicts cumulative project risk severity over time. The likelihoods of the various Risks are plotted on top of each other to show cumulative risk on the y-axis. The initial identification and evaluation of risks on the project and the creation of the Risk Burndown Chart are done initially. Then, at predetermined time intervals, new risks may be identified and assessed and remaining risks should be re-evaluated and updated accordingly on the chart. An appropriate time to do this is during the Sprint Planning Meeting. Tracking risks in this manner allows the team to recognize trends in risk exposure and take appropriate action, as necessary.

Figure 7-5 shows a sample Risk Burndown Chart.

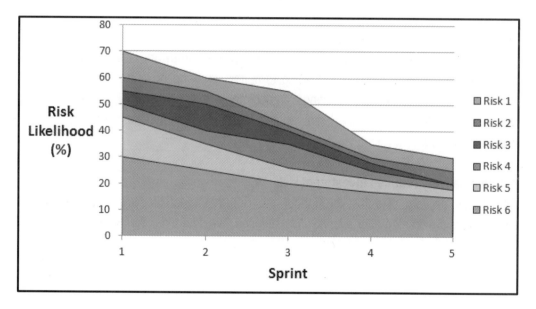

Figure 7-5: Sample Risk Burndown Chart

7.5   Minimizing Risks through Scrum

Being an Agile, iterative process, the Scrum framework inherently minimizes risk. The following Scrum practices facilitate the effective management of risk:

1. **Flexibility reduces business-environment-related risk**

   Risk is largely minimized in Scrum due to the flexibility in adding or modifying requirements at any time in the project lifecycle. This enables the organization to respond to threats or opportunities from the business environment and unforeseen requirements whenever they arise, with usually low cost of managing such risks.

2. **Regular feedback reduces expectations-related risk**

   Being iterative, the Scrum framework gives ample opportunities to obtain feedback and set expectations throughout the project lifecycle. This ensures that the project stakeholders, as well as the team, are not caught off guard by miscommunicated requirements.

3. **Team ownership reduces estimation risk**

   The Scrum Team estimates and takes ownership of the Sprint Backlog Items, which leads to more accurate estimation and timely delivery of product increments

4. **Transparency reduces non-detection risk**

   The Scrum principle of transparency around which the framework is built ensures that risks are detected and communicated early, leading to better risk handling and mitigation. Moreover, when conducting Scrum of Scrums Meetings, Impediments that one team is currently facing may be deemed a risk for other Scrum Teams in the future. This should be recognized in the Updated Impediments Log.

5. **Iterative delivery reduces investment risk**

   Continuous delivery of value throughout the Scrum project lifecycle, as potentially shippable Deliverables are created after every Sprint, reduces investment risk for the customer.

7.6 Risks in Portfolios and Programs

While some risks are specifically related to individual projects, others may originate in programs or portfolios and will generally be managed there itself. However, risks related to a portfolio or program will also impact projects that are part of the respective portfolio or program. During risk assessment in portfolios and programs, if it is determined that a risk may affect an individual project, relevant information about the risk must be communicated to the Product Owner and Scrum Team.

Depending on the severity or priority, when the program or portfolio team communicates a risk that will impact an individual project, the Scrum Team may have to stop and re-plan the current Sprint to address the risk. For less urgent risks, the team can continue the current Sprint and address the risk in a subsequent Sprint.

7.6.1 In Portfolio

1. When risks in Portfolio are identified, the Portfolio Product Owner will need to capture them and assess the proximity, probability, and impact of each identified risk in order to prioritize it and determine the appropriate response for the portfolio.

2. The Portfolio Product Owner will also need to communicate the risks to the relevant stakeholders, the program teams, and the project teams. In some cases, the portfolio team may have to assume the ownership of specific risks.

7.6.2 In Program

1. When program risks are identified, the Program Product Owner should enter them in the program Risk Adjusted Prioritized Product Backlog, assess the proximity, probability, and impact of each identified risk in order to prioritize it and determine the appropriate responses for programs.

2. The Program Product Owner will also need to communicate the risks to relevant stakeholders and the project teams. In some cases, the program team would have to assume ownership of specific risks.

Figure 7-6 demonstrates how risks can be managed within the Scrum flow for both portfolios and programs.

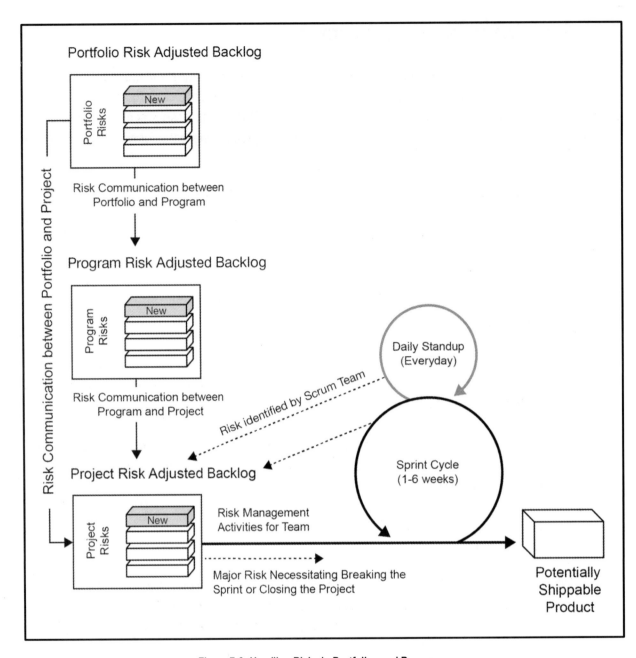

Figure 7-6: Handling Risks in Portfolios and Programs

7.7   Summary of Responsibilities

In Scrum, the risk management activities are divided among various roles with some responsibility resting with everyone in the Scrum Team and the Scrum Master facilitating the process.

Role	Responsibilities
Scrum Guidance Body	• Provides overall guidance for the risk management procedure to be followed throughout the project
Portfolio Product Owner	• Captures and assesses risks for portfolios • Prioritizes and communicates risks to relevant stakeholders, program, and project teams
Portfolio Scrum Master	• Facilitates identification, assessment and communication of risks portfolios
Program Product Owner	• Captures and assesses risks for programs • Prioritizes and communicates risks to relevant stakeholders and project teams
Program Scrum Master	• Facilitates identification, assessment and escalation of risks for programs
Stakeholder(s)	• Interfaces with the Scrum Core Team to provide them inputs on management of risks that affect the achievement of expected outcomes and benefits from the project
Product Owner	• Captures and assesses risks for project • Prioritizes and communicates risks to relevant stakeholders, program, and portfolio teams • Ensures project risk levels are within acceptable limits
Scrum Master	• Facilitates identification and escalation of risks by the Scrum Team
Scrum Team	• Identifies risks during development of the product during the *Create Deliverables* process • Implements risk management activities as advised by the Product Owner

Table 7-1: Summary of Responsibilities Relevant to Risk

7.8   Scrum vs. Traditional Project Management

Scrum and most of the traditional project management methods define risk as 'uncertain event(s) that could positively or negatively affect the achievement of project objectives.' Also, risks are identified, assessed, planned for, and communicated continually.

In Traditional project management models, there is emphasis on detailed upfront planning to identify, assess, and determine risk responses for all project risks. During project execution, any project team member can identify risks and the project manager or the project management office or project support staff can update them in the Risk Log or Risk Register. The project manager regularly monitors and controls all risks and usually identifies specific individuals in the team to take responsibility for different aspects of risks.

In Scrum, any Scrum Team member can identify risks and the Product Owner can update the identified risks in the Risk Adjusted Prioritized Product Backlog. The Scrum principles of Empirical Process Control and Iterative Development enable the Scrum Team to constantly keep identifying risks and adding them to the Prioritized Product Backlog, where such risks are prioritized with other existing User Stories in the backlog, to be mitigated in subsequent Sprints. The Scrum Team has collective responsibilities for managing all risks for the Sprint.

8. INITIATE

This chapter includes the processes related to initiation of a project: *Create Project Vision*, *Identify Scrum Master and Stakeholder(s)*, *Form Scrum Team*, *Develop Epic(s)*, *Create Prioritized Product Backlog*, and *Conduct Release Planning*.

Initiate, as defined in *A Guide to the Scrum Body of Knowledge* (SBOK™ *Guide*), is applicable to the following:

- Portfolios, programs, and/or projects in *any* industry
- Products, services, or any other results to be delivered to stakeholders
- Projects of any size or complexity

The term "product" in the SBOK™ *Guide* may refer to a product, service, or other deliverable. Scrum can be applied effectively to any project in any industry—from small projects or teams with as few as six team members to large, complex projects with up to several hundred team members.

To facilitate the best application of the Scrum framework, this chapter identifies inputs, tools, and outputs for each process as either "mandatory" or "optional." Inputs, tools, and outputs denoted by asterisks (*) are mandatory, whereas those with no asterisks are optional.

It is recommended that the Scrum Team and those individuals being introduced to the Scrum framework and processes focus primarily on the mandatory inputs, tools, and outputs; while Product Owners, Scrum Masters, and other more experienced Scrum practitioners strive to attain a more thorough knowledge of the information in this entire chapter. It is also important to realize that although all processes are defined uniquely in the SBOK™ *Guide*, they are not necessarily performed sequentially or separately. At times, it may be more appropriate to combine some processes, depending on the specific requirements of each project.

This chapter is written from the perspective of one Scrum Team working on one Sprint to produce potentially shippable Deliverables as part of a larger project. However, the information described is equally applicable to entire projects, programs, and portfolios. Additional information pertaining to the use of Scrum for projects, programs, and portfolios is available in chapters 2 through 7, which cover Scrum principles and Scrum aspects.

8

Figure 8-1 provides an overview of the Initiate phase processes, which are as follows:

8.1 Create Project Vision—In this process, the Project Business Case is reviewed to create a Project Vision Statement that will serve as the inspiration and provide focus for the entire project. The Product Owner is identified in this process.

8.2 Identify Scrum Master and Stakeholder(s)—In this process, the Scrum Master and Stakeholders are identified using specific Selection Criteria.

8.3 Form Scrum Team—In this process, Scrum Team members are identified. Normally the Product Owner has the primary responsibility of selecting team members, but often does so in collaboration with the Scrum Master.

8.4 Develop Epic(s)—In this process, the Project Vision Statement serves as the basis for developing Epics. User Group Meetings may be held to discuss appropriate Epics.

8.5 Create Prioritized Product Backlog—In this process, Epic(s) are refined, elaborated, and then prioritized to create a Prioritized Product Backlog for the project. The Done Criteria is also established at this point.

8.6 Conduct Release Planning—In this process, the Scrum Core Team reviews the User Stories in the Prioritized Product Backlog to develop a Release Planning Schedule, which is essentially a phased deployment schedule that can be shared with the project stakeholders. The Length of Sprints is also determined in this process.

8.1 Create Project Vision

INPUTS
1. Project Business Case*
2. Program Product Owner
3. Program Scrum Master
4. Program Stakeholder(s)
5. Chief Product Owner
6. Program Product Backlog
7. Trial Project
8. Proof of Concept
9. Company Vision
10. Company Mission
11. Market Study
12. Scrum Guidance Body Recommendations

TOOLS
1. Project Vision Meeting*
2. JAD Sessions
3. SWOT Analysis
4. Gap Analysis

OUTPUTS
1. Identified Product Owner*
2. Project Vision Statement*
3. Project Charter
4. Project Budget

8.2 Identify Scrum Master and Stakeholder(s)

INPUTS
1. Product Owner*
2. Project Vision Statement*
3. Program Product Owner
4. Program Scrum Master
5. Chief Product Owner
6. Chief Scrum Master
7. Program Stakeholder(s)
8. People Requirements
9. People Availability and Commitment
10. Organizational Resource Matrix
11. Skills Requirement Matrix
12. Scrum Guidance Body Recommendations

TOOLS
1. Selection Criteria*
2. Expert Advice from HR
3. Training and Training Costs
4. Resource Costs

OUTPUTS
1. Identified Scrum Master*
2. Identified Stakeholder(s)*

8.3 Form Scrum Team

INPUTS
1. Product Owner*
2. Scrum Master*
3. Project Vision Statement*
4. Chief Product Owner
5. People Requirements
6. People Availability and Commitment
7. Organizational Resource Matrix
8. Skills Requirement Matrix
9. Resource Requirements
10. Scrum Guidance Body Recommendations

TOOLS
1. Scrum Team Selection*
2. Expert Advice from HR
3. People Costs
4. Training and Training Costs
5. Resource Costs

OUTPUTS
1. Identified Scrum Team*
2. Back-up Persons
3. Collaboration Plan
4. Team Building Plan

8.4 Develop Epic(s)

INPUTS
1. Scrum Core Team*
2. Project Vision Statement*
3. Stakeholder(s)
4. Program Product Backlog
5. Approved Change Requests
6. Unapproved Change Requests
7. Program and Portfolio Risks
8. Laws and Regulations
9. Applicable Contracts
10. Previous Project Information
11. Scrum Guidance Body Recommendations

TOOLS
1. User Group Meetings*
2. User Story Workshops
3. Focus Group Meetings
4. User or Customer Interviews
5. Questionnaires
6. Risk Identification Techniques
7. Scrum Guidance Body Expertise

OUTPUTS
1. Epic(s)*
2. Personas*
3. Approved Changes
4. Identified Risks

8.5 Create Prioritized Product Backlog

INPUTS
1. Scrum Core Team*
2. Epic(s)*
3. Personas*
4. Stakeholder(s)
5. Project Vision Statement
6. Program Product Backlog
7. Business Requirements
8. Approved Change Requests
9. Identified Risks
10. Applicable Contracts
11. Scrum Guidance Body Recommendations

TOOLS
1. User Story Prioritization Methods*
2. User Story Workshops
3. Planning for Value
4. Risk Assessment Techniques
5. Estimation of Project Value
6. User Story Estimation Methods
7. Scrum Guidance Body Expertise

OUTPUTS
1. Prioritized Product Backlog*
2. Done Criteria*

8.6 Conduct Release Planning

INPUTS
1. Scrum Core Team*
2. Stakeholder(s)*
3. Project Vision Statement*
4. Prioritized Product Backlog*
5. Done Criteria*
6. Program Product Owner
7. Program Scrum Master
8. Chief Product Owner
9. Program Product Backlog
10. Business Requirements
11. Holiday Calendar
12. Scrum Guidance Body Recommendations

TOOLS
1. Release Planning Sessions*
2. Release Prioritization Methods*

OUTPUTS
1. Release Planning Schedule*
2. Length of Sprint*
3. Target Customers for Release
4. Refined Prioritized Product Backlog

8

Figure 8-1: Initiate Overview

Note: Asterisks (*) denote a "mandatory" input, tool, or output for the corresponding process.

Figure 8-2 below shows the mandatory inputs, tools, and outputs for processes in Initiate phase.

8.1 Create Project Vision

INPUTS
1. Project Business Case*

TOOLS
1. Project Vision Meeting*

OUTPUTS
1. Identified Product Owner*
2. Project Vision Statement*

8.2 Identify Scrum Master and Stakeholder(s)

INPUTS
1. Product Owner*
2. Project Vision Statement*

TOOLS
1. Selection Criteria*

OUTPUTS
1. Identified Scrum Master*
2. Identified Stakeholder(s)*

8.3 Form Scrum Team

INPUTS
1. Product Owner*
2. Scrum Master*
3. Project Vision Statement*

TOOLS
1. Scrum Team Selection*

OUTPUTS
1. Identified Scrum Team*

8.4 Develop Epic(s)

INPUTS
1. Scrum Core Team*
2. Project Vision Statement*

TOOLS
1. User Group Meetings*

OUTPUTS
1. Epic(s)*
2. Personas*

8.5 Create Prioritized Product Backlog

INPUTS
1. Scrum Core Team*
2. Epic(s)*
3. Personas*

TOOLS
1. User Story Prioritization Methods*

OUTPUTS
1. Prioritized Product Backlog*
2. Done Criteria*

8.6 Conduct Release Planning

INPUTS
1. Scrum Core Team*
2. Stakeholders*
3. Project Vision Statement*
4. Prioritized Product Backlog*
5. Done Criteria*

TOOLS
1. Release Planning Sessions*
2. Release Prioritization Methods*

OUTPUTS
1. Release Planning Schedule*
2. Length of Sprint*

Figure 8-2: Initiate Overview (Essentials)

Note: Asterisks (*) denote a "mandatory" input, tool, or output for the corresponding process.

8.1   Create Project Vision

Figure 8-3 shows all the inputs, tools, and outputs for *Create Project Vision* process.

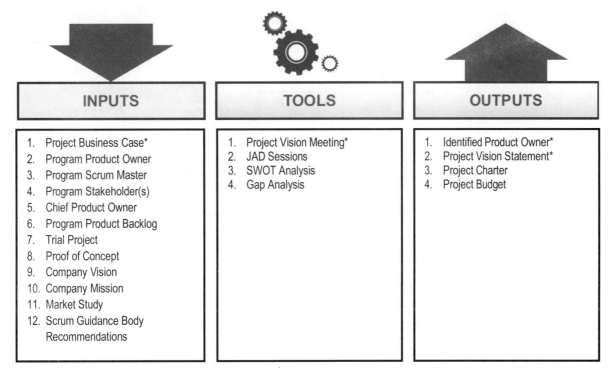

INPUTS

1. Project Business Case*
2. Program Product Owner
3. Program Scrum Master
4. Program Stakeholder(s)
5. Chief Product Owner
6. Program Product Backlog
7. Trial Project
8. Proof of Concept
9. Company Vision
10. Company Mission
11. Market Study
12. Scrum Guidance Body
    Recommendations

TOOLS

1. Project Vision Meeting*
2. JAD Sessions
3. SWOT Analysis
4. Gap Analysis

OUTPUTS

1. Identified Product Owner*
2. Project Vision Statement*
3. Project Charter
4. Project Budget

Figure 8-3: Create Project Vision—Inputs, Tools, and Outputs

Note: Asterisks (*) denote a "mandatory" input, tool, or output for the corresponding process.

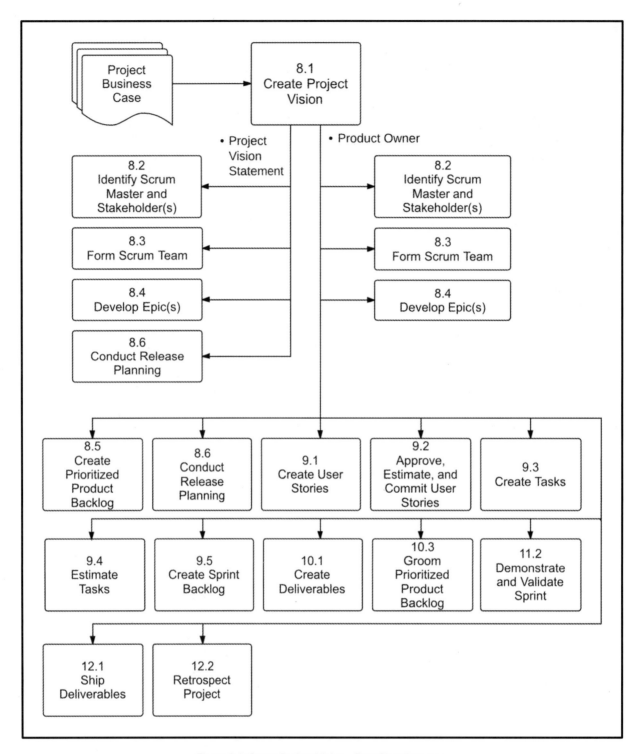

Figure 8-4: Create Project Vision—Data Flow Diagram

8.1.1 Inputs

8.1.1.1 Project Business Case*

A business case may be a well-structured document or simply a verbal statement that expresses the rationale for initiating a project. It may be formal and comprehensive, or informal and brief. Regardless of format, it often includes substantial information on the background of the project, the intended business purpose and desired outcomes, a SWOT and Gap analysis report, a list of identified risks, and estimations of time, effort, and cost.

The project commences with the presentation of the Project Business Case. A business case is presented to the stakeholders and sponsors. The stakeholders understand the expected business benefits of the project and the sponsors confirm that they will provide the financial resources for the project.

8.1.1.2 Program Product Owner

The Program Product Owner is the person responsible for maximizing business value for a program. He or she is responsible for articulating customer requirements and maintaining business justification for the program and can provide valuable inputs into what and how the projects in a program should be envisioned. The Program Product Owner also manages the Program Product Backlog.

The Program Product Owner interfaces with the Portfolio Product Owner to ensure alignment of the program with the goals and objectives of the portfolio. He or she is also involved with appointing Product Owners for individual projects, and ensuring that the vision, objectives, outcomes, and releases of individual projects in the program align with that of the program.

8.1.1.3 Program Scrum Master

The Program Scrum Master is a facilitator who ensures that all project teams in the program are provided with an environment conducive to completing their projects successfully. The Program Scrum Master guides, facilitates, and teaches Scrum practices to everyone involved in the program; provides guidance to Scrum Masters of individual projects; clears impediments for the different project teams; coordinates with the Scrum Guidance Body to define objectives related to quality, government regulations, security, and other key organizational parameters; and, ensures that Scrum processes are being effectively followed throughout the program.

The Program Scrum Master interfaces with the Portfolio Scrum Master to ensure alignment of the program with the goals and objectives of the portfolio. He or she is also involved with appointing Scrum Masters for individual projects and ensuring that the vision, objectives, outcomes, and releases of individual projects in the program align with that of the program.

8.1.1.4   Program Stakeholder(s)

Program Stakeholder(s) is a collective term that includes customers, users, and sponsors for a program. They influence all the projects in the program throughout the project's development. Program Stakeholder(s) can also help define the project vision and provide guidance regarding business value.

Program Stakeholder(s) interface with Portfolio Stakeholder(s) to ensure alignment of the program with the goals and objectives of the portfolio. They are also involved with appointing Stakeholder(s) for individual projects and ensuring that the vision, objectives, outcomes, and releases of individual projects in the program align with that of the program.

8.1.1.5   Chief Product Owner

In the case of large projects with numerous Scrum Teams, having a Chief Product Owner may be a necessity. This role is responsible for coordinating the work of multiple Product Owners. The Chief Product Owner prepares and maintains the overall Prioritized Product Backlog for the large project, using it to coordinate work through the Product Owners of the Scrum Teams. The Product Owners, in turn, manage their respective parts of the Prioritized Product Backlog.

The Chief Product Owner also interfaces with the Program Product Owner to ensure alignment of the large project with the goals and objectives of the program.

8.1.1.6   Program Product Backlog

The Program Product Owner develops the Program Product Backlog which contains a prioritized list of high level business and project requirements preferably written in the form of large Program Backlog Items. These are later refined by the Product Owners of individual projects as they create and prioritize Product Backlogs for their projects. These Prioritized Product Backlogs have much smaller but detailed User Stories that can be approved, estimated, and committed by individual Scrum Teams.

The Program Product Backlog is continuously groomed by the Program Product Owner to ensure that new business requirements are added and existing requirements are properly documented and prioritized. This ensures that the most valuable requirements in meeting the program's objectives are prioritized as high and the remaining are given a lower priority.

The Program Product Backlog created for the program presents a larger picture of all projects that are part of the program. Therefore, it can provide significant guidance regarding project goals, scope, objectives, and the expected business benefits.

8.1.1.7   Trial Project

If feasible, a small scale demo or trial project could be run as an experiment to predict and evaluate viability, time and cost, risks, and possible effects of the actual project. This helps evaluate the practical environment and guides the actual project design prior to the initiation of the project on a full scale.

8.1.1.8   Proof of Concept

A Proof of Concept demonstrates and verifies that the idea behind the current project is potentially viable in the real world environment. Often in the form of a prototype, it is designed to determine financial and technical viability, help understand requirements, and assist in assessment of design decisions early in the process. However, the Proof of Concept does not need to necessarily represent actual project Deliverables.

8.1.1.9   Company Vision

Understanding the Company Vision helps the project keep its focus on the organization's objectives and the future potential of the company. The Product Owner can take guidance and direction from the Company Vision to create the Project Vision Statement.

8.1.1.10   Company Mission

The Company Mission provides a framework for formulating the strategies of the company and guides overall decision making in the company. Project Vision must be framed such that its fulfillment helps the organization fulfill its mission.

8.1.1.11   Market Study

Market Study refers to the organized research, gathering, collation, and analysis of data related to customers' preferences for products. It often includes extensive data on market trends, market segmentation, and marketing processes. Market study could also include an analytical study of competitors which provides better understanding of competitors' strengths and weaknesses and can help decision makers formulate better positioned products.

8.1.1.12 Scrum Guidance Body Recommendations

The Scrum Guidance Body (SGB) is an optional role. It generally consists of a group of documents and/or a group of experts who are typically involved with defining objectives related to quality, government regulations, security, and other key organizational parameters. These objectives guide the work carried out by the Product Owner, Scrum Master, and Scrum Team. The Scrum Guidance Body also helps capture the best practices that should be used across all Scrum projects in the organization.

The Scrum Guidance Body does not make decisions related to the project. Instead it acts as a consulting or guidance structure for all the hierarchy levels in the project organization—the portfolio, program, and project. Scrum Teams have the option of asking the Scrum Guidance Body for advice as required.

It is important to ensure that the project vision aligns with recommendations provided by the Scrum Guidance Body and that processes comply with any standards and guidelines established by the Body.

8.1.2 Tools

8.1.2.1 Project Vision Meeting*

A Project Vision Meeting is a meeting with the Program Stakeholder(s), Program Product Owner, Program Scrum Master, and Chief Product Owner. It helps identify the business context, business requirements, and stakeholder expectations in order to develop an effective Project Vision Statement. Scrum believes in closely engaging and collaborating with all business representatives to get their buy-in for the project and to deliver greater value.

8.1.2.2 JAD Sessions

A Joint Application Design (JAD) Session is a requirements gathering technique. It is a highly structured facilitated workshop which hastens the *Create Project Vision* process as it enables the Stakeholder(s) and other decision makers to come to a consensus on the scope, objectives, and other specifications of the project.

It consists of methods for increasing user participation, speeding development, and improving specifications. Relevant Program Stakeholder(s), Program Product Owner, Program Scrum Master and Chief Product Owner could meet to outline and analyze desired business outcomes and visualize their vision for the Scrum project.

8.1.2.3 SWOT Analysis

SWOT is a structured approach to project planning that helps evaluate the **S**trengths, **W**eaknesses, **O**pportunities, and **T**hreats related to a project. This type of analysis helps identify both the internal and the external factors that could impact the project. Strengths and weaknesses are internal factors, whereas opportunities and threats are external factors. Identification of these factors helps stakeholders and decision makers finalize the processes, tools, and techniques to be used to achieve the project objectives. Conducting a SWOT Analysis allows the early identification of priorities, potential changes, and risks.

8.1.2.4 Gap Analysis

Gap Analysis is a technique used to compare the current, actual state with some desired state. In an organization, it involves determining and documenting the difference between current business capabilities and the final desired set of capabilities. A project is normally initiated to bring an organization to the desired state, so conducting a Gap Analysis would help decision makers determine the need for a project.

The main steps involved in Gap Analysis are presented in Figure 8-5.

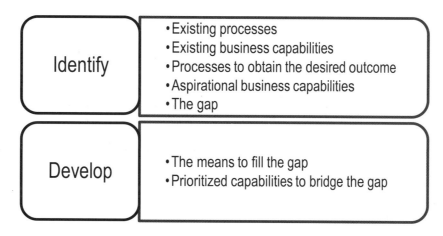

Figure 8-5: The Gap Analysis Process

8.1.3 Outputs

8.1.3.1 Identified Product Owner*

One of the outputs of this process is the identification of the Product Owner. The Product Owner is the person responsible for achieving maximum business value for the project. He or she is also responsible for articulating customer requirements and maintaining business justification for the project. The Product Owner represents the Voice of the Customer.

Each Scrum Team will have a designated Product Owner. A small project may have only one Product Owner, whereas larger projects may have several. These Product Owners are responsible for managing their sections of the Prioritized Product Backlog. Product Owners write the User Stories and manage and groom the Prioritized Product Backlog.

The Product Owner role is described in more detail in section 3.4.

8.1.3.2　Project Vision Statement*

The key output of the *Create Project Vision* process is a well-structured Project Vision Statement. A good project vision explains the business need the project is intended to meet rather than how it will meet the need.

The Project Vision Statement should not be too specific and should have room for flexibility. It is possible that the current understanding of the project may be based on assumptions that will change as the project progresses, so it is important that the project vision is flexible enough to accommodate these changes. The project vision should focus on the problem rather than the solution.

> *Example:*
>
> VMFoods, an offline grocery chain, wants to expand with an online e-commerce portal and has contacted your firm to create the product.
>
> Project Vision: Develop an easy to use and aesthetically pleasing online sales channel for VMFoods.

8.1.3.3　Project Charter

A Project Charter is an official statement of the desired objectives and outcomes of the project. In several organizations, the Project Charter is the document that officially and formally authorizes the project, providing the team with written authority to begin project work.

8.1.3.4　Project Budget

The Project Budget is a financial document which includes the cost of people, materials, and other related expenses in a project. The Project Budget is typically signed off by the sponsor(s) to ensure that sufficient funds are available. Once signed off, Product Owner and Scrum Master would be involved with managing the Project Budget on a regular basis and also ensuring that people and other resources required for project activities are available.

8.2   Identify Scrum Master and Stakeholder(s)

Figure 8-6 shows all the inputs, tools, and outputs for *Identify Scrum Master and Stakeholder(s)* process.

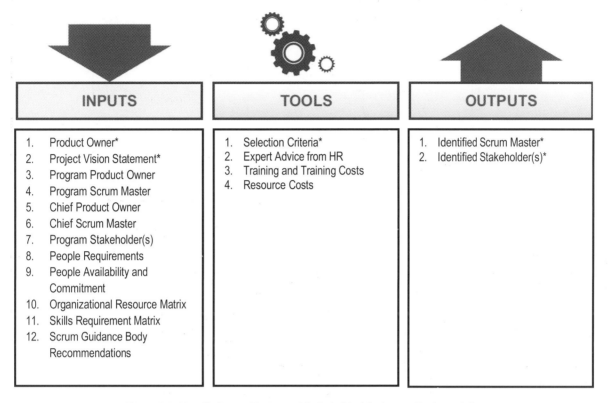

INPUTS	TOOLS	OUTPUTS
1. Product Owner* 2. Project Vision Statement* 3. Program Product Owner 4. Program Scrum Master 5. Chief Product Owner 6. Chief Scrum Master 7. Program Stakeholder(s) 8. People Requirements 9. People Availability and Commitment 10. Organizational Resource Matrix 11. Skills Requirement Matrix 12. Scrum Guidance Body Recommendations	1. Selection Criteria* 2. Expert Advice from HR 3. Training and Training Costs 4. Resource Costs	1. Identified Scrum Master* 2. Identified Stakeholder(s)*

Figure 8-6: Identify Scrum Master and Stakeholder(s)—Inputs, Tools, and Outputs

8

Note: Asterisks (*) denote a "mandatory" input, tool, or output for the corresponding process.

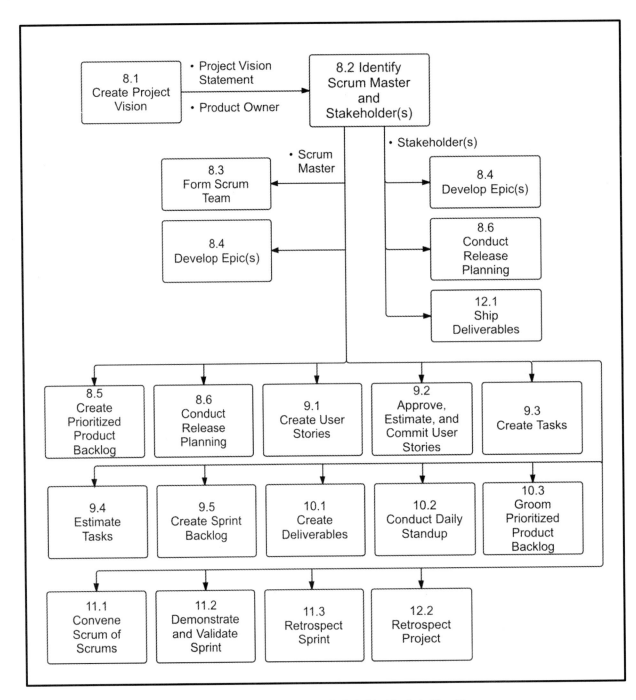

Figure 8-7: Identify Scrum Master and Stakeholder(s)—Data Flow Diagram

8.2.1   Inputs

8.2.1.1   Product Owner*

Described in section 8.1.3.1.

8.2.1.2   Project Vision Statement*

Described in section 8.1.3.2.

8.2.1.3   Program Product Owner

Described in section 8.1.1.2.

8.2.1.4   Program Scrum Master

Described in section 8.1.1.3.

8.2.1.5   Chief Product Owner

Described in section 8.1.1.5.

8.2.1.6   Chief Scrum Master

Large projects require multiple Scrum Teams to work in parallel. Information gathered from one team may need to be appropriately communicated to other teams—the Chief Scrum Master is responsible for this activity.

Coordination across various Scrum Teams working on a project is typically done through the Scrum of Scrums (SoS) Meeting (see section 3.7.2.1). This is analogous to the Daily Standup Meeting and is facilitated by the Chief Scrum Master. The Chief Scrum Master is typically responsible for addressing impediments that impact more than one Scrum Team.

8.2.1.7   Program Stakeholder(s)

Described in section 8.1.1.4.

8.2.1.8   People Requirements

Identifying People Requirements is one of the initial steps in selecting the Scrum Master and the Stakeholder(s). It is important to document the roles and responsibilities of all those who would be involved in completing the tasks in the project. This includes all individuals involved in the project in any capacity, regardless of whether their role is core or non-core.

Usually, the Product Owner or the Scrum Master work with the Human Resource Department of the company to determine and finalize the People Requirements for a project.

8.2.1.9   People Availability and Commitment

Prior to selecting the Scrum Master and Stakeholder(s), their availability must be confirmed. Only team members who will be available and can fully commit to the project should be selected. People Availability and Commitment are commonly depicted in the form of calendars showing when human resources will be available to work throughout the duration of the project.

To be effective, Scrum Teams should ideally have six to ten members; and replacing persons or changing team members is not advisable in Scrum Core Teams. So, it is important to have persons in the Scrum Core Team who are available and fully committed to the project.

8.2.1.10   Organizational Resource Matrix

The Organizational Resource Matrix is a hierarchical depiction of a combination of a functional organizational structure and a projectized organizational structure. Matrix organizations bring together team members for a project from different functional departments such as information technology, finance, marketing, sales, manufacturing, and other departments - and create cross-functional teams.

Team members in a matrix organization fulfill two objectives—functional and project. Team members are directed by Product Owner(s) with respect to project related activities, while the functional managers perform managerial activities related to their departments such as performance appraisals and approving leaves.

8.2.1.11   Skills Requirement Matrix

The Skills Requirement Matrix, also known as a competency framework, is used to assess skill gaps and training requirements for team members. A skills matrix maps the skills, capabilities, and interest level of team members in using those skills and capabilities on a project. Using this matrix, the organization can assess any skill gaps in team members and identify the employees who will need further training in a particular area or competency.

8.2.1.12   Scrum Guidance Body Recommendations

Described in section 8.1.1.12.

8.2.2   Tools

8.2.2.1   Selection Criteria*

Selecting appropriate Scrum Master(s) and identifying relevant Stakeholder(s) is crucial to the success of any project. In some projects, there may have been pre-conditions stipulating certain team members and their roles.

When there is flexibility in choosing the Scrum Master(s), the following are important Selection Criteria:

1. *Problem-solving skills*—This is one of the primary criteria to be considered while selecting Scrum Master(s). The Scrum Master(s) should have the necessary skills and experience to help remove any impediments for the Scrum Team.
2. *Availability*—The Scrum Master should be available to schedule, oversee, and facilitate various meetings, including the Release Planning Meeting, Daily Standup Meeting, and other Sprint-related meetings.
3. *Commitment*—The Scrum Master should be highly committed to ensure that the Scrum Team is provided with a conducive work environment to ensure successful delivery of Scrum projects.
4. *Servant Leadership Style*—For more details, please refer to section 3.10.4.1

When identifying the Stakeholder(s), it is important to remember that stakeholders are all the customers, users, and sponsors, who frequently interface with the Product Owner, Scrum Master, and Scrum Team to provide inputs and facilitate creation of the project's products. The stakeholders influence the project throughout its lifecycle.

8

8.2.2.2   Expert Advice from HR

Expert Advice from Human Resource managers can be valuable in identifying the Scrum Master and the Stakeholder(s). The HR department possesses specialized knowledge about the employees of an organization and various techniques that might help in identifying the Scrum Master and Stakeholder(s).

8.2.2.3   Training and Training Costs

Scrum is a radically different framework from traditional methods of project management. Team members may not always possess the required knowledge or skills to work in the Scrum environment. The Product Owner should evaluate the training needs of potential team members and facilitate training to bridge any knowledge gaps in the team. The Product Owner is normally responsible for evaluating and selecting team members, but often does this in consultation with the Scrum Master who may have additional knowledge of the resources from working with them on other projects.

Appropriate training should be provided to the Scrum Team members both prior to the commencement of work and also while they are working on their projects. Scrum Team members should also be ready to learn from each other and from more experienced persons in the team.

8.2.2.4   Resource Costs

One of the primary considerations in selecting people has to do with the trade-offs related to experience versus salary. There are other people related factors impacting cost that may also need to be considered. Ideally, the Scrum Master(s), team members, and Stakeholder(s) should be colocated, so that they can communicate frequently and easily. If colocation is not possible and there are distributed teams, additional resources will have to be devoted to facilitate communications, understand cultural differences, synchronize work, and foster knowledge sharing.

8.2.3　Outputs

8.2.3.1　Identified Scrum Master*

A Scrum Master is a facilitator and 'servant leader' who ensure that the Scrum Team is provided with an environment conducive to completing the project successfully. The Scrum Master guides, facilitates, and teaches Scrum practices to everyone involved in the project; clears impediments for the team; and, ensures that Scrum processes are being followed. It is the responsibility of the Product Owner to identify the Scrum Master for a Scrum project.

The Scrum Master role is described in more detail in section 3.4.

8.2.3.2　Identified Stakeholder(s)*

Stakeholder(s), which is a collective term that includes customers, users, and sponsors, frequently interface with the Scrum Core Team and influence the project throughout the product development process. It is for the stakeholders that the project produces the collaborative benefits.

The Stakeholder(s) role is described in section 3.3.2.

8

8.3 Form Scrum Team

Figure 8-8 shows all the inputs, tools, and outputs for *Form Scrum Team* process.

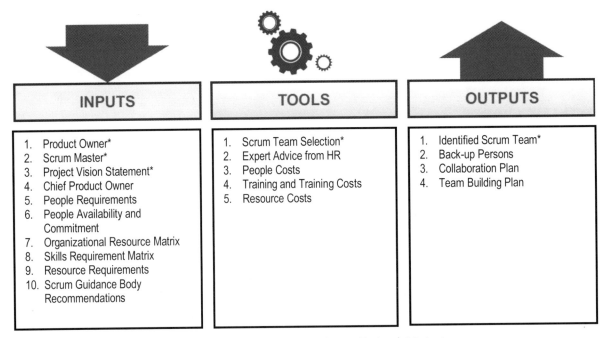

INPUTS

1. Product Owner*
2. Scrum Master*
3. Project Vision Statement*
4. Chief Product Owner
5. People Requirements
6. People Availability and Commitment
7. Organizational Resource Matrix
8. Skills Requirement Matrix
9. Resource Requirements
10. Scrum Guidance Body Recommendations

TOOLS

1. Scrum Team Selection*
2. Expert Advice from HR
3. People Costs
4. Training and Training Costs
5. Resource Costs

OUTPUTS

1. Identified Scrum Team*
2. Back-up Persons
3. Collaboration Plan
4. Team Building Plan

Figure 8-8: Form Scrum Team—Inputs, Tools, and Outputs

Note: Asterisks (*) denote a "mandatory" input, tool, or output for the corresponding process.

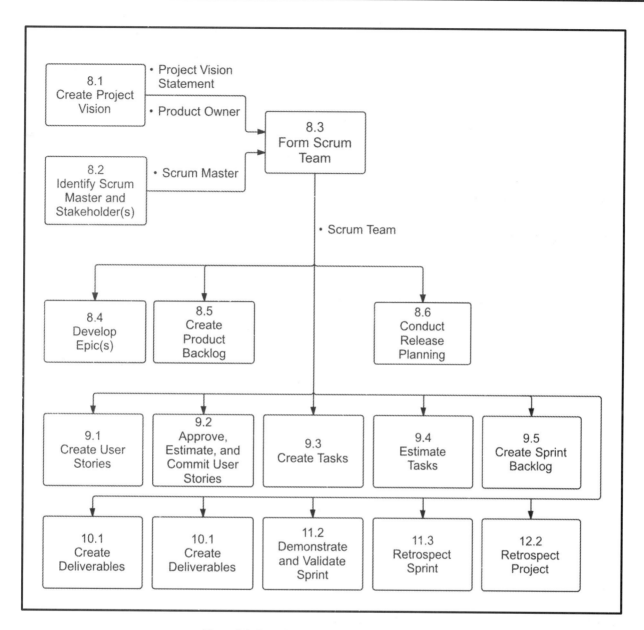

Figure 8-9: Form Scrum Team—Data Flow Diagram

8.3.1 Inputs

8.3.1.1 Product Owner*

Described in section 8.1.3.1.

8.3.1.2 Scrum Master*

Described in section 8.2.3.1.

8.3.1.3 Project Vision Statement*

Described in section 8.1.3.2.

8.3.1.4 Chief Product Owner

Described in section 8.1.1.5.

8.3.1.5 People Requirements

Described in section 8.2.1.8.

8.3.1.6 People Availability and Commitment

Described in section 8.2.1.9.

8.3.1.7 Organizational Resource Matrix

Described in section 8.2.1.10.

8.3.1.8 Skills Requirement Matrix

Described in section 8.2.1.11.

8.3.1.9   Resource Requirements

These requirements include all resources—other than people—required for the Scrum Team to function effectively. These resources include office infrastructure, meeting spaces, work equipment, Scrumboards, etc. In the case of virtual teams, additional resources such as collaboration tools, video conferencing, shared document repositories, translation services, etc. have to be considered.

8.3.1.10   Scrum Guidance Body Recommendations

Described in section 8.1.1.12.

8.3.2   Tools

8.3.2.1   Scrum Team Selection*

The Scrum Team is the core of any Scrum project and getting the right team members is important for successful delivery of Scrum projects. Scrum Team members are generalists/specialists in that they have knowledge of various fields and are experts in at least one. Beyond their subject-matter expertise, it is the soft skills of team members that determine the success of self-organizing teams.

Ideal members of the Scrum Team are independent, self-motivated, customer-focused, responsible, and collaborative. The team should be able to foster an environment of independent thinking and group decision-making in order to extract the most benefits from the structure.

8.3.2.2   Expert Advice from HR

Expert Advice from Human Resource (HR) managers can be valuable while forming a Scrum Team. The HR department possesses specialized knowledge about the employees of an organization and of the numerous techniques that might help Product Owners, Scrum Masters, and sponsors identify the right team members.

8.3.2.3   People Costs

All costs associated with people requirements need to be assessed, analyzed, approved, and budgeted for.

8

8.3.2.4   Training and Training Costs

Team members may not possess the required skills or knowledge to carry out specialized tasks. The Product Owner should evaluate the training needs of potential team members and provide training, when any skill or knowledge gaps are found.

For a truly effective Scrum implementation, there must be a significant level of awareness within the organization of Scrum principles and values. This awareness will aid in the successful execution of Scrum. The Scrum Team has to be sensitized and trained in the practices of Scrum and the Scrum Master should play the role of a coach for the team. Because planning Sprints is a major success factor, training will help teams understand how to discuss and identify achievable Sprint goals. The Scrum Master needs to bring out the best from the Scrum Team by motivating them and facilitating the development process. By training and coaching team members, the Scrum Master can help them articulate issues and challenges they face. Normally any issues or conflicts experienced within the team are solved by the team with coaching and assistance from the Scrum Master as required. The Scrum Master should address issues such as low morale or lack of coordination within the team. He or she is responsible for removing impediments for the team. When required, the Scrum Master can escalate external issues and impediments to management for resolution or removal.

Training and Training Costs are also discussed in the *Identify Scrum Master and Stakeholder(s)* process, section 8.2.2.3.

8.3.2.5   Resource Costs

The costs associated with all non-people requirements must be assessed, analyzed, approved, and budgeted for. A resource in the project environment is anything used to perform a task or activity including—but not limited to—equipment, material, outside services, and physical space.

8.3.3   Outputs

8.3.3.1   Identified Scrum Team*

The Scrum Team, sometimes referred to as the Development Team, is a group or team of people who are responsible for understanding the business requirements specified by the Product Owner, estimating User Stories, and final creation of the project Deliverables. Scrum Teams are cross-functional and self-organizing. The team decides the amount of work to commit to in a Sprint and determines the best way to perform the work. The Scrum Team consists of cross-functional team members, who carry out all the work involved in creating potentially shippable Deliverables including development, testing, quality assurance, etc.

Identifying the Scrum Team is the responsibility of the Product Owner, often in consultation with the Scrum Master.

The Scrum Team role is described in more detail in section 3.6.

8.3.3.2   Back-up Persons

When selecting teams, another important aspect is to create backups for each Scrum Team member. Although people availability and commitment is confirmed for team members in advance, issues may arise such as an illness, family emergency, or a team member leaving the organization. Scrum Teams work in small groups of six to ten persons. Having Back-up Persons ensures that there is no major decrease in productivity due to the loss of a team member.

8.3.3.3   Collaboration Plan

Collaboration is a very important element in Scrum. Planning for how the various decision makers, stakeholders, and team members engage and collaborate with each other is vital. The Collaboration Plan is an optional output that may be formal or informal. At times, it may simply be an oral understanding between the various stakeholders, since Scrum avoids any unnecessary documentation. However, for larger, more complex projects, especially those with distributed teams, a more formal agreement may need to be put in place. The plan may address how the Scrum Core Team members, Stakeholder(s) and others involved in the Scrum project will communicate and collaborate throughout the project and may also define specific tools or techniques to be used for that purpose. For example, in distributed teams, there may be a need for an agreement on when and how meetings will be conducted, what type of communication tools will be used, and who should be involved in each type of meeting.

8.3.3.4   Team Building Plan

Since a Scrum Team is cross-functional, each member needs to participate actively in all aspects of the project. The Scrum Master should identify issues with team members and address them diligently in order to maintain an effective team.

To build team cohesion, the Scrum Master should ensure that relationships among the team members are positive and that the team members are unified in achieving the overall project and organizational goals, thus leading to greater efficiency and increased productivity.

In this context, it is important to study section 3.10, which discusses popular HR theories and their relevance to Scrum.

8.4 Develop Epic(s)

Figure 8-10 shows all the inputs, tools, and outputs for *Develop Epic(s)* process.

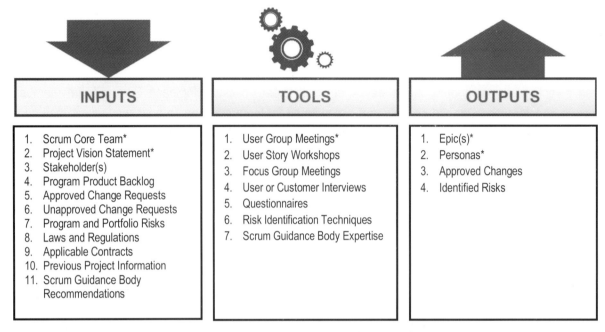

INPUTS	TOOLS	OUTPUTS
1. Scrum Core Team*	1. User Group Meetings*	1. Epic(s)*
2. Project Vision Statement*	2. User Story Workshops	2. Personas*
3. Stakeholder(s)	3. Focus Group Meetings	3. Approved Changes
4. Program Product Backlog	4. User or Customer Interviews	4. Identified Risks
5. Approved Change Requests	5. Questionnaires	
6. Unapproved Change Requests	6. Risk Identification Techniques	
7. Program and Portfolio Risks	7. Scrum Guidance Body Expertise	
8. Laws and Regulations		
9. Applicable Contracts		
10. Previous Project Information		
11. Scrum Guidance Body Recommendations		

Figure 8-10: Develop Epic(s)—Inputs, Tools, and Outputs

Note: Asterisks (*) denote a "mandatory" input, tool, or output for the corresponding process.

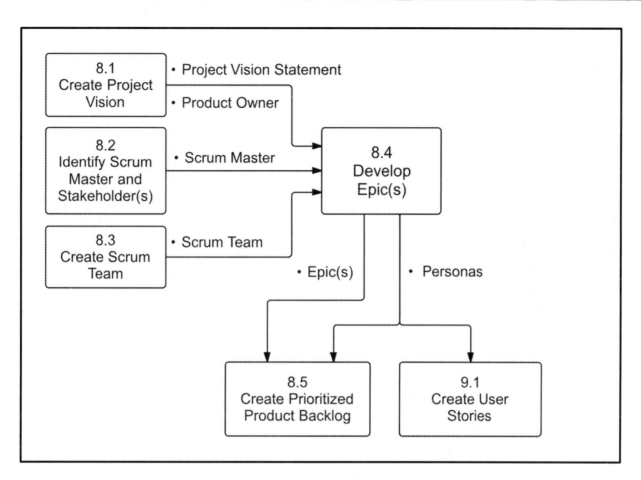

Figure 8-11: Develop Epic(s)—Data Flow Diagram

8.4.1   Inputs

8.4.1.1   Scrum Core Team*

The Scrum Core Team consists of the Scrum Team, the Scrum Master and the Product Owner as described in section 3.3.1.

8.4.1.2   Project Vision Statement*

Described in section 8.1.3.2.

8.4.1.3   Stakeholder(s)

Described in section 8.2.3.2.

8.4.1.4   Program Product Backlog

Described in section 8.1.1.6.

8.4.1.5   Approved Change Requests

Approved Change Requests originating from the program or portfolio are inputs to be added to the list of approved project changes for implementation in future Sprints. Each change can require its own Epic or User Story and could become an input to the *Develop Epic(s)* process. Approved Change Requests to this process could also result from other Scrum processes

Change Requests and Approved Change Requests are discussed in sections 6.3.1, 6.4.2.1 and 6.6.

8.4.1.6   Unapproved Change Requests

Request for changes are usually submitted as Change Requests and remain in an unapproved status until they are formally approved. Unapproved Change Requests to *Develop Epic(s)* process could come from *Create Deliverables*, *Conduct Daily Standup* and other processes.

Change Requests and Unapproved Change Requests are discussed in sections 6.3.1, 6.4.2.1 and 6.6.

8.4.1.7　Program and Portfolio Risks

Risks related to a portfolio or program will also impact projects that are part of the respective portfolio or program. During risk assessment in portfolios and programs, if it is determined that a risk may affect an individual project, relevant information about the risk must be communicated to the Product Owner and Scrum Team. Program and Portfolio Risks could be inputs to the *Develop Epic(s)* process and can have an overall impact on how this process is conducted.

Program and Portfolio Risks are described in section 7.5.1.

8.4.1.8　Laws and Regulations

Depending on the project, there may be Laws and Regulations, imposed by governing bodies, which impact planning and execution. Laws are external to the organization and imposed by a governmental entity. Regulations can either be internal or external. Internal regulations are those that are applicable within the company, typically based on policies. These regulations might relate to quality management systems, financial regulations, staff regulations, etc. External regulations are those relating to government established standards, norms, and requirements.

Laws and Regulations must be considered while developing Epics. Epics are based on business requirements. To meet those requirements the project team has to abide by both internal and external Laws and Regulations.

At times, some of the Laws and Regulations impacting multiple Scrum projects may be included as part of Scrum Guidance Body Recommendations, as discussed in section 8.1.1.12.

8.4.1.9　Applicable Contracts

If the entire project or portions of it are being completed under a contract, the contract defines the scope of work and the specific terms of the contract. The type of contract used influences project risk.

Some of the most common types of contracts used in Scrum projects are as follows:

Incremental Delivery Contract—This contract includes inspection points at regular intervals. It helps the customer or stakeholders make decisions regarding product development periodically throughout the project at each inspection point. The customer can either accept the development of the product, decide to stop the development of the product, or request product modifications.

Joint Venture Contract—This contract is generally used when two or more parties partner to accomplish the work of a project. The parties involved in the project will both achieve some Return on Investment because the revenues or benefits generated will be shared between the parties.

Development in Phases Contract—This contract makes funding available each month or each quarter after a release is successfully completed. It gives incentive to both customer and supplier and ensures that the monetary risk for the customer is limited to that particular time period since unsuccessful releases are not funded.

Incentive and Penalty Contract—These contracts are based on the agreement that the supplier will be rewarded with a financial incentive if the project's products are delivered on time, but will incur financial penalties if the delivery is late.

Other popular contract types include paying by features contract, time and materials contract, fixed price and fixed scope contract, and fixed profit contract.

Epics should be developed keeping in mind the terms and conditions of the contract type being used.

8.4.1.10   Previous Project Information

Information and insights gained from previous similar projects within the organization are valuable inputs for developing Epics and assessing risk. Previous Project Information could include project manager's notes, project logs, and stakeholder comments.

Some information and best practices related to previous project information may be available through Scrum Guidance Body Recommendations.

8.4.1.11   Scrum Guidance Body Recommendations

Discussed in section 8.1.1.12

Scrum Guidance Body Recommendations may include information on rules, regulations, standards, and best practices for developing Epics.

8.4.2 Tools

8.4.2.1 User Group Meetings*

User Group Meetings involve relevant stakeholders (primarily users or customers of the product). They provide the Scrum Core Team with firsthand information about user expectations. This helps in formulating the Acceptance Criteria for the product and provides valuable insights for developing Epics. User Group Meetings are vital in the prevention of expensive rework that may result from a lack of clarity regarding expectations and requirements. These meetings also promote buy-in for the project and create a common understanding among the Scrum Core Team and relevant Stakeholder(s).

8.4.2.2 User Story Workshops

User Story Workshops are held as part of the *Develop Epic(s)* process. The Scrum Master facilitates these sessions, where the entire Scrum Core Team is involved, and at times, it is desirable to include other Stakeholder(s). These workshops help the Product Owner to prioritize requirements and enable the Scrum Core Team to have a shared perspective of the Acceptance Criteria. They ensure that the Epics and User Stories describe the functionality from the users' point of view, are easy to understand, and can be reliably estimated. User Story Workshops are useful in understanding user expectations for the deliverables and are excellent for team building. They also facilitate preparation for the planning of the next Sprint. A User Story Workshop is a good platform to discuss and clarify every element of a product and often delve into the smallest details to ensure clarity.

8.4.2.3 Focus Group Meetings

Focus groups assemble individuals in a guided session to provide their opinions, perceptions, or ratings of a product, service, or desired result. Focus group members have the freedom to ask questions to each other and to get clarifications on particular subjects or concepts. Through questioning, constructive criticism, and feedback, focus groups lead to a better quality product and thereby contribute to meeting the expectations of the users. In these meetings, the focus group members sometimes reach consensus in certain areas, while in other areas their opinions may differ. Where group members have differing opinions or perspectives, every effort is made to resolve the differences in order to reach consensus.

Focus group sessions can help teams come up with innovative ideas, solve problems, and give suggestions for improvement. These meetings facilitate fact finding and generate ideas and feedback from potential users and product developers. These meetings are usually conducted for planning, evaluating, or improving a product or service. Insights obtained from these meetings can also help develop Epics and User Stories. At times, Focus Group Meetings are conducted to resolve issues that may arise during the development of Epics.

8.4.2.4 User or Customer Interviews

Engaging stakeholders, including the sponsor, users, and customers of the product, is important to gain the necessary context and insight required to develop Epics. Quality time spent interviewing users and customers will result in ensuring that the requirements in Epics align with the overall Project Vision, thereby delivering greater value.

These interviews help to:

* Identify and understand stakeholder needs and expectations
* Gather opinions and facts
* Understand stakeholders' perspective of the end product
* Gather feedback about the iterated or partially developed product

8.4.2.5 Questionnaires

A cost effective way to gain quantitative and qualitative statistical insight from a large number of users or customers is to use surveys or Questionnaires. A Questionnaire is a research instrument that contains questions to be asked to a respondent in order to collect information about a specific issue or topic. Questionnaires can be self-administered or administered by an interviewer.

Great care must be exercised in the design of Questionnaires, selecting the right target audience, and determining an appropriate method of survey deployment to avoid errors and bias.

While developing Epics, the Product Owner or the Scrum Master might conduct a survey to gather relevant information from stakeholders or the Scrum Team.

8.4.2.6 Risk Identification Techniques

Described in section 7.4.1.1

8.4.2.7 Scrum Guidance Body Expertise

Described in section 3.3.2

While creating Epics, Scrum Guidance Body Expertise could relate to documented rules and regulations; or standards and best practices for creating Epics. There may also be a team of subject matter experts who may assist the Product Owner to create Epics. This team could include Business Analysts, Lead Architects, Senior Developers, Scrum Experts, or other experienced persons. This expert group is usually not the same team that will stay on and work on a particular project, as they tend to move from project to project during the 'selling phase' or 'phase zero' with the customers or users.

8.4.3   Outputs

8.4.3.1   Epic(s)*

Epics are written in the initial stages of the project when most User Stories are high-level functionalities or product descriptions and requirements are broadly defined. They are large, unrefined User Stories in the Prioritized Product Backlog.

Once these Epics come up in the Prioritized Product Backlog for completion in an upcoming Sprint, they are then broken down into smaller, more granular User Stories. These smaller User Stories are generally simple, short, and easy to implement functionalities or blocks of tasks to be completed in a Sprint.

8.4.3.2   Personas*

Personas are highly detailed fictional characters, representative of the majority of users and of other stakeholders who may not directly use the end product. Personas are created to identify the needs of the target user base. Creating specific Personas can help the team better understand users and their requirements and goals. Based on a Persona, the Product Owner can more effectively prioritize features to create the Prioritized Product Backlog.

Creating a Persona: This involves assigning a fictional name and preferably a picture, like a stock image, to the character. The Persona will include highly specific attributes such as age, gender, education, environment, interests, and goals. A quote illustrating the Persona's requirements can be included as well. Below is an example of a Persona for a travel website.

> *Example:*
>
> Vanessa is a 39 year old resident of San Francisco. She is pursuing her passion for traveling after having a highly successful career as an attorney. She likes to have options while picking air travel and accommodation services so that she can choose the best and the most affordable. She gets frustrated with slow and cluttered websites.

8.4.3.3 Approved Changes

Unapproved Change Requests may be approved by the Product Owner during the *Develop Epic(s)* process, at times with suggestions provided by relevant stakeholders. Such changes are categorized as Approved Changes and can be prioritized and implemented in future Sprints.

Change Requests and Approved Change Requests are discussed in sections 6.3.1, 6.4.2.1 and 6.6.

8.4.3.4 Identified Risks

When creating Epics, new risks may be identified and these Identified Risks form an important output of this stage. These risks contribute to the development of the Prioritized Product Backlog (also be referred to as the Risk Adjusted Product Backlog).

Risk Identification is described in section 7.4.1.

8.5 Create Prioritized Product Backlog

Figure 8-12 shows all the inputs, tools, and outputs for *Create Prioritized Product Backlog* process.

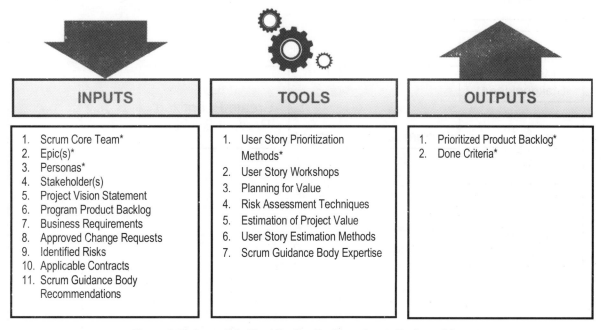

INPUTS	TOOLS	OUTPUTS
1. Scrum Core Team*	1. User Story Prioritization Methods*	1. Prioritized Product Backlog*
2. Epic(s)*	2. User Story Workshops	2. Done Criteria*
3. Personas*	3. Planning for Value	
4. Stakeholder(s)	4. Risk Assessment Techniques	
5. Project Vision Statement	5. Estimation of Project Value	
6. Program Product Backlog	6. User Story Estimation Methods	
7. Business Requirements	7. Scrum Guidance Body Expertise	
8. Approved Change Requests		
9. Identified Risks		
10. Applicable Contracts		
11. Scrum Guidance Body Recommendations		

Figure 8-12: Create Prioritized Product Backlog—Inputs, Tools, and Outputs

8

Note: Asterisks (*) denote a "mandatory" input, tool, or output for the corresponding process.

© 2013 SCRUMstudy™. *A Guide to the Scrum Body of Knowledge (SBOK™ Guide)*   **167**

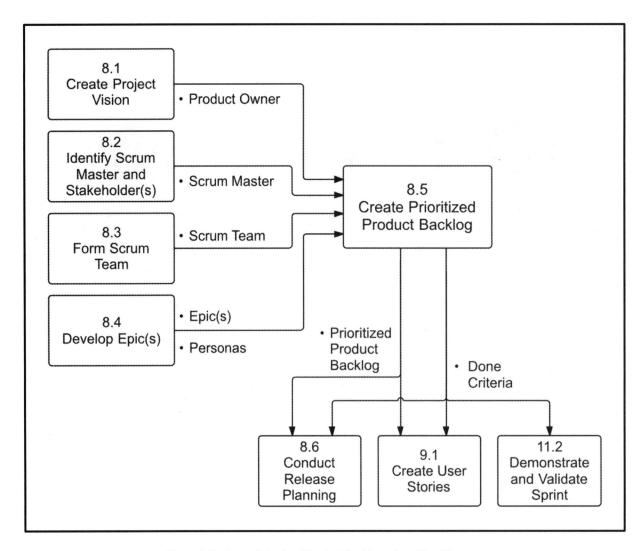

Figure 8-13: Create Prioritized Product Backlog—Data Flow Diagram

8.5.1 Inputs

8.5.1.1 Scrum Core Team*

Described in section 8.4.1.1.

8.5.1.2 Epic(s)*

Described in section 8.4.3.1.

8.5.1.3 Personas*

Described in section 8.4.3.2.

8.5.1.4 Stakeholder(s)

Described in section 8.2.3.2.

8.5.1.5 Project Vision Statement

Described in section 8.1.3.2.

8.5.1.6 Program Product Backlog

Described in section 8.1.1.6.

8.5.1.7 Business Requirements

The sum of all the insights gained through various tools such as user or customer interviews, Questionnaires, JAD Sessions, Gap Analysis, SWOT Analysis, and other meetings, helps develop a better perspective about the business requirements and aids in creating the Prioritized Product Backlog.

8.5.1.8   Approved Change Requests

Described in section 8.4.3.3.

8.5.1.9   Identified Risks

Described in section 8.4.3.4.

8.5.1.10   Applicable Contracts

Described in section 8.4.1.9.

8.5.1.11   Scrum Guidance Body Recommendations

Discussed in section 8.1.1.12.

While creating the Prioritized Product Backlog, Scrum Guidance Body Recommendations may include information on rules, regulations, standards, and best practices for developing the Prioritized Product Backlog.

8.5.2   Tools

8.5.2.1   User Story Prioritization Methods*

Some techniques used to prioritize the User Stories or requirements in the Prioritized Product Backlog, on the basis of business value are presented below:

- **MoSCoW Prioritization scheme**—The MoSCoW prioritization scheme derives its name from the first letters of the phrases "Must have," "Should have," "Could have," and "Won't have". This prioritization method is generally more effective than simple schemes. The labels are in decreasing order of priority with "Must have" User Stories being those without which the product will have no value and "Won't have" User Stories being those that, although they would be nice to have, are not necessary to be included.

- **Paired Comparison**—In this technique, a list of all the User Stories in the Prioritized Product Backlog is prepared. Next, each User Story is taken individually and compared with the other User Stories in the list, one at a time. Each time two User Stories are compared, a decision is made regarding which of the two is more important. Through this process, a prioritized list of User Stories can be generated.

- **100-Point Method**—The 100-Point Method was developed by Dean Leffingwell and Don Widrig (2003). It involves giving the customer 100 points they can use to vote for the User Stories that are most important. The objective is to give more weight to the User Stories that are of higher priority when compared to the other available User Stories. Each group member allocates points to the various User Stories, giving more points to those they feel are more important. On completion of the voting process, prioritization is determined by calculating the total points allocated to each User Story.

- **Kano Analysis**

   Described in section 4.5.2

8.5.2.2   User Story Workshops

Described in section 8.4.2.2.

8.5.2.3   Planning for Value

Described in section 4.5.2

8.5.2.4   Risk Assessment Techniques

Described in section 7.4.2.1.

8.5.2.5   Estimation of Project Value

Described in section 4.5.1.

8.5.2.6   User Story Estimation Methods

All the tools used for the *Approve, Estimate, and Commit User Stories* process (as described in section 9.2.2) can be used for creating high level estimates for Epic(s) when we create the Prioritized Product Backlog. Some important tools are:

1. User Group Meetings
2. Planning Poker
3. Fist of Five
4. Points for Cost Estimation
5. Other Estimation Techniques

8.5.2.7   Scrum Guidance Body Expertise

Described in section 8.4.2.7

While creating the Prioritized Product Backlog, the Scrum Guidance Body Expertise could relate to documented rules and regulations or standards and best practices for creating Epics. There may also be a team of subject matter experts who could assist the Product Owner in the *Create Prioritized Product Backlog* process. This team could include Business Analysts, Lead Architects, Senior Developers, Scrum Experts, and/or other experienced persons. This expert group is usually not the same team that will stay on and work on this project, as they tend to move from project to project during the 'selling phase' or 'phase zero' with the customers or users.

8.5.3   Outputs

8.5.3.1   Prioritized Product Backlog*

The Product Owner develops a Prioritized Product Backlog which contains a prioritized list of business and project requirements written in the form of Epic(s), which are high level User Stories. The Prioritized Product Backlog is based on three primary factors: value, risk or uncertainty, and dependencies. It is also referred to as the Risk Adjusted Product Backlog since it includes identified and assessed risks related to the project. It also encompasses all Approved Changes that can be appropriately prioritized in the Prioritized Product Backlog (as described in section 6.3.1).

- **Value**—It is the Product Owner's responsibility to ensure delivery of those products that provide the highest level of business value first. Even an extremely valuable product may not be part of the first release if there are other products of even higher value that are sufficient for a first release.

- **Risk and Uncertainty**—The more uncertainty that exists, the riskier the project is. Therefore, it is important that riskier products in the Prioritized Product Backlog are given higher priority. Products carrying a higher level of risk will also require risk mitigation actions. When these risk mitigation actions are prioritized against the backlog, the result is a Risk Adjusted Product Backlog. Dealing with risks early in the project does not guarantee that the project will be successful, but it does enhance the team's ability to deal with risk. This is described in section 7.4.3.

- **Dependencies**—It is usually not possible to create a Prioritized Product Backlog in which there are no dependencies between User Stories. Functional requirements often depend on other functional and even non-functional requirements. These dependencies can impact how the User Stories in the Prioritized Product Backlog are prioritized. Two of the most common ways to resolve dependencies are to either split a single story into multiple parts or combine interdependent stories.

- **Estimates**—High level estimates for Epic(s) are also available in the Prioritized Product Backlog.

8.5.3.2 Done Criteria*

Done Criteria are a set of rules that are applicable to all User Stories. A clear definition of Done is critical, because it removes ambiguity from requirements and helps the team adhere to mandatory quality norms. This clear definition is used to create the Done Criteria that are an output of the *Create Prioritized Product Backlog* process. A User Story is considered Done when it is demonstrated to and approved by the Product Owner who judges it on the basis of the Done Criteria and the User Story Acceptance Criteria.

Example of Done Criteria:

Project: Designing the new variants of a popular sports car at LRA Ltd.

Done Criteria:

- The design is approved by the Technical Excellence division.
- The prototype passes all wind tunnel tests mandated by the Aerodynamics division.
- The design is cleared for production by the Intellectual Property division.
- The design's safety expectations are corroborated by the Safety Division's Design Safety report.
- The Cost Estimation report for the design is approved by the Finance division.

8.6   Conduct Release Planning

Figure 8-14 shows all the inputs, tools, and outputs for *Conduct Release Planning* process.

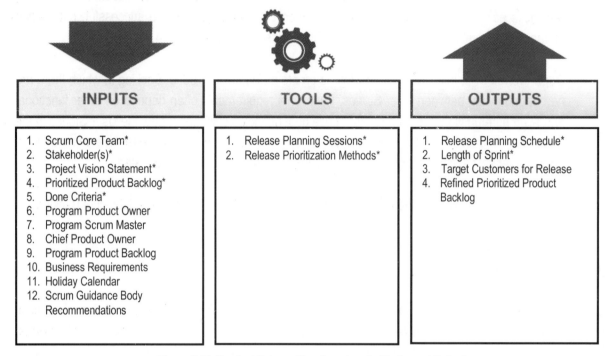

INPUTS

1. Scrum Core Team*
2. Stakeholder(s)*
3. Project Vision Statement*
4. Prioritized Product Backlog*
5. Done Criteria*
6. Program Product Owner
7. Program Scrum Master
8. Chief Product Owner
9. Program Product Backlog
10. Business Requirements
11. Holiday Calendar
12. Scrum Guidance Body Recommendations

TOOLS

1. Release Planning Sessions*
2. Release Prioritization Methods*

OUTPUTS

1. Release Planning Schedule*
2. Length of Sprint*
3. Target Customers for Release
4. Refined Prioritized Product Backlog

Figure 8-14: Conduct Release Planning—Inputs, Tools, and Outputs

Note: Asterisks (*) denote a "mandatory" input, tool, or output for the corresponding process.

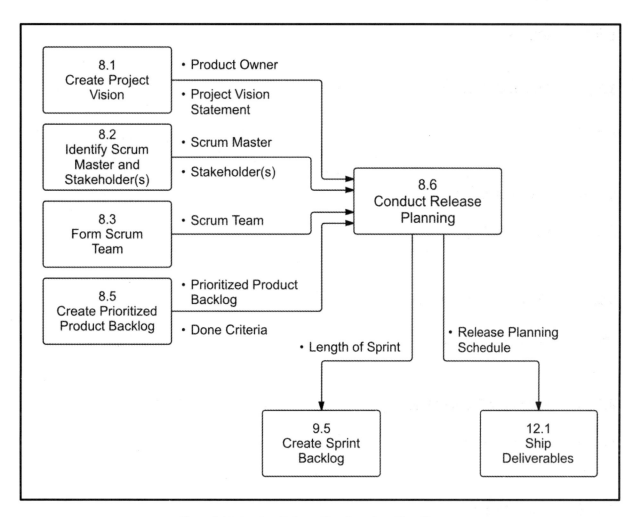

Figure 8-15: Conduct Release Planning—Data Flow Diagram

8.6.1 Inputs

8.6.1.1 Scrum Core Team*

Described in section 8.4.1.1.

8.6.1.2 Stakeholder(s)*

Described in section 8.2.3.2.

8.6.1.3 Project Vision Statement*

Described in section 8.1.3.2.

8.6.1.4 Prioritized Product Backlog*

Described in section 8.5.3.1.

8.6.1.5 Done Criteria*

Described in section 8.5.3.2.

8.6.1.6 Program Product Owner

Described in section 8.1.1.2.

8.6.1.7 Program Scrum Master

Described in section 8.1.1.3.

8.6.1.8 Chief Product Owner

Described in section 8.1.1.5.

8.6.1.9   Program Product Backlog

Described in section 8.1.1.6.

8.6.1.10   Business Requirements

Described in section 8.5.1.7.

8.6.1.11   Holiday Calendar

It is important for the Scrum Team to keep track of key dates and availability of all team members. This can be accomplished through the use of a shared calendar that provides information on official holidays, leaves, travel plans, events, etc. This calendar will help the team in planning and executing Sprints.

8.6.1.12   Scrum Guidance Body Recommendations

Described in section 8.1.1.12

In the *Conduct Release Planning* process, Scrum Guidance Body Recommendations can relate to rules, regulations, standards, and best practices for developing the Release Plan. The Guidance Body may be the best authority for defining guidelines related to business value, release expectations, deployment strategies, quality, and security.

8.6.2   Tools

8.6.2.1   Release Planning Sessions*

Release Planning Sessions are conducted to develop a Release Plan. The plan defines when various sets of usable functionality or products will be delivered to the customer. In Scrum, the major objective of a Release Planning Meeting is to enable the Scrum Team to have an overview of the releases and delivery schedule for the product they are developing so that they can align with the expectations of the Product Owner and relevant stakeholders (primarily the project sponsor).

Many organizations have a strategy regarding release of products. Some organizations prefer continuous deployment, where there is a release after creation of specified usable functionality. Other organizations prefer phased deployment, where releases are made at predefined intervals. Depending on the organization's strategy, Release Planning Sessions in projects may be driven by functionality, in which the objective is to deliver a release once a predetermined set of functionality has been developed; or the planning may be driven by date, in which the release happens on a predefined date.

Since Scrum framework promotes information based, iterative decision making over the detailed upfront planning practiced in traditional waterfall style project management, Release Planning Sessions need not produce a detailed Release Plan for the entire project. The Release Plan can be updated continually as relevant information is available.

8.6.2.2   Release Prioritization Methods*

Release Prioritization Methods are used to develop a Release Plan. These methods are industry and organization specific and are usually determined by the organization's senior management.

8.6.3   Outputs

8.6.3.1   Release Planning Schedule*

A Release Planning Schedule is one of the key outputs of the *Conduct Release Planning* process. A Release Planning Schedule states which deliverables are to be released to the customers, along with planned intervals, and dates for releases. There may not be a release scheduled at the end of every Sprint iteration. At times, a release may be planned after a group of Sprint iterations are completed. Depending on the organization's strategy, Release Planning sessions in projects may be driven by functionality, in which the objective is to deliver once a predetermined set of functionality has been developed, or the planning may be driven by date, in which the release happens on a predefined date. The deliverable should be released when it offers sufficient business value to the customer.

8.6.3.2   Length of Sprint*

Based on the various inputs including business requirements and Release Planning Schedule, the Product Owner and the Scrum Team decide on the Length of Sprint for the project. Once determined, the Length of Sprint often remains the same throughout the project.

However, the Length of Sprint may be changed if and as the Product Owner and the Scrum Team deem appropriate. Early in the project they may still be experimenting to find the best Sprint length. Later in the project a change in the Length of Sprint normally means it can be reduced due to improvements in the project environment.

A Sprint could be Time-boxed from 1 to 6 weeks. However, to get maximum benefits from a Scrum project, it is always recommended to keep the Sprint Time-boxed to 4 weeks, unless there are projects with very stable requirements, where Sprints can extend up to 6 weeks.

Impact of Expected Change on the Length of Sprint is described in section 6.5.1

8.6.3.3   Target Customers for Release

Not every release will target all stakeholders or users. The Stakeholder(s) may choose to limit certain releases to a subset of users. The Release Plan should specify the target customers for the release.

8.6.3.4   Refined Prioritized Product Backlog

The Prioritized Product Backlog, developed in the *Create Prioritized Product Backlog* process, may be refined in this process. There may be additional clarity about the User Stories in the Prioritized Product Backlog after the Scrum Core Team conducts Release Planning Sessions with Stakeholder(s).

8

8.7   Phase Data Flow Diagram

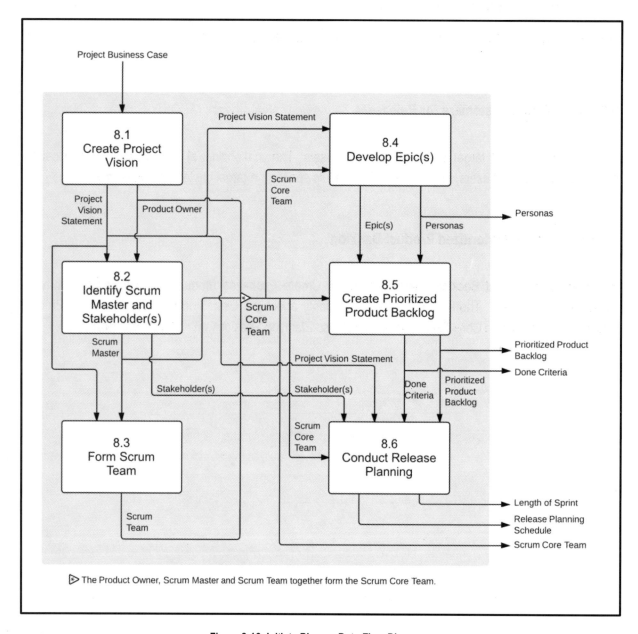

Figure 8-16: Initiate Phase—Data Flow Diagram

9. PLAN AND ESTIMATE

The Plan and Estimate phase consists of processes related to planning and estimating tasks, which include *Create User Stories, Approve, Estimate, and Commit User Stories, Create Tasks, Estimate Tasks,* and *Create Sprint Backlog.*

Plan and Estimate, as defined in *A Guide to the Scrum Body of Knowledge (SBOK™ Guide)*, is applicable to the following:

- Portfolios, programs, and/or projects in *any* industry
- Products, services, or any other results to be delivered to stakeholders
- Projects of any size or complexity

The term "product" in the *SBOK™ Guide* may refer to a product, service, or other deliverable. Scrum can be applied effectively to any project in any industry—from small projects or teams with as few as six team members to large, complex projects with up to several hundred team members.

To facilitate the best application of the Scrum framework, this chapter identifies inputs, tools, and outputs for each process as either "mandatory" or "optional." Inputs, tools, and outputs denoted by asterisks (*) are mandatory, whereas those with no asterisks are optional.

It is recommended that the Scrum Team and those individuals being introduced to the Scrum framework and processes focus primarily on the mandatory inputs, tools, and outputs; while Product Owners, Scrum Masters, and other more experienced Scrum practitioners strive to attain a more thorough knowledge of the information in this entire chapter. It is also important to realize that although all processes are defined uniquely in the *SBOK™ Guide*, they are not necessarily performed sequentially or separately. At times, it may be more appropriate to combine some processes, depending on the specific requirements of each project.

This chapter is written from the perspective of one Scrum Team working on one Sprint to produce potentially shippable Deliverables as part of a larger project. However, the information described is equally applicable to entire projects, programs, and portfolios. Additional information pertaining to the use of Scrum for projects, programs, and portfolios is available in chapters 2 through 7, which cover Scrum principles and Scrum aspects.

9

Figure 9-1 provides an overview of the Plan and Estimate phase processes, which are as follows:

9.1 Create User Stories—In this process, User Stories and their related User Story Acceptance Criteria are created. User Stories are usually written by the Product Owner and are designed to ensure that the customer's requirements are clearly depicted and can be fully understood by all stakeholders. User Story Writing Workshops may be held which involves Scrum Team members creating the User Stories. User Stories are incorporated into the Prioritized Product Backlog.

9.2 Approve, Estimate, and Commit User Stories—In this process, the Product Owner approves User Stories for a Sprint. Then, the Scrum Master and Scrum Team estimate the effort required to develop the functionality described in each User Story. Finally, the Scrum Team commits to deliver the customer requirements in the form of Approved, Estimated, and Committed User Stories.

9.3 Create Tasks—In this process, the Approved, Estimated, and Committed User Stories are broken down into specific tasks and compiled into a Task List. Often, a Task Planning Meeting is held for this purpose.

9.4 Estimate Tasks—In this process, the Scrum Core Team, in Task Estimation Meetings, estimate the effort required to accomplish each task in the Task List. The result of this process is an Effort Estimated Task List.

9.5 Create Sprint Backlog—In this process, the Scrum Core Team holds Sprint Planning Meetings where the group creates a Sprint Backlog containing all tasks to be completed in the Sprint.

9.1 Create User Stories

INPUTS
1. Scrum Core Team*
2. Prioritized Product Backlog*
3. Done Criteria*
4. Personas*
5. Stakeholder(s)
6. Epic(s)
7. Business Requirements
8. Laws and Regulations
9. Applicable Contracts
10. Scrum Guidance Body Recommendations

TOOLS
1. User Story Writing Expertise*
2. User Story Workshops
3. User Group Meetings
4. Focus Group Meetings
5. Customer or User Interviews
6. Questionnaires
7. User Story Estimation Methods
8. Scrum Guidance Body Expertise

OUTPUTS
1. User Stories*
2. User Story Acceptance Criteria*
3. Updated Prioritized Product Backlog
4. Updated or Refined Personas

9.2 Approve, Estimate, and Commit User Stories

INPUTS
1. Scrum Core Team*
2. User Stories*
3. User Story Acceptance Criteria*
4. Scrum Guidance Body Recommendations

TOOLS
1. User Group Meetings*
2. Planning Poker
3. Fist of Five
4. Points for Cost Estimation
5. Other Estimation Techniques
6. Scrum Guidance Body Expertise

OUTPUTS
1. Approved, Estimated, and Committed User Stories*

9.3 Create Tasks

INPUTS
1. Scrum Core Team*
2. Approved, Estimated, and Committed User Stories*

TOOLS
1. Task Planning Meetings*
2. Index Cards
3. Decomposition
4. Dependency Determination

OUTPUTS
1. Task List*
2. Updated Approved, Estimated, and Committed User Stories
3. Dependencies

9.4 Estimate Tasks

INPUTS
1. Scrum Core Team*
2. Task List*
3. User Story Acceptance Criteria
4. Dependencies
5. Identified Risks
6. Scrum Guidance Body Recommendations

TOOLS
1. Task Estimation Meetings*
2. Estimation Criteria*
3. Planning Poker
4. Fist of Five
5. Other Task Estimation Techniques

OUTPUTS
1. Effort Estimated Task List*
2. Updated Task List

9.5 Create Sprint Backlog

INPUTS
1. Scrum Core Team*
2. Effort Estimated Task List*
3. Length of Sprint*
4. Previous Sprint Velocity
5. Dependencies
6. Team Calendar

TOOLS
1. Sprint Planning Meetings*
2. Sprint Tracking Tools
3. Sprint Tracking Metrics

OUTPUTS
1. Sprint Backlog*
2. Sprint Burndown Chart*

Figure 9-1: Plan and Estimate Overview

Note: Asterisks (*) denote a "mandatory" input, tool, or output for the corresponding process.

Figure 9-2 below shows the mandatory inputs, tools, and outputs for processes in Plan and Estimate phase.

9.1 Create User Stories

INPUTS
1. Scrum Core Team*
2. Prioritized Product Backlog*
3. Done Criteria*
4. Personas*

TOOLS
1. User Story Writing Expertise*

OUTPUTS
1. User Stories*
2. User Story Acceptance Criteria*

9.2 Approve, Estimate, and Commit User Stories

INPUTS
1. Scrum Core Team*
2. User Stories*
3. User Story Acceptance Criteria*

TOOLS
1. User Story Meetings*

OUTPUTS
1. Approved, Estimated, and Committed User Stories*

9.3 Create Tasks

INPUTS
1. Scrum Core Team*
2. Approved, Estimated and Committed User Stories*

TOOLS
1. Task Planning Meetings*

OUTPUTS
1. Task List*

9.4 Estimate Tasks

INPUTS
1. Scrum Core Team*
2. Task List*

TOOLS
1. Task Estimation Meetings*
2. Estimation Criteria*

OUTPUTS
1. Effort Estimated Task List*

9.5 Create Sprint Backlog

INPUTS
1. Scrum Core Team*
2. Effort Estimated Task List*
3. Length of Sprint*

TOOLS
1. Sprint Planning Meetings*

OUTPUTS
1. Sprint Backlog*
2. Sprint Burndown Chart*

Figure 9-2: Plan and Estimate Overview (Essentials)

Note: Asterisks (*) denote a "mandatory" input, tool, or output for the corresponding process.

9.1 Create User Stories

Figure 9-3 shows all the inputs, tools, and outputs for *Create User Stories* process.

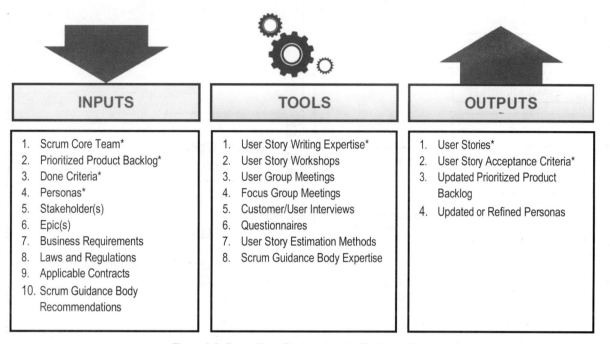

INPUTS

1. Scrum Core Team*
2. Prioritized Product Backlog*
3. Done Criteria*
4. Personas*
5. Stakeholder(s)
6. Epic(s)
7. Business Requirements
8. Laws and Regulations
9. Applicable Contracts
10. Scrum Guidance Body Recommendations

TOOLS

1. User Story Writing Expertise*
2. User Story Workshops
3. User Group Meetings
4. Focus Group Meetings
5. Customer/User Interviews
6. Questionnaires
7. User Story Estimation Methods
8. Scrum Guidance Body Expertise

OUTPUTS

1. User Stories*
2. User Story Acceptance Criteria*
3. Updated Prioritized Product Backlog
4. Updated or Refined Personas

9

Figure 9-3: Create User Stories—Inputs, Tools, and Outputs

Note: Asterisks (*) denote a "mandatory" input, tool, or output for the corresponding process.

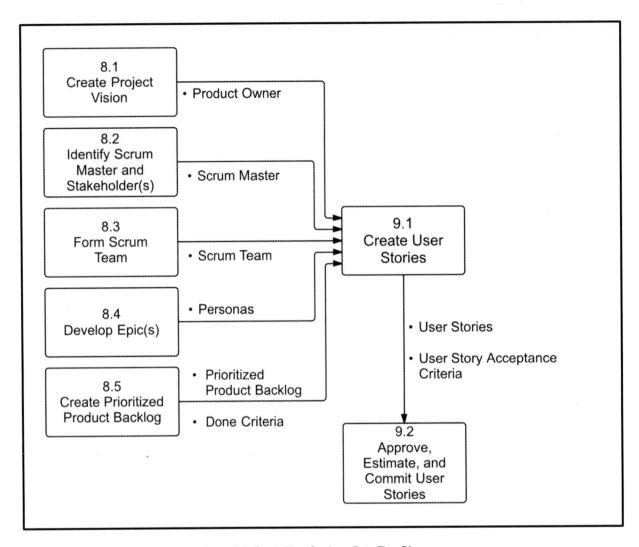

Figure 9-4: Create User Stories—Data Flow Diagram

9.1.1   Inputs

9.1.1.1   Scrum Core Team*

Described in section 8.4.1.1.

9.1.1.2   Prioritized Product Backlog*

Described in section 8.5.3.1.

9.1.1.3   Done Criteria*

Described in section 8.5.3.2.

9.1.1.4   Personas*

Described in section 8.4.3.2.

9.1.1.5   Stakeholder(s)

Described in section 8.2.3.2.

9.1.1.6   Epic(s)

Described in section 8.4.3.1.

9.1.1.7   Business Requirements

Described in section 8.5.1.7.

9.1.1.8   Laws and Regulations

Described in section 8.4.1.8.

9.1.1.9 Applicable Contracts

Described in section 8.4.1.9.

9.1.1.10 Scrum Guidance Body Recommendations

Described in section 8.1.1.12.

In *Create User Stories* process, Scrum Guidance Body Recommendations may include information on rules, regulations, standards, and best practices required to create effective User Stories.

9.1.2 Tools

9.1.2.1 User Story Writing Expertise*

The Product Owner, based on his or her interaction with the stakeholders, business knowledge and expertise, and inputs from the team, develops User Stories that will form the initial Prioritized Product Backlog for the project. The Prioritized Product Backlog represents the total sum of what must be completed for the project. The objective of this exercise is to create elaborated and refined User Stories that can be approved, estimated, and committed to by the Scrum Team. At times, the Product Owner may bring a Business Analyst to assist with writing User Stories.

Although the Product Owner has the primary responsibility for writing User Stories and often carries out this exercise on his or her own, a User Story Writing Workshop can be held if desired.

9.1.2.2 User Story Workshops

Described in section 8.4.2.2.

9.1.2.3 User Group Meetings

Described in section 8.4.2.1.

9.1.2.4   Focus Group Meetings

Focus Group Meetings are a qualitative technique to gauge and understand user needs and expectations about a proposed product. A small group of users are selected to form the focus group. This group may be selected randomly from a large pool of users or can be selected specifically to represent all the major Personas being targeted. Focus Group Meetings normally adhere to a certain format in which the group is asked questions that they then discuss among themselves. Each Focus Group Meeting can have its own rules of discussion as decided by the organizers. These meetings are usually held in the presence of a moderator.

9.1.2.5   Customer or User Interviews

Described in section 8.4.2.4.

9.1.2.6   Questionnaires

Described in section 8.4.2.5.

9.1.2.7   User Story Estimation Methods

All the tools used for *Approve, Estimate, and Commit User Stories* process (as described in section 9.2.2) can be used for creating high level estimates for Epic(s) when we create the Prioritized Product Backlog. Some important tools are:

1. User Group Meetings
2. Planning Poker
3. Fist of Five
4. Points for Cost Estimation
5. Other Estimation Techniques

9.1.2.8   Scrum Guidance Body Expertise

Described in section 8.4.2.7.

While creating User Stories, Scrum Guidance Body Expertise could relate to documented rules and regulations; or standards and best practices for creating User Stories. There may also be a team of subject matter experts who may assist the Product Owner or provide guidance on how to create User Stories. This team could include Business Analysts, Lead Architects, Senior Developers, Scrum Experts, or other experienced persons. This expert group is usually not the same team that will stay on and work on this project, as they tend to move from project to project and provide guidance to Scrum Teams if required.

9.1.3   Outputs

9.1.3.1   User Stories*

User Stories adhere to a specific, predefined structure and are a simplistic way of documenting the requirements and desired end-user functionality. A User Story tells you three things about the requirement: Who, What, and Why. The requirements expressed in User Stories are short, simple, and easy-to-understand statements. The predefined, standard format results in enhanced communication among the stakeholders and better estimations by the team. Some User Stories may be too large to handle within a single Sprint. These large User Stories are often called Epics. Once Epics come up in the Prioritized Product Backlog to be completed in an upcoming Sprint, they are further decomposed into smaller User Stories.

The Prioritized Product Backlog is a dynamic list that is continuously updated because of reprioritization and new, updated, refined, and sometimes, deleted User Stories. These updates to the backlog are typically the result of changing business requirements.

Also refer to section 8.5.3.1 to know more about the Prioritized Product Backlog.

User Story Format:

As a <role/persona>, I should be able to <requirement> so that <benefit>.

User Story Example:

As a Database Administrator, I should be able to revert a selected number of database updates so that the desired version of the database is restored.

9.1.3.2   User Story Acceptance Criteria*

Every User Story has an associated Acceptance Criteria. User Stories are subjective, so the Acceptance Criteria provide the objectivity required for the User Story to be considered as Done or not Done during the Sprint Review. Acceptance Criteria provide clarity to the team on what is expected of a User Story, remove ambiguity from requirements, and help in aligning expectations. The Product Owner defines and communicates the Acceptance Criteria to the Scrum Team. In the Sprint Review Meetings, the Acceptance Criteria provide the context for the Product Owner to decide if a User Story has been completed satisfactorily. It is important and the responsibility of the Scrum Master to ensure that the Product Owner does not change the Acceptance Criteria of a committed User Story in the middle of a Sprint.

9.1.3.3   Updated Prioritized Product Backlog

The Prioritized Product Backlog created in the *Create Prioritized Product Backlog* process is updated with information on User Stories, Epic(s), estimates for User Stories, and User Story Acceptance Criteria.

Prioritized Product Backlog is described in section 8.5.3.1.

9.1.3.4   Updated or Refined Personas

Personas are initially created in the *Develop Epic(s)* process. While writing User Stories, the Scrum Team may come to a collective decision that some of those initial Personas are inadequate and need refinement. If refining Personas is required, it is normally done near the end of the *Create User Stories* process.

Personas are described in section 8.4.3.2.

9

9.2 Approve, Estimate, and Commit User Stories

Figure 9-5 shows all the inputs, tools, and outputs for *Approve, Estimate, and Commit User Stories* process.

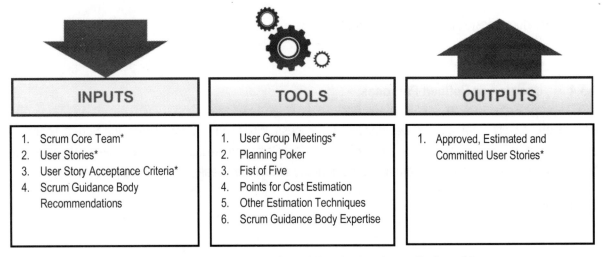

INPUTS	TOOLS	OUTPUTS
1. Scrum Core Team* 2. User Stories* 3. User Story Acceptance Criteria* 4. Scrum Guidance Body Recommendations	1. User Group Meetings* 2. Planning Poker 3. Fist of Five 4. Points for Cost Estimation 5. Other Estimation Techniques 6. Scrum Guidance Body Expertise	1. Approved, Estimated and Committed User Stories*

Figure 9-5: Approve, Estimate, and Commit User Stories—Inputs, Tools, and Outputs

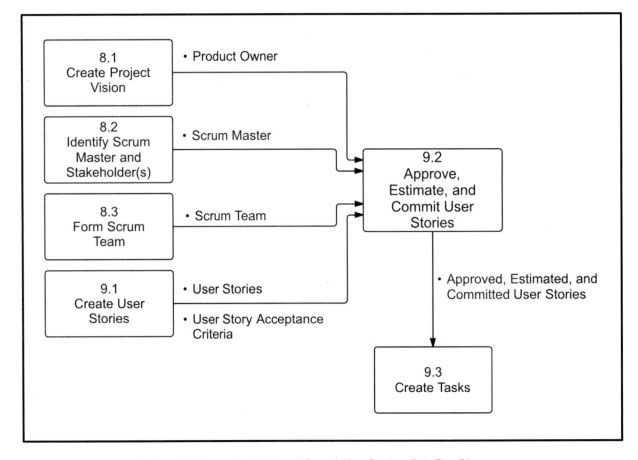

Figure 9-6: Approve, Estimate, and Commit User Stories—Data Flow Diagram

Note: Asterisks (*) denote a "mandatory" input, tool, or output for the corresponding process.

9.2.1   Inputs

9.2.1.1   Scrum Core Team*

Described in section 8.4.1.1.

9.2.1.2   User Stories*

Described in section 9.1.3.1.

The User Stories have high-level estimates from the *Create Prioritized Product Backlog* and *Create User Stories* processes. These estimates would be used by the Product Owner to create a list of approved User Stories which would be more accurately estimated by the Scrum Team. Such estimated User Stories are then committed to be completed by the Scrum Team in the Sprint.

9.2.1.3   User Story Acceptance Criteria*

Described in section 9.1.3.2.

9.2.1.4   Scrum Guidance Body Recommendations

Described in section 8.1.1.12.

In *Approve, Estimate, and Commit User Stories* process, Scrum Guidance Body Recommendations may include information on rules, regulations, standards, and best practices required to effectively Approve, Estimate, and Commit User Stories.

9.2.2   Tools

9.2.2.1   User Group Meetings*

Described in section 8.4.2.1.

9.2.2.2   Planning Poker

Planning Poker, also called Estimation Poker, is an estimation technique which uses consensus to estimate relative sizes of User Stories or the effort required to create them.

In Planning Poker, each team member is assigned a deck of cards. Each card is numbered in a sequence and the numbers represent complexity of the problem, in terms of time or effort, as estimated by the team member. The Product Owner chooses a User Story from the Prioritized Product Backlog and presents it to the team. The Scrum Team members assess the User Story and try to understand it better before providing their estimate for developing it. Then, each member picks a card from the deck that represents their estimate for the User Story. If the majority or all team members select the same card then the estimate indicated by that card will be the estimate for that User Story. If there is no consensus, then the team members discuss reasons for selecting different cards or estimates. After this discussion they pick cards again. This sequence continues until all the assumptions are understood, misunderstandings are resolved, and consensus or agreement is reached.

Planning Poker advocates greater interaction and enhanced communication among the participants. It facilitates independent thinking by participants, thus avoiding the phenomenon of group think.

9.2.2.3   Fist of Five

Fist of Five is a simple and fast mechanism to achieve consensus in a group and drive discussion. After initial discussion on a given proposal or a pending decision, the Scrum Team members are each asked to vote on a scale of 1 to 5 using their fingers. The value in using this technique is not only consensus building but also driving discussion because each team member is asked to explain the reason for their ranking. They are also given the opportunity to express any issues or concerns. Once the team has discussed it, a collective decision will be made.

The number of fingers used to vote indicates the level of agreement and desire for discussion:

1. One finger: I disagree with the group's conclusion and have major concerns.
2. Two fingers: I disagree with the group's conclusion and would like to discuss some minor issues.
3. Three fingers: I am not sure and would like to go with the group's consensus conclusion.
4. Four fingers: I agree with the group's conclusion and would like to discuss some minor issues.
5. Five fingers: I wholeheartedly agree with the group's conclusion.

9.2.2.4   Points for Cost Estimation

Cost estimation can be accomplished through the use of relative units (e.g., effort estimates) rather than absolute units (i.e., actual costs incurred). In order to estimate the cost to implement a User Story, the Scrum Team can use story points. When this is done, the cost estimated for each task will be in the form of story points, rather than monetary units. In order to do this successfully, the Scrum Team should identify a baseline User Story that all team members can relate to. Once this baseline is identified, all cost estimates for User Stories should be done compared to that baseline. These estimates remain fixed throughout a Sprint because teams are not supposed to change during a Sprint.

9.2.2.5 Other Estimation Techniques

9.2.2.5.1 Wideband Delphi

Wideband Delphi is a group-based estimation technique for determining how much work is involved and how long it will take to complete. Individuals within a team anonymously provide estimations for each feature and the initial estimates are plotted on a chart. The team then discusses the factors that influenced their estimates and proceed to a second round of estimation. This process is repeated until the estimates of individuals are close to each other and a consensus for the final estimate can be reached.

Planning poker (as described in section 9.2.2.2) is one example of a Wideband Delphi technique. It is also important to note that it is the individual input collected by a mechanism that avoids the group thinking. Then the individual inputs are used for a group decision.

9

9.2.2.5.2 Relative Sizing/Story Points

In addition to being used for estimating cost, story points can also be used for estimating the overall size of a User Story or feature. This approach assigns a story point value based on an overall assessment of the size of a User Story with consideration given to risk, amount of effort required, and level of complexity. This assessment will be conducted by the Scrum Team and a story point value will be assigned. Once an evaluation is done on one User Story in the Prioritized Product Backlog, the Scrum Team can then evaluate other User Stories relative to that first story. For example, a feature with a 2-point story value must be twice as difficult to complete as a feature with a 1-point story; a 3-point story should be three times as difficult to complete as a 1-point story.

9.2.2.5.3 Affinity Estimation

Affinity Estimation is a technique used to quickly estimate a large number of User Stories. Using sticky notes or index cards and tape, the team places User Stories on a wall or other surface, in order from small to large. For this, each team member begins with a subset of User Stories from the overall Prioritized Product Backlog to place by relative size. This initial placement is done in silence. Once everyone has placed their User Stories on the wall, the team reviews all of the placements and may move User Stories around as appropriate. This second part of the exercise involves discussion. Finally, the Product Owner will indicate some sizing categories on the wall. These categories can be small, medium, or large, or they may be numbered using story point values to indicate relative size. The team will then move User Stories into these categories as the final step in the process. Some key benefits of this approach are that the process is very transparent, visible to everyone, and is easy to conduct.

9.2.2.5.4 Estimate Range

Estimates for projects should be presented in ranges. Precise figures may give an impression of being highly accurate when in fact they may not be. In fact, estimates by definition are understood not to be precisely accurate. Estimate ranges should be based on the level of confidence the team has in each estimate. The range can be narrow when the team is confident and wide when the team is less confident.

9.2.2.6 Scrum Guidance Body Expertise

Described in section 8.4.2.7.

Conflicts with respect to estimates for completing certain User Stories may arise during this process because team member perspectives may differ and because the team may not yet have enough experiences to estimate Sprints. In these situations, the Guidance Body's experience and expertise can assist in resolving conflicts.

9.2.3 Outputs

9.2.3.1 Approved, Estimated, and Committed User Stories*

The User Stories which are input to this process have high-level estimates from the *Create Prioritized Product Backlog* and *Create User Stories* processes. These estimates are used by the Product Owner to approve User Stories for the Sprint.

It must be noted that it is the Product Owner's responsibility to ensure that approved User Stories deliver value and meet the needs and requirements of the project stakeholders. Once approved, the User Stories are estimated by the team using the various estimation techniques discussed in this section. After estimation, the team commits to a subset of approved and estimated User Stories that they believe they can complete in the next Sprint. These User Stories are Approved, Estimated, and Committed User Stories which will become part of the Sprint Backlog.

Although the Product Owner approves the initial User Stories for a Sprint, the final decision about which specific User Stories (among those approved by the Product Owner) should be chosen for the Sprint lies with the Scrum Team. The Scrum Team (with consultation from the Product Owner, if required) finalizes which User Stories they will be working on during the Sprint.

9.3 Create Tasks

Figure 9-7 shows all the inputs, tools, and outputs for *Create Tasks* process.

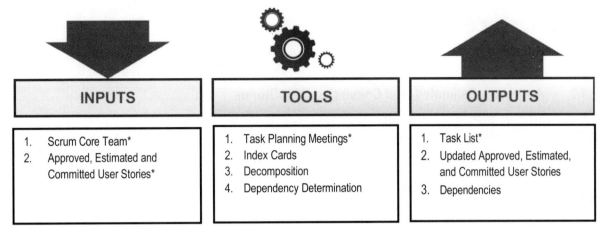

Figure 9-7: Create Tasks—Inputs, Tools, and Outputs

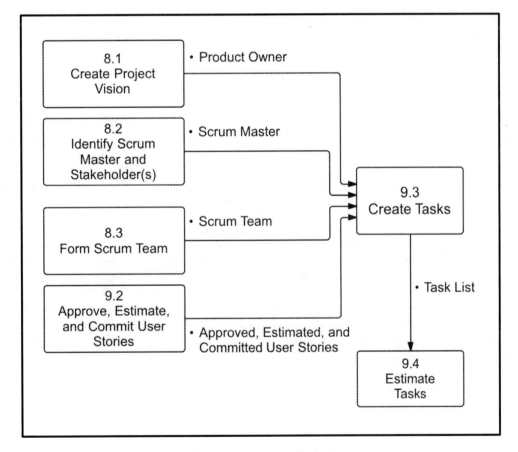

Figure 9-8: Create Tasks—Data Flow Diagram

Note: Asterisks (*) denote a "mandatory" input, tool, or output for the corresponding process.

9.3.1 Inputs

9.3.1.1 Scrum Core Team*

Described in sections 8.4.1.1.

9.3.1.2 Approved, Estimated, and Committed User Stories*

Described in section 9.2.3.1.

9.3.2 Tools

9.3.2.1 Task Planning Meetings*

In Task Planning Meetings, the Scrum Team gets together to plan the work to be done in the Sprint. The team reviews the committed User Stories at the top of the Prioritized Product Backlog. The Product Owner is present during this meeting in case clarification is required related to User Stories in the Prioritized Product Backlog and to help the team make design decisions. To help ensure that the group stays on topic, this meeting should be Time-boxed, with the standard length limited to two hours per week of Sprint duration. This assists in preventing the tendency to stray into discussions that should actually occur in other meetings, like the Release Planning or Sprint Review Meetings. By the end of the meeting, the entire Scrum Team will have fully committed to deliver a subset of User Stories from the Prioritized Product Backlog in the Sprint.

The Task Planning Meeting is normally divided into two sections, with a designated purpose and broad agenda for each (see Figure 9-9)

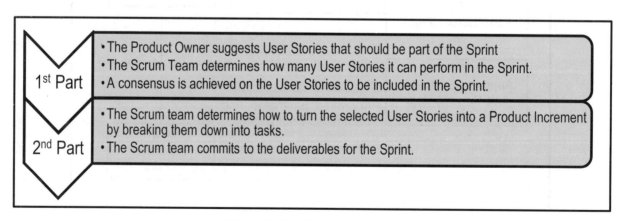

Figure 9-9: Task Planning Meetings

The Task Planning Meetings may at times also be referred to as "Sprint Planning Meetings" - such meetings may also be combined with Task Estimation Meetings as described in section 9.4.2.1

9.3.2.2   Index Cards

In Scrum, User Stories are written on small Index Cards. Only essential details are documented on the cards, which can be used by the Scrum Team to collaborate and discuss. These Index Cards, often described as Story Cards, increase visibility and transparency, and facilitate early discovery of any problems that may arise.

9.3.2.3   Decomposition

Decomposition is a tool whereby high-level tasks are broken down into lower level, more detailed tasks. The User Stories are decomposed into tasks by members of the Scrum Team. Prioritized Product Backlog User Stories should be sufficiently decomposed to a level that provides the Scrum Team adequate information to create deliverables from the tasks mentioned in the Task List.

9.3.2.4   Dependency Determination

Once the Scrum Team has selected User Stories for a given Sprint, they should then consider any dependencies, including those related to the availability of people as well as any technical dependencies. Properly documenting dependencies helps the Scrum Teams determine the relative order in which Tasks should be executed to create the Sprint Deliverables. Dependencies also highlight the relationship and interaction between Tasks both within the Scrum Team working on a given Sprint and with other Scrum Teams in the project.

There are numerous types of dependencies: mandatory and discretionary, internal and external, or some combination of these dependencies. For example, a dependency may be both mandatory and external.

- **Mandatory dependencies**—Dependencies that are either inherent in the nature of the work, like a physical limitation, or that may be due to contractual obligations or legal requirements. For example, work on the first floor cannot begin until the foundation of the building is complete. Mandatory dependencies are also commonly described as hard logic.

- **Discretionary dependencies**—Dependencies that are placed into the workflow by choice. Typically, discretionary dependencies are determined by the Scrum Team based on past experiences or best practices in a particular field or domain. For example, the team can decide to complete one task before working on another because it is a best practice, but not required. For example, the team may choose to build the door and window frames before the full structure of the wall is in place.

- **External dependencies**—External dependencies are those related to tasks, activities, or products that are outside the scope of the work to be executed by the Scrum Team, but are needed to complete a project task or create a project deliverable. External dependencies are usually outside the Scrum Team's control. For example, if the Scrum Team is not responsible for procuring the materials required for building the walls, then those materials and tasks related to their procurement are considered external dependencies.

- **Internal dependencies**—Internal dependencies are those dependencies between tasks, products, or activities that are under the control of the Scrum Team. For example, installing drywall must be completed before painting the wall can begin. This is an example of an internal dependency because both tasks are part of the project. In this case, it is also mandatory because it is based on a physical limitation. It is not possible to paint the wall before it is dry-walled.

9.3.3   Outputs

9.3.3.1   Task List*

This is a comprehensive list that contains all the tasks to which the Scrum Team has committed for the current Sprint. It contains descriptions of each task along with estimates derived during the *Create Tasks* process. The Task List must include any testing and integration efforts so that the Product Increment from the Sprint can be successfully integrated into the deliverables from previous Sprints.

Even though tasks are often activity based, the level of granularity to which the tasks are decomposed is decided by the Scrum Team.

9.3.3.2   Updated Approved, Estimated, and Committed User Stories

The User Stories are updated during this process. Updates can include revisions to the original User Story estimates based on tasks creation and complexity factors discussed during the Sprint Planning Meeting. Approved, Estimated, and Committed User Stories are described in section 9.2.3.1.

9.3.3.3   Dependencies

Dependencies describe the relationship and interaction between different tasks in a project and can be classified as mandatory or discretionary; or internal or external; as discussed in section 9.3.2.4.

There are numerous ways to identify, define, and present the tasks and their dependencies. Two common methods involve the use of product flow diagrams and Gantt charts.

9.4 Estimate Tasks

Figure 9-10 shows all the inputs, tools, and outputs for *Estimate Tasks* process.

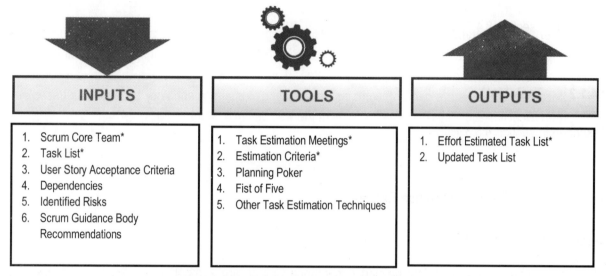

INPUTS

1. Scrum Core Team*
2. Task List*
3. User Story Acceptance Criteria
4. Dependencies
5. Identified Risks
6. Scrum Guidance Body Recommendations

TOOLS

1. Task Estimation Meetings*
2. Estimation Criteria*
3. Planning Poker
4. Fist of Five
5. Other Task Estimation Techniques

OUTPUTS

1. Effort Estimated Task List*
2. Updated Task List

Figure 9-10: Estimate Tasks—Inputs, Tools, and Outputs

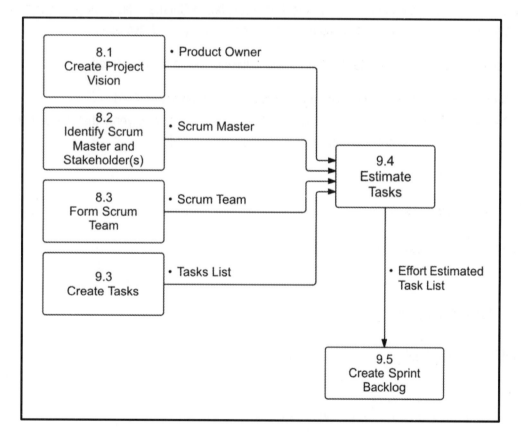

Figure 9-11: Estimate Tasks—Data Flow Diagram

Note: Asterisks (*) denote a "mandatory" input, tool, or output for the corresponding process.

9.4.1   Inputs

9.4.1.1   Scrum Core Team*

Described in section 8.4.1.1.

9.4.1.2   Task List*

Described in section 9.3.3.1.

9.4.1.3   User Story Acceptance Criteria

Described in section 9.1.3.2.

The Scrum Team must ensure that defined Acceptance Criteria are appropriate for the User Stories and provide clarity regarding the requirements to the Scrum Team. Acceptance testing refers to the assessment of the ability of the completed deliverable to meet its Acceptance Criteria. This provides information to the Product Owner to help make a decision about approving or rejecting the Deliverable.

When developing User Story Acceptance Criteria, the following should be considered:

*   Acceptance Criteria should not be vague, ambiguous, or too generalized.
*   Defined Acceptance Criteria should ensure that the team is able to verify that the outcomes are in alignment with the sponsor organization's goals and objectives.

9.4.1.4   Dependencies

Described in section 9.3.3.3

9.4.1.5   Identified Risks

Described in section 8.4.3.4.

9.4.1.6   Scrum Guidance Body Recommendations

Described in section 8.1.1.12.

In the *Estimate Tasks* process, Scrum Guidance Body Recommendations may include information on rules, regulations, standards, and best practices required to effectively estimate tasks in the Task List.

9.4.2   Tools

9.4.2.1   Task Estimation Meetings*

Task Estimation Meetings enable the Scrum Team to estimate the effort required to complete a task or set of tasks and to estimate the people effort and other resources required to carry out the tasks within a given Sprint. In Task Estimation Meetings, the Scrum Team members use the Task List to estimate the duration and effort for the User Stories to be completed in the Sprint.

One of the key benefits of this technique is that it enables the team to have a shared perspective of the User Stories and requirements so that they can reliably estimate the effort required. The information developed in the Task Estimation Meetings is included in the Effort Estimated Task List and it is used to determine the velocity for the Sprint.

In this workshop, the Scrum Team may use various techniques such as decomposition, expert judgment, analogous estimation, and parametric estimation.

Task Estimation Meetings are sometimes also referred to as "Sprint Planning Meetings" - such meetings may also be combined with Task Planning Meetings as described in section 9.3.2.1.

9.4.2.2   Estimation Criteria*

The primary objective of using Estimation Criteria is to maintain relative estimation sizes and minimize the need for re-estimation. Estimation Criteria can be expressed in numerous ways, with two common examples being story points and ideal time. For example, an ideal time normally describes the number of hours a Scrum Team member works exclusively on developing the project's deliverables, without including any time spent on other activities or work that is outside the project. Estimation Criteria make it easier for the Scrum Team to estimate effort and enable them to evaluate and address inefficiencies when necessary.

9.4.2.3   Planning Poker

Described in section 9.2.2.2.

9.4.2.4   Fist of Five

Described in section 9.2.2.3.

9.4.2.5   Other Task Estimation Techniques

Described in section 9.2.2.5.

9.4.3   Outputs

9.4.3.1   Effort Estimated Task List*

The Effort Estimated Task List is a list of tasks associated with the Committed User Stories included in a Sprint. Typically the accuracy of estimates varies with team skills. Estimated effort is expressed in terms of the Estimation Criteria agreed on by the team. The Effort Estimated Task List is used by the Scrum Team during Sprint Planning Meetings to create the Sprint Backlog and Sprint Burndown Chart. It is also used to determine when the team needs to reduce its commitment, or can take on additional User Stories during Sprint Planning.

9.4.3.2   Updated Task List

The Task List, developed as part of the *Create Tasks* process, includes the initial User Story estimations that need to be revised based on the more detailed estimation activities undertaken in the *Estimate Tasks* process. There may also be re-estimations resulting from a review of early Sprints, or change in the Scrum Team's collective understanding of User Stories and requirements.

9.5 Create Sprint Backlog

Figure 9-12 shows all the inputs, tools, and outputs for *Create Sprint Backlog* process.

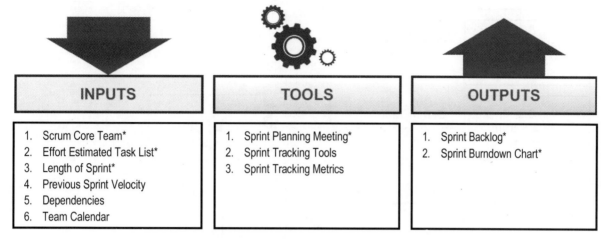

INPUTS	TOOLS	OUTPUTS
1. Scrum Core Team*	1. Sprint Planning Meeting*	1. Sprint Backlog*
2. Effort Estimated Task List*	2. Sprint Tracking Tools	2. Sprint Burndown Chart*
3. Length of Sprint*	3. Sprint Tracking Metrics	
4. Previous Sprint Velocity		
5. Dependencies		
6. Team Calendar		

Figure 9-12: Create Sprint Backlog—Inputs, Tools, and Outputs

Note: Asterisks (*) denote a "mandatory" input, tool, or output for the corresponding process.

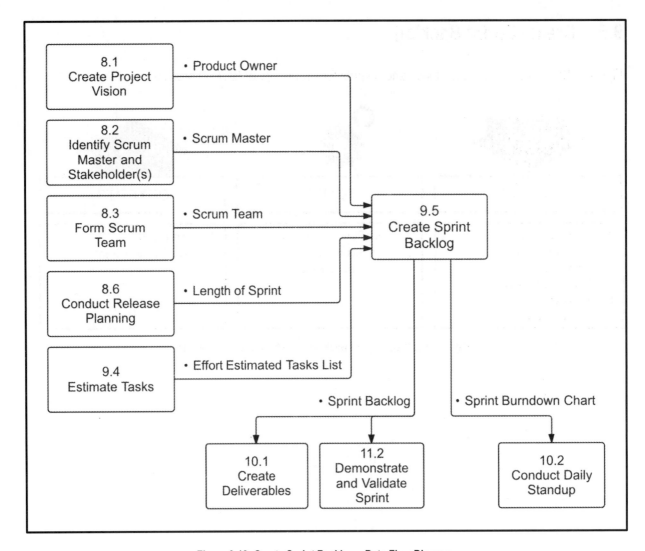

Figure 9-13: Create Sprint Backlog—Data Flow Diagram

9.5.1 Inputs

9.5.1.1 Scrum Core Team*

Described in section 8.4.1.1.

9.5.1.2 Effort Estimated Task List*

Described in section 9.4.3.1.

9.5.1.3 Length of Sprint*

Described in section 8.6.3.2.

9.5.1.4 Previous Sprint Velocity

Sprint Velocity is the rate at which the team can complete the work in a Sprint. It is usually expressed in the same units as those used for estimation, normally story points or ideal time. A record of the Sprint Velocity of the team for each Sprint is maintained and used as a reference in future Sprints. The Previous Sprint Velocity becomes the most important factor in determining the amount of work the team can commit to in a subsequent Sprint. Any changes in the situation or conditions since the last Sprint are accounted for to ensure accurate estimation of Sprint velocity for the upcoming Sprint.

9.5.1.5 Dependencies

Described in section 9.3.3.3.

9.5.1.6 Team Calendar

A Team Calendar contains information regarding availability of team members including information related to employee vacation, leaves, important events, and holidays.

One of the major objectives of using a Team Calendar is to track what each team member is working on throughout the project. It helps the team not only in planning and executing the Sprints efficiently but also in aligning the Sprints with release dates.

9.5.2   Tools

9.5.2.1   Sprint Planning Meetings*

During Sprint Planning Meetings, the User Stories, which are approved, estimated, and committed during the *Approve, Estimate, and Commit User Stories* process, are taken up for discussion by the Scrum Team. Each Scrum Team member also uses Effort Estimated Task List to select the tasks they plan to work on in the Sprint, based on their skills and experience. The Scrum Team also creates the Sprint Backlog and Sprint Burndown Chart using the User Stories and the Effort Estimated Task List during the Sprint Planning Meetings.

9.5.2.2   Sprint Tracking Tools

It is important to track the progress of a Sprint and to know where the Scrum Team stands in terms of completing the tasks in the Sprint Backlog. A variety of tools can be used to track the work in a Sprint, but one of the most common is a Scrumboard, also known as a task board or a progress chart. The Scrumboard is divided into sections: To Do (sometimes referred to as Work Not Started), Work In Progress, and Completed Work. Sticky notes representing each task or User Story are placed in the appropriate category to reflect the status of the work. They are moved forward to the next category as the work progresses.

9.5.2.3   Sprint Tracking Metrics

Metrics used in Scrum projects include velocity, business value delivered, and number of stories.

Velocity—represents the number of User Stories or number of functionalities delivered in a single Sprint.

Business value delivered—measures the value of the User Stories delivered from the business perspective.

Number of stories—refers to how many User Stories are delivered as part of a single Sprint. It can be expressed in terms of simple count or weighted count.

9.5.3   Outputs

9.5.3.1   Sprint Backlog*

The list of the tasks to be executed by the Scrum Team in the upcoming Sprint is called the Sprint Backlog.

It is common practice that the Sprint Backlog is represented on a Scrumboard or task board, which provides a constantly visible depiction of the status of the User Stories in the backlog. Also included in the Sprint Backlog are any risks associated with the various tasks. Any mitigating activities to address the identified risks would also be included as tasks in the Sprint Backlog.

Once the Sprint Backlog is finalized and committed to by the Scrum Team, new User Stories should not be added; however, tasks that might have been missed or overlooked from the committed User Stories may need to be added. If new requirements arise during a Sprint, they will be added to the overall Prioritized Product Backlog and included in a future Sprint.

9.5.3.2   Sprint Burndown Chart*

The Sprint Burndown Chart is a graph that depicts the amount of work remaining in the ongoing Sprint. The initial Sprint Burndown Chart is accompanied by a planned burndown. The Sprint Burndown Chart should be updated at the end of each day as work is completed. This chart shows the progress that has been made by the Scrum Team and also allows for the detection of estimates that may have been incorrect. If the Sprint Burndown Chart shows that the Scrum Team is not on track to finish the tasks in the Sprint on time, the Scrum Master should identify any obstacles or impediments to successful completion and try to remove them.

A related chart is a Sprint Burnup Chart. Unlike the Sprint Burndown Chart which shows the amount of work remaining, the Sprint Burnup Chart depicts the work completed as part of the Sprint.

9.6 Phase Data Flow Diagram

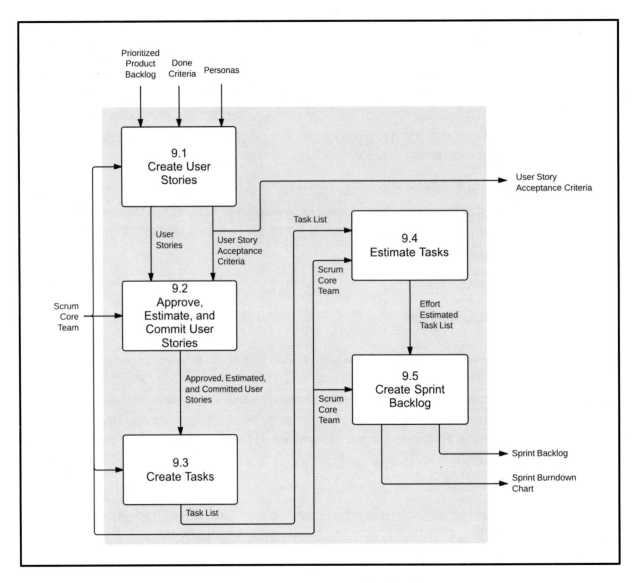

Figure 9-14: Plan and Estimate Phase—Data Flow Diagram

10. IMPLEMENT

The Implement phase is related to the execution of the tasks and activities to create a project's product. These activities include creating various deliverables, conducting Daily Standup Meetings, and grooming (i.e., reviewing, fine-tuning, and regularly updating) the Product Backlog at regular intervals.

Implement, as defined in *A Guide to the Scrum Body of Knowledge* (*SBOK™ Guide*), is applicable to the following:

- Portfolios, programs, and/or projects in *any* industry
- Products, services, or any other results to be delivered to stakeholders
- Projects of any size or complexity

The term "product" in the *SBOK™ Guide* may refer to a product, service, or other deliverable. Scrum can be applied effectively to any project in any industry—from small projects or teams with as few as six team members to large, complex projects with up to several hundred team members.

To facilitate the best application of the Scrum framework, this chapter identifies inputs, tools, and outputs for each process as either "mandatory" or "optional." Inputs, tools, and outputs denoted by asterisks (*) are mandatory, whereas those with no asterisks are optional.

It is recommended that the Scrum Team and those individuals being introduced to the Scrum framework and processes focus primarily on the mandatory inputs, tools, and outputs; while Product Owners, Scrum Masters, and other more experienced Scrum practitioners strive to attain a more thorough knowledge of the information in this entire chapter. It is also important to realize that although all processes are defined uniquely in the *SBOK™ Guide*, they are not necessarily performed sequentially or separately. At times, it may be more appropriate to combine some processes, depending on the specific requirements of each project.

This chapter is written from the perspective of one Scrum Team working on one Sprint to produce potentially shippable Deliverables as part of a larger project. However, the information described is equally applicable to entire projects, programs, and portfolios. Additional information pertaining to the use of Scrum for projects, programs, and portfolios is available in chapters 2 through 7, which cover Scrum principles and Scrum aspects.

10

Figure 10-1 provides an overview of the Implement phase processes, which are as follows:

10.1 Create Deliverables—In this process, the Scrum Team works on the tasks in the Sprint Backlog to create Sprint Deliverables. A Scrumboard is often used to track the work and activities being carried out. Issues or problems being faced by the Scrum Team could be updated in an Impediment Log.

10.2 Conduct Daily Standup—In this process, everyday a highly focused, Time-boxed meeting is conducted referred to as the Daily Standup Meeting. This is the forum for the Scrum Team to update each other on their progress and any impediments they may be facing.

10.3 Groom Prioritized Product Backlog—In this process, the Prioritized Product Backlog is continuously updated and maintained. A Prioritized Product Backlog Review Meeting may be held, in which any changes or updates to the backlog are discussed and incorporated into the Prioritized Product Backlog as appropriate.

10.1 Create Deliverables

INPUTS
1. Scrum Core Team*
2. Sprint Backlog*
3. Scrumboard*
4. Impediment Log*
5. Release Planning Schedule
6. Dependencies
7. Scrum Guidance Body Recommendations

TOOLS
1. Team Expertise*
2. Software
3. Other Development Tools
4. Scrum Guidance Body Expertise

OUTPUTS
1. Sprint Deliverables*
2. Updated Scrumboard*
3. Updated Impediment Log*
4. Unapproved Change Requests
5. Identified Risks
6. Mitigated Risks
7. Updated Dependencies

10.2 Conduct Daily Standup

INPUTS
1. Scrum Team*
2. Scrum Master*
3. Sprint Burndown Chart*
4. Impediment Log*
5. Product Owner
6. Previous Work Day Experience
7. Scrumboard
8. Dependencies

TOOLS
1. Daily Standup Meeting*
2. Three Daily Questions*
3. War Room
4. Video Conferencing

OUTPUTS
1. Updated Sprint Burndown Chart*
2. Updated Impediment Log*
3. Motivated Scrum Team
4. Updated Scrumboard
5. Unapproved Change Requests
6. Identified Risks
7. Mitigated Risks
8. Updated Dependencies

10.3 Groom Prioritized Product Backlog

INPUTS
1. Scrum Core Team*
2. Prioritized Product Backlog*
3. Rejected Deliverables
4. Approved Change Requests
5. Unapproved Change Requests
6. Identified Risks
7. Updated Program Product Backlog
8. Retrospect Sprint Log(s)
9. Dependencies
10. Release Planning Schedule
11. Scrum Guidance Body Recommendations

TOOLS
1. Prioritized Product Backlog Review Meetings*
2. Communication Techniques
3. Other Prioritized Product Backlog Grooming Techniques

OUTPUTS
1. Updated Prioritized Product Backlog*
2. Updated Release Planning Schedule

10

Figure 10-1: Implement Overview

Note: Asterisks (*) denote a "mandatory" input, tool, or output for the corresponding process.

Figure 10-2 below shows the mandatory inputs, tools, and outputs for processes in Implement phase.

10.1 Create Deliverables

INPUTS
1. Scrum Core Team*
2. Sprint Backlog*
3. Scrumboard*
4. Impediment Log*

TOOLS
1. Team Expertise*

OUTPUTS
1. Sprint Deliverables*
2. Updated Scrumboard*
3. Updated Impediment Log*

10.2 Conduct Daily Standup

INPUTS
1. Scrum Team*
2. Scrum Master*
3. Sprint Burndown Chart*
4. Impediment Log*

TOOLS
1. Daily Standup Meeting*
2. Three Daily Questions*

OUTPUTS
1. Updated Sprint Burndown Chart*
2. Updated Impediment Log*

10.3 Groom Prioritized Product Backlog

INPUTS
1. Scrum Core Team*
2. Prioritized Product Backlog*

TOOLS
1. Prioritized Product Backlog Review Meeting*

OUTPUTS
1. Updated Prioritized Product Backlog*

Figure 10-2: Implement Overview (Essentials)

Note: Asterisks (*) denote a "mandatory" input, tool, or output for the corresponding process.

10.1 Create Deliverables

Figure 10-3 shows all the inputs, tools, and outputs for *Create Deliverables* process.

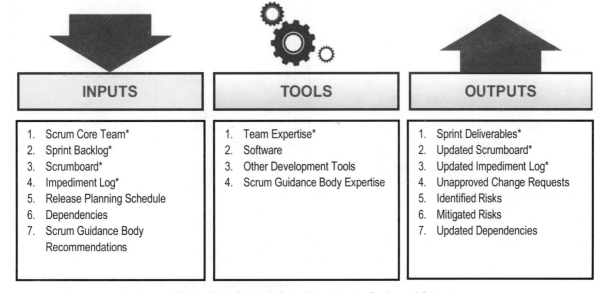

INPUTS	TOOLS	OUTPUTS
1. Scrum Core Team*	1. Team Expertise*	1. Sprint Deliverables*
2. Sprint Backlog*	2. Software	2. Updated Scrumboard*
3. Scrumboard*	3. Other Development Tools	3. Updated Impediment Log*
4. Impediment Log*	4. Scrum Guidance Body Expertise	4. Unapproved Change Requests
5. Release Planning Schedule		5. Identified Risks
6. Dependencies		6. Mitigated Risks
7. Scrum Guidance Body Recommendations		7. Updated Dependencies

Figure 10-3: Create Deliverables—Inputs, Tools, and Outputs

10

Note: Asterisks (*) denote a "mandatory" input, tool, or output for the corresponding process.

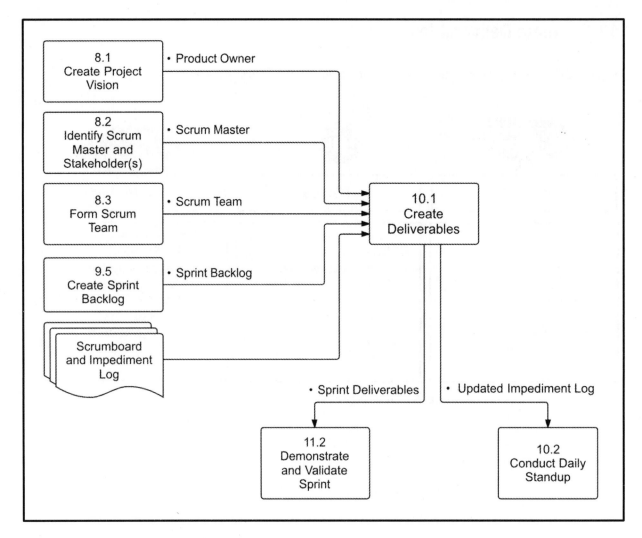

Figure 10-4: Create Deliverables—Data Flow Diagram

10.1.1 Inputs

10.1.1.1 Scrum Core Team*

Described in section 8.4.1.1.

10.1.1.2 Sprint Backlog*

Described in section 9.5.3.1.

10.1.1.3 Scrumboard*

Scrum's transparency comes from openly viewable information tools like the Scrumboard, which shows the progress of the team. The team uses a Scrumboard to plan and track progress during each Sprint. The Scrumboard contains four columns to indicate the progress of the estimated tasks for the Sprint: a 'To Do' column for tasks not yet started, an 'In Progress' column for the tasks started but not yet completed, a 'Testing' column for tasks completed but in the process of being tested, and a 'Done' column for the tasks that have been completed and successfully tested. At the beginning of a Sprint, all tasks for that Sprint are placed in the 'To Do' column and are subsequently moved forward according to their progress.

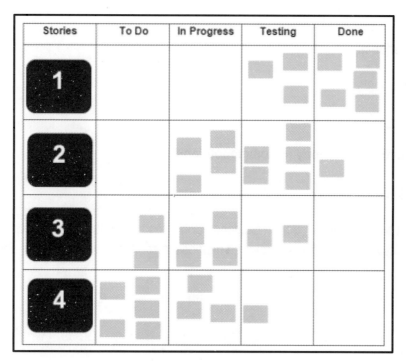

Figure 10-5: Scrumboard

The Scrumboard should preferably be maintained manually on paper or a white board, but can also be maintained electronically in a spreadsheet.

The Scrum Team should change or add to the Scrumboard as required so that the Scrumboard provides visual information and control about the work going on as agreed and committed by the team.

10.1.1.4 Impediment Log*

An impediment is any hindrance or hurdle that reduces the productivity of the Scrum Team. Impediments must be identified, resolved and removed if the team is to continue working effectively. Impediments can be internal to the team, such as inefficient workflow or lack of communication, or they can be external. Examples of external impediments might include software license issues or unnecessary documentation requirements. The Scrum framework, with its inherent transparency, facilitates the swift and easy identification of impediments. Failure to identify or deal with impediments can be very costly. Impediments should be formally recorded by the Scrum Master in an Impediment Log, and can be discussed during Daily Standup Meetings and Sprint Review Meetings as appropriate.

10.1.1.5 Release Planning Schedule

Described in section 8.6.3.1.

10.1.1.6 Dependencies

Described in section 9.3.3.3.

10.1.1.7 Scrum Guidance Body Recommendations

Described in section 8.1.1.12.

In the *Create Deliverables* process, Scrum Guidance Body Recommendations may include best practices to effectively create deliverables, including preferred methods to conduct reviews, testing, documentation, etc.

10.1.2 Tools

10.1.2.1 Team Expertise*

This refers to the collective expertise of the Scrum Team members to understand the User Stories and tasks in the Sprint Backlog in order to create the final deliverables. Team Expertise is used to assess the inputs needed to execute the planned work of the project. This judgment and expertise are applied to all technical and management aspects of the project during the *Create Deliverables* process. Scrum Team members have the authority and responsibility to determine the best means for converting the Prioritized Product Backlog Items into finished products, without requiring involvement of any stakeholders outside the team. Additional expertise is available from the Scrum Guidance Body, as required.

10.1.2.2 Software

Automated Software tools can be used for scheduling, information collection, and distribution. Virtual collaboration tools are also essential in projects where the Scrum Team is not colocated. A variety of automated software-based tools are available, which enable tracking progress, data collection, and distribution, and contribute to speeding up processes.

10.1.2.3 Other Development Tools

Based on the specific requirements of the project and industry specifications, other development tools can be used accordingly.

1. **Refactoring**

   Refactoring is a tool specific to software projects. The aim of this technique is to improve the maintainability of the existing code and make it simpler, more concise, and more flexible. Refactoring means improving the design of the present code without changing how the code behaves. It involves the following:

   - Eliminating repetitive and redundant code
   - Breaking methods and functions into smaller routines
   - Clearly defining variables and method names
   - Simplifying the code design
   - Making the code easier to understand and modify

   Regular refactoring optimizes code design a little at a time, over a period of time. Ultimately, refactoring results in cleaner, more maintainable code, while preserving all functionalities.

2. **Design Patterns**

    Design Patterns provide a formal way of recording a resolution to a design problem in a specific field of expertise. These patterns record both the process used and the actual resolution, which can later be reused to improve decision making and productivity.

10.1.2.4   Scrum Guidance Body Expertise

Described in section 8.4.2.7.

In *Create Deliverables* and *Approve, Estimate and Commit User Stories* processes, Scrum Guidance Body Expertise could relate to documented rules and regulations, development guidelines; or standards and best practices (e.g., guidance on how to conduct reviews or testing). There may also be a team of subject matter experts who may provide guidance to the Scrum Team in creating deliverables. This team could include Lead Architects, Senior Developers, Security Experts, or other experienced persons.

10.1.3   Outputs

10.1.3.1   Sprint Deliverables*

At the end of each Sprint, a product increment or deliverable is completed. The deliverable should possess all features and functionality defined in the User Stories included in the Sprint and should have been tested successfully.

10.1.3.2   Updated Scrumboard*

The Scrumboard is updated regularly as the team keeps completing tasks. However, at the end of the Sprint, the Scrumboard will be reset or wiped off and a new Scrumboard is created for the next Sprint.

10.1.3.3   Updated Impediment Log

Described in section 10.1.1.4.

10.1.3.4   Unapproved Change Requests

Described in section 8.4.1.6.

10.1.3.5   Identified Risks

Described in section 8.4.3.4.

10.1.3.6   Mitigated Risks

As the Scrum Team executes the work of creating deliverables according to the User Stories in the Product Backlog, they carry out the mitigating actions that have been defined to address any previously Identified Risks. Throughout the *Create Deliverables* process, the team documents any newly Identified Risks and mitigating actions taken. The record of project risks is a living document, continuously updated throughout the project by the team to reflect the current status of all risks.

Additional information about Managing Risks is described in section 7.4.3

10.1.3.7   Updated Dependencies

Described in section 9.3.3.3.

10.2 Conduct Daily Standup

Figure 10-6 shows all the inputs, tools, and outputs for *Conduct Daily Standup* process.

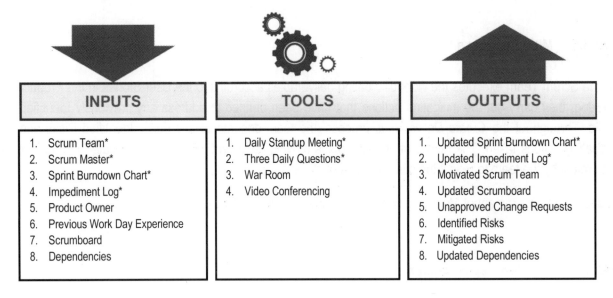

INPUTS	TOOLS	OUTPUTS
1. Scrum Team*	1. Daily Standup Meeting*	1. Updated Sprint Burndown Chart*
2. Scrum Master*	2. Three Daily Questions*	2. Updated Impediment Log*
3. Sprint Burndown Chart*	3. War Room	3. Motivated Scrum Team
4. Impediment Log*	4. Video Conferencing	4. Updated Scrumboard
5. Product Owner		5. Unapproved Change Requests
6. Previous Work Day Experience		6. Identified Risks
7. Scrumboard		7. Mitigated Risks
8. Dependencies		8. Updated Dependencies

Figure 10-6: Conduct Daily Standup—Inputs, Tools, and Outputs

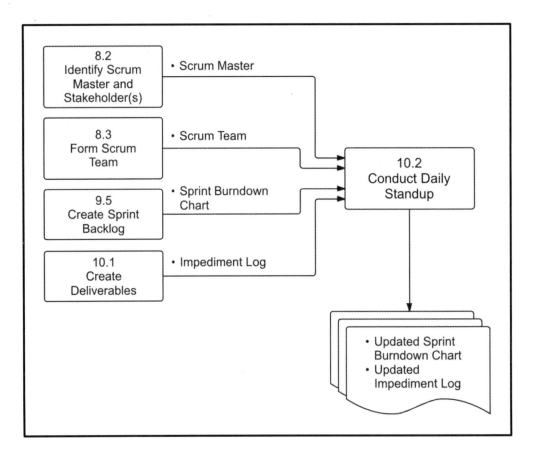

Figure 10-7: Conduct Daily Standup—Data Flow Diagram

Note: Asterisks (*) denote a "mandatory" input, tool, or output for the corresponding process.

10.2.1   Inputs

10.2.1.1   Scrum Team*

Described in section 8.3.3.1.

10.2.1.2   Scrum Master*

Described in section 8.2.3.1.

10.2.1.3   Sprint Burndown Chart*

Described in section 9.5.3.2.

10.2.1.4   Impediment Log*

Described in section 10.1.1.4.

10.2.1.5   Product Owner

Described in section 8.1.3.1.

10.2.1.6   Previous Work Day Experience

The Scrum Team members give status updates to fellow team members in the Daily Standup Meeting. This session is called a Standup because members stand throughout the meeting. Team members discuss achievements and experience from the previous work day. This experience is an important input to the Daily Standup Meeting.

10.2.1.7   Scrumboard

Described in section 10.1.1.3.

10.2.1.8 Dependencies

Described in section 9.3.3.3.

10.2.2 Tools

10.2.2.1 Daily Standup Meeting*

The Daily Standup Meeting is a short daily meeting, Time-boxed to 15 minutes. Team members assemble to report their progress in the Sprint and plan the day's activities. The meeting duration is very short and all members of the Scrum Team are expected to attend. However, the meeting is not cancelled or delayed if one or more members are not able to attend.

In the meeting, each Scrum Team member provides answers to the Three Daily Questions as mentioned in section 10.2.2.2. Discussions between the Scrum Master and the team or between some Scrum Team members are encouraged, but such discussions happen after the meeting to ensure that the Daily Standup Meeting is short.

10.2.2.2 Three Daily Questions*

In the Daily Standup Meeting, facilitated by the Scrum Master, each Scrum Team member provides information in the form of answers to three specific questions:

- What did I complete yesterday?
- What will I complete today?
- What impediments or obstacles (if any) am I currently facing?

By focusing on these three questions, the entire team can have a clear understanding of the work status. Occasionally, other items may be discussed, but this is kept to a minimum in light of the Time-boxed nature of the meeting.

It is highly recommended that the first two questions should be answered by team members in a quantifiable manner if possible, instead of qualitative lengthy answers. Team members can organize additional meetings after the daily Standup Meeting to address items that need additional discussion.

10.2.2.3   War Room

In Scrum, it is preferable for the team to be colocated, with all team members working in the same location. The term commonly used to describe this place is the War Room. Normally, it is designed in such a way that team members can move around freely, work, and communicate easily because they are located in close proximity to each other. Typically index cards, sticky notes, and other low-tech, high-touch tools are made available in the room to facilitate workflow, collaboration, and problem solving.

The room is sometimes noisy due to team conversations, but these conversations contribute to the team's progress. A good War Room is cubicle free and allows the entire team to sit together ensuring face-to-face communication, which leads to team building and openness. The War Room is ideal for conducting Daily Standup Meetings as well.

Stakeholder(s) members from other Scrum Teams could also walk by the War Room and discuss relevant issues.

10.2.2.4   Video Conferencing

In real-life situations, it may not always be possible for the entire Scrum Team to be colocated. In such cases, it becomes imperative to use video conferencing tools to enable face-to-face communication.

10

10.2.3   Outputs

10.2.3.1   Updated Sprint Burndown Chart*

Described in section 9.5.3.2.

10.2.3.2   Updated Impediment Log*

Described in section 10.1.1.4.

10.2.3.3   Motivated Scrum Team

Daily Standup Meetings propagate the idea that each member of the team is important and is a major contributor, which improves individual and team morale. This, along with the concept of self-organizing teams, improves overall motivation, leads to enhanced performance of the team and improved quality of deliverables produced.

Scrum Team is described in section 8.3.3.1.

10.2.3.4   Updated Scrumboard

Described in section 10.1.1.3.

10.2.3.5   Unapproved Change Requests

Described in section 8.4.1.6.

10.2.3.6   Identified Risks

Described in section 8.4.3.4.

10.2.3.7   Mitigated Risks

Described in section 10.1.3.6.

10.2.3.8   Updated Dependencies

Described in section 9.3.3.3.

10.3 Groom Prioritized Product Backlog

Figure 10-8 shows all the inputs, tools, and outputs for *Groom Prioritized Product Backlog* process.

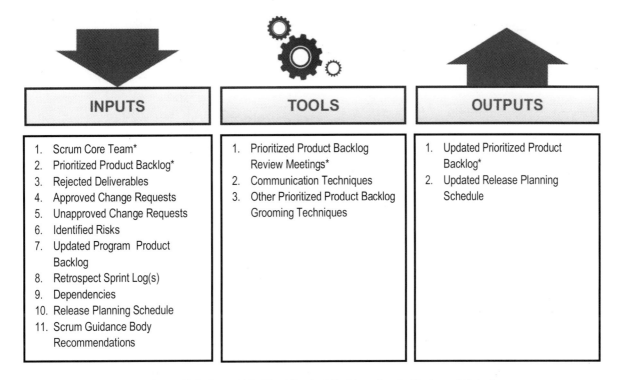

INPUTS	TOOLS	OUTPUTS
1. Scrum Core Team*	1. Prioritized Product Backlog Review Meetings*	1. Updated Prioritized Product Backlog*
2. Prioritized Product Backlog*	2. Communication Techniques	2. Updated Release Planning Schedule
3. Rejected Deliverables	3. Other Prioritized Product Backlog Grooming Techniques	
4. Approved Change Requests		
5. Unapproved Change Requests		
6. Identified Risks		
7. Updated Program Product Backlog		
8. Retrospect Sprint Log(s)		
9. Dependencies		
10. Release Planning Schedule		
11. Scrum Guidance Body Recommendations		

Figure 10-8: Groom Prioritized Product Backlog—Inputs, Tools, and Outputs

10

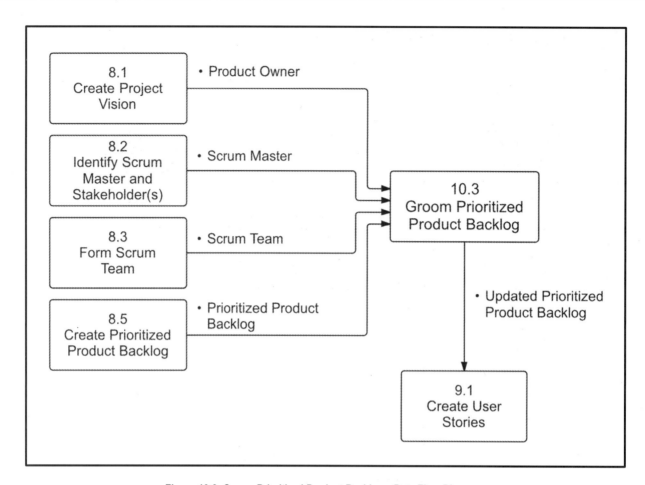

Figure 10-9: Groom Prioritized Product Backlog—Data Flow Diagram

10.3.1 Inputs

10.3.1.1 Scrum Core Team*

Described in sections 8.1.3.1, 8.2.3.1, and 8.3.3.1.

10.3.1.2 Prioritized Product Backlog*

Described in section 8.5.3.1.

10.3.1.3 Rejected Deliverables

In cases where a deliverable does not meet the Acceptance Criteria, it is considered a Rejected Deliverable. The Rejected Deliverables are normally not kept in a separate list. They simply remain in the Prioritized Product Backlog and don't get marked as done so that they can be reprioritized in the *Groom Prioritized Product Backlog* process and be considered for development in the next Sprint.

10.3.1.4 Approved Change Requests

Described in section 8.4.1.5.

10.3.1.5 Unapproved Change Requests

Described in section 8.4.1.6.

10.3.1.6 Identified Risks

Described in section 8.4.3.4.

10.3.1.7   Updated Program Product Backlog

Similar to the Project Product Backlog, the Program Product Backlog may also undergo periodic grooming to incorporate changes and new requirements. Changes to the Program Product Backlog can result from changes in either external or internal conditions. External conditions might include changing business scenarios, technology trends, or legal compliance requirements. Internal factors affecting the Program Product Backlog could be related to modifications in organizational strategy or policies, Identified Risks and other factors. Changes in requirements in the Program Product Backlog often impact the Project Product Backlogs of underlying projects, so they should be taken into account during the *Groom Prioritized Product Backlog* process.

10.3.1.8   Retrospect Sprint Log(s)

Described in section 11.3.3.4.

10.3.1.9   Dependencies

Described in section 9.3.3.3.

10.3.1.10   Release Planning Schedule

Described in section 8.6.3.1.

10.3.1.11   Scrum Guidance Body Recommendations

Described in section 8.1.1.12.

In the *Groom Prioritized Product Backlog* process, Scrum Guidance Body Recommendations may include best practices on how to systematically understand and collate requirements from Stakeholder(s) and Scrum Teams and then properly prioritize the Product Backlog and communicate updates to all relevant persons involved with the Scrum project.

10.3.2   Tools

10.3.2.1   Prioritized Product Backlog Review Meetings*

The Product Owner may have multiple and separate meetings with relevant Stakeholder(s), the Scrum Master, and the Scrum Team to ensure that he or she has enough information to make updates to the Prioritized Product Backlog during the *Groom Prioritized Product Backlog* process.

The intent of the Prioritized Product Backlog Review Meetings is to ensure that User Stories and Acceptance Criteria are understood and are written properly by the Product Owner so that they reflect the actual stakeholder (customer) requirements and priorities; User Stories are understood by everyone in the Scrum Team; and that high priority User Stories are well-refined so that the Scrum Team can properly estimate and commit to such User Stories.

The Prioritized Product Backlog Review Meetings also ensure that irrelevant User Stories are removed and any Approved Change Requests or Identified Risks are incorporated into the Prioritized Product backlog.

10.3.2.2   Communication Techniques

Scrum promotes accurate and effective communication primarily through colocation of the Scrum Team. Scrum also favors informal, face-to-face interactions over formal written communications. When a Scrum Team needs to be distributed, the Scrum Master should ensure that effective communication techniques are available so that teams can self-organize and work effectively.

10.3.2.3   Other Prioritized Product Backlog Grooming Techniques

Some other Prioritized Product Backlog Grooming tools include many of the same tools used for the following processes:

- *Develop Epic(s)*—Described in section 8.4.2.
- *Create Prioritized Product Backlog*—Described in section 8.5.2.
- *Conduct Release Planning*—Described in section 8.6.2.
- *Create User Stories*—Described in section 9.1.2.
- *Approve, Estimate, and Commit User Stories*—Described in section 9.2.2.
- *Create Tasks*—Described in section 9.3.2.
- *Estimate Tasks*—Described in section 9.4.2.

10.3.3   Outputs

10.3.3.1   Updated Prioritized Product Backlog*

Described in section 8.5.3.1.

Prioritized Product Backlog may be updated with new User Stories, new Change Requests, new Identified Risks, updated User Stories, or reprioritization of existing User Stories.

10.3.3.2   Updated Release Planning Schedule

Described in section 8.6.3.1.

The Release Planning Schedule may be updated to reflect the impact of new or changed User Stories in the Prioritized Product Backlog.

10.4 Phase Data Flow Diagram

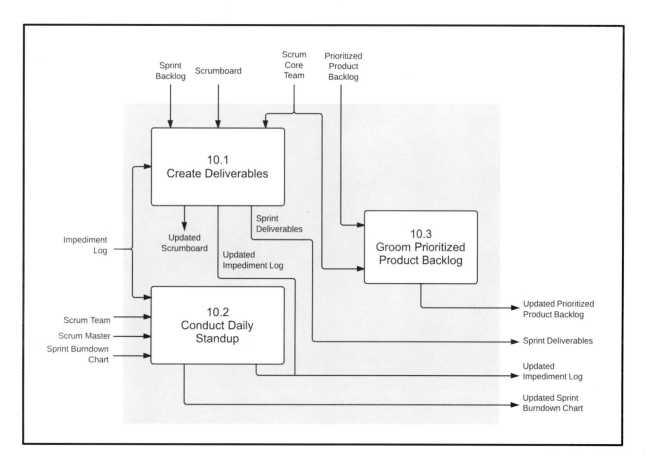

Figure 10-10: Implement Phase—Data Flow Diagram

11. REVIEW AND RETROSPECT

The Review and Retrospect phase is concerned with reviewing the deliverables and the work that has been done and determining ways to improve the practices and methods used to do project work. In large organizations the *Review* and *Retrospect* processes may also include convening Scrum of Scrums Meetings.

Review and Retrospect, as defined in *A Guide to the Scrum Body of Knowledge* (SBOK™ *Guide*), is applicable to the following:

- Portfolios, programs, and/or projects in *any* industry
- Products, services, or any other results to be delivered to stakeholders
- Projects of any size or complexity

The term "product" in the SBOK™ *Guide* may refer to a product, service, or other deliverable. Scrum can be applied effectively to any project in any industry—from small projects or teams with as few as six team members to large, complex projects with up to several hundred team members.

To facilitate the best application of the Scrum framework, this chapter identifies inputs, tools, and outputs for each process as either "mandatory" or "optional." Inputs, tools, and outputs denoted by asterisks (*) are mandatory, whereas those with no asterisks are optional.

It is recommended that the Scrum Team and those individuals being introduced to the Scrum framework and processes focus primarily on the mandatory inputs, tools, and outputs; while Product Owners, Scrum Masters, and other more experienced Scrum practitioners strive to attain a more thorough knowledge of the information in this entire chapter. It is also important to realize that although all processes are defined uniquely in the SBOK™ *Guide*, they are not necessarily performed sequentially or separately. At times, it may be more appropriate to combine some processes, depending on the specific requirements of each project.

This chapter is written from the perspective of one Scrum Team working on one Sprint to produce potentially shippable Deliverables as part of a larger project. However, the information described is equally applicable to entire projects, programs, and portfolios. Additional information pertaining to the use of Scrum for projects, programs, and portfolios is available in chapters 2 through 7, which cover Scrum principles and Scrum aspects.

11

Figure 11-1 provides an overview of the Review and Retrospect phase processes, which are as follows:

11.1 Convene Scrum of Scrums—In this process, Scrum Team representatives convene Scrum of Scrums (SoS) Meetings in predetermined intervals or whenever required to collaborate and track their respective progress, impediments, and dependencies across teams. This is relevant only for large projects where multiple Scrum Teams are involved.

11.2 Demonstrate and Validate Sprint—In this process, the Scrum Team demonstrates the Sprint Deliverables to the Product Owner and relevant stakeholders in a Sprint Review Meeting. The purpose of this meeting is to secure approval and acceptance of the product or service by the Product Owner.

11.3 Retrospect Sprint—In this process, the Scrum Master and Scrum Team meet to discuss the lessons learned throughout the Sprint. This information is documented as lessons learned which can be applied to future Sprints. Often, as a result of this discussion, there may be Agreed Actionable Improvements or Updated Scrum Guidance Body Recommendations.

11.1 Convene Scrum of Scrums

INPUTS
1. Scrum Master or Scrum Team Representatives*
2. Chief Scrum Master
3. Chief Product Owner
4. Meeting Agenda
5. Impediment Log
6. Dependencies
7. Outputs from *Retrospect Sprint*

TOOLS
1. Scrum of Scrums Meeting*
2. Four Questions per Team*
3. Video Conferencing
4. Meeting Room
5. Scrum Guidance Body Expertise

OUTPUTS
1. Better Team Coordination*
2. Resolved Issues
3. Updated Impediment Log
4. Updated Dependencies

11.2 Demonstrate and Validate Sprint

INPUTS
1. Scrum Core Team*
2. Sprint Deliverables*
3. Sprint Backlog*
4. Done Criteria*
5. User Story Acceptance Criteria*
6. Stakeholder(s)
7. Release Planning Schedule
8. Identified Risks
9. Dependencies
10. Scrum Guidance Body Recommendations

TOOLS
1. Sprint Review Meetings*
2. Earned Value Analysis
3. Scrum Guidance Body Expertise

OUTPUTS
1. Accepted Deliverables*
2. Rejected Deliverables
3. Updated Risks
4. Earned Value Analysis Results
5. Updated Release Planning Schedule
6. Updated Dependencies

11.3 Retrospect Sprint

INPUTS
1. Scrum Master*
2. Scrum Team*
3. Outputs from *Demonstrate and Validate Sprint*
4. Product Owner
5. Scrum Guidance Body Recommendations

TOOLS
1. Retrospect Sprint Meeting*
2. ESVP
3. Speed Boat
4. Metrics and Measuring Techniques
5. Scrum Guidance Body Expertise

OUTPUTS
1. Agreed Actionable Improvements*
2. Assigned Action Items and Due Dates
3. Proposed Non-Functional Items for Prioritized Product Backlog
4. Retrospect Sprint Log(s)
5. Scrum Team Lessons Learned
6. Updated Scrum Guidance Body Recommendations

11

Figure 11-1: Review and Retrospect Overview

Note: Asterisks (*) denote a "mandatory" input, tool, or output for the corresponding process.

Figure 11-2 below shows the mandatory inputs, tools, and outputs for processes in Review and Retrospect phase.

11.1 Convene Scrum of Scrums	**11.2 Demonstrate and Validate Sprint**	**11.3 Retrospect Sprint**
INPUTS 1. Scrum Master or Scrum Team Representatives* **TOOLS** 1. Scrum of Scrums Meeting* 2. Four Questions per Team* **OUTPUTS** 1. Better Team Coordination*	**INPUTS** 1. Scrum Core Team* 2. Sprint Deliverables* 3. Sprint Backlog* 4. Done Criteria* 5. User Story Acceptance Criteria* **TOOLS** 1. Sprint Review Meetings* **OUTPUTS** 1. Accepted Deliverables*	**INPUTS** 1. Scrum Master* 2. Scrum Team* 3. Outputs from *Demonstrate and Validate Sprint* **TOOLS** 1. Retrospect Sprint Meeting* **OUTPUTS** 1. Agreed Actionable Improvements*

Figure 11-2: Review and Retrospect Overview (Essentials)

Note: Asterisks (*) denote a "mandatory" input, tool, or output for the corresponding process.

11.1 Convene Scrum of Scrums

Figure 11-3 shows all the inputs, tools, and outputs for *Convene Scrum of Scrums* process.

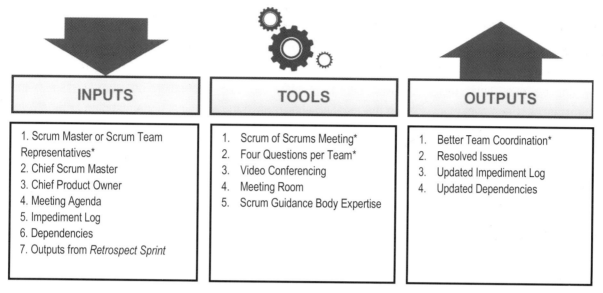

INPUTS

1. Scrum Master or Scrum Team Representatives*
2. Chief Scrum Master
3. Chief Product Owner
4. Meeting Agenda
5. Impediment Log
6. Dependencies
7. Outputs from *Retrospect Sprint*

TOOLS

1. Scrum of Scrums Meeting*
2. Four Questions per Team*
3. Video Conferencing
4. Meeting Room
5. Scrum Guidance Body Expertise

OUTPUTS

1. Better Team Coordination*
2. Resolved Issues
3. Updated Impediment Log
4. Updated Dependencies

Figure 11-3: Convene Scrum of Scrums—Inputs, Tools, and Outputs

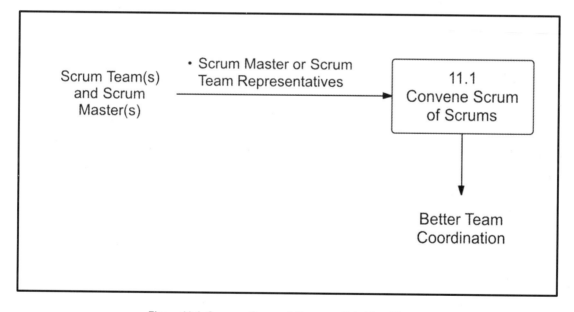

Figure 11-4: Convene Scrum of Scrums—Data Flow Diagram

Note: Asterisks (*) denote a "mandatory" input, tool, or output for the corresponding process.

11.1.1 Inputs

11.1.1.1 Scrum Master or Scrum Team Representatives*

Normally, one member from each Scrum Team will represent his or her team in the Scrum of Scrums (SoS) Meeting. In most cases, this is the Scrum Master, but at times someone else may represent the team. A single person may be nominated by the team to represent them in every SoS Meeting, or the representative may change over time, based on who can best fulfill the role depending on current issues and circumstances. Each person involved in the meeting should have the technical understanding to be able to identify instances in which teams could cause each other impediments or delays.

11.1.1.2 Chief Scrum Master

Described in section 8.2.1.6.

11.1.1.3 Chief Product Owner(s)

Described in section 8.1.1.5

11.1.1.4 Meeting Agenda

The main purpose of the Scrum of Scrums (SoS) Meeting is to communicate progress between multiple teams. The Chief Scrum Master (or any Scrum Master who would facilitate the SoS Meeting) may announce an agenda prior to the meeting. This allows individual teams to consider the agenda items in preparation for the SoS Meeting. Any impediments being faced by a team that may also affect other teams, should be indicated so they can be conveyed at the SoS Meeting. In addition, if a team becomes aware of a large scale issue, change or risk that may affect other teams, it should be communicated at the SoS Meeting.

11.1.1.5 Impediment Log

Described in section to 10.1.1.4.

11.1.1.6 Dependencies

Described in section 9.3.3.3.

11.1.1.7 Outputs from Retrospect Sprint

Outputs from the *Retrospect Sprint* process may have issues that could impact multiple Scrum Teams and could be used an input to effective Scrum of Scrums (SoS) Meeting.

11.1.2 Tools

11.1.2.1 Scrum of Scrums Meeting*

These are preferably short meetings (but usually not Time-boxed to allow for more sharing of information between teams) where a representative from each Scrum Team meets to share status of the respective teams. The Scrum of Scrums (SoS) Meeting is held at predetermined intervals or when required by Scrum Teams to facilitate the sharing of information among different Scrum Teams. Issues, dependencies, and risks impacting multiple Scrum Teams can be closely monitored, which helps the various teams working on a large project better coordinate and integrate their work. It is the responsibility of the Chief Scrum Master (or another Scrum Master who facilitates the SoS Meetings) to ensure that all representatives have an environment conducive to open and honest sharing of information, including feedback to other team representatives. For larger projects, involving a significant number of teams, multiple levels of these meetings may be convened to share the status of the respective teams.

The SoS Meeting is described in more detail in section 3.7.2.

11

11.1.2.2 Four Questions per Team*

Each Scrum Team representative will provide updates from his or her team in turn. These updates are usually provided in the form of answers to four specific questions.

1) What has my team been working on since the last meeting?
2) What will my team do until the next meeting?
3) What were other teams counting on our team to finish that remains undone?
4) What is our team planning on doing that might affect other teams?

The answers to these four questions provide information that allows each team to clearly understand the work status of all other teams.

11.1.2.3   Video Conferencing

Described in section to 10.2.2.4

It is very likely that the Scrum of Scrums (SoS) Meeting is not face-to-face. Video conferencing is usually needed for large projects where there is a higher possibility of distributed teams.

11.1.2.4   Meeting Room

It is recommended that a dedicated conference room be made available for the SoS Meeting, where all the Scrum Team Representatives are comfortable.

11.1.2.5   Scrum Guidance Body Expertise

Also described in section 8.4.2.7.

In the *Convene Scrum of Scrums* process, Scrum Guidance Body Expertise could relate to documented best practices about how to conduct Scrum of Scrum (SoS) Meetings and incorporate suggestions from such meetings in project work of individual Scrum Teams. There may also be a team of subject matter experts who may help the Chief Scrum Master facilitate the SoS Meeting.

11.1.3 Outputs

11.1.3.1 Better Team Coordination*

The Scrum of Scrums (SoS) Meeting facilitates coordination of work across multiple Scrum Teams. This is especially important when there are tasks involving inter-team dependencies. Incompatibilities and discrepancies between the work and deliverables of different teams are quickly exposed. This forum also gives teams the opportunity to showcase their achievements and give feedback to other teams. By using the SoS Meeting, there is collaboration across the organization as opposed to people working in closed teams concerned primarily with their individual responsibilities.

11.1.3.2 Resolved Issues

The Scrum of Scrums (SoS) Meeting is a forum where Scrum Team members have the opportunity to transparently discuss issues impacting their project. The need to deliver every Sprint on time forces the teams to actively confront such issues early instead of postponing seeking resolution. This timely discussion and resolution of issues in the SoS Meeting greatly improve coordination between different Scrum Teams and also reduces the need for redesign and rework. Risks related to dependencies and delivery time tables are mitigated as well.

The SoS Meeting is described in more detail in section 3.7.2.1.

11

11.1.3.3 Updated Impediment Log

Described in section to 10.1.3.3.

11.1.3.4 Updated Dependencies

Described in section to 9.3.3.3.

11.2 Demonstrate and Validate Sprint

Figure 11-5 shows all the inputs, tools, and outputs for *Demonstrate and Validate Sprint* process.

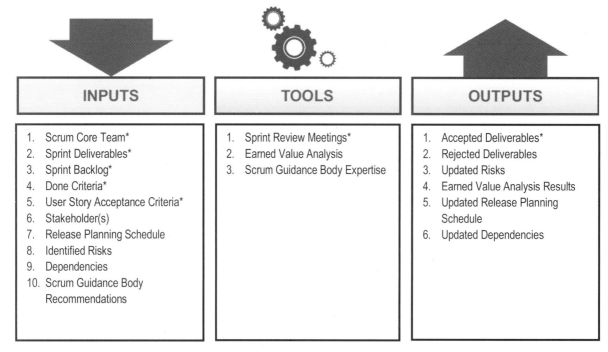

INPUTS	TOOLS	OUTPUTS
1. Scrum Core Team*	1. Sprint Review Meetings*	1. Accepted Deliverables*
2. Sprint Deliverables*	2. Earned Value Analysis	2. Rejected Deliverables
3. Sprint Backlog*	3. Scrum Guidance Body Expertise	3. Updated Risks
4. Done Criteria*		4. Earned Value Analysis Results
5. User Story Acceptance Criteria*		5. Updated Release Planning Schedule
6. Stakeholder(s)		6. Updated Dependencies
7. Release Planning Schedule		
8. Identified Risks		
9. Dependencies		
10. Scrum Guidance Body Recommendations		

Figure 11-5: Demonstrate and Validate Sprint—Inputs, Tools, and Outputs

Note: Asterisks (*) denote a "mandatory" input, tool, or output for the corresponding process.

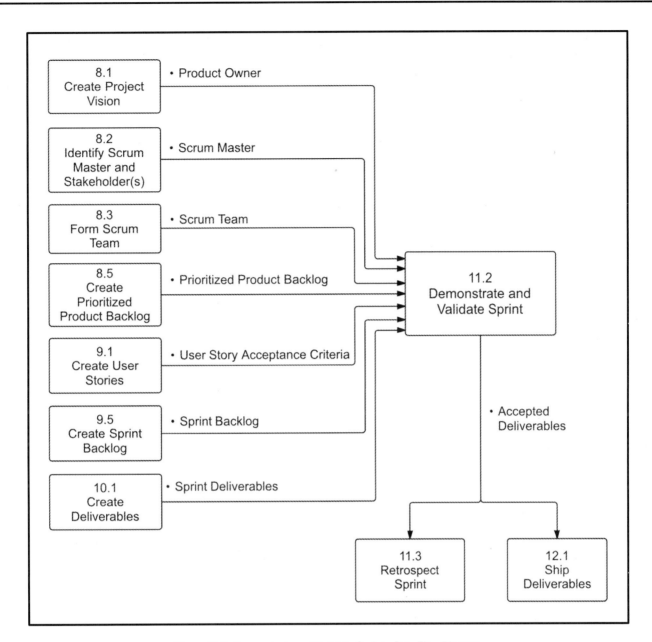

Figure 11-6: Demonstrate and Validate Sprint—Data Flow Diagram

11

11.2.1 Inputs

11.2.1.1 Scrum Core Team*

Described in section 8.4.1.1.

11.2.1.2 Sprint Deliverables*

Described in section 10.1.3.1

11.2.1.3 Sprint Backlog*

Described in section to 9.5.3.1.

11.2.1.4 Done Criteria*

Described in section 8.5.3.2.

11.2.1.5 User Stories Acceptance Criteria*

Described in section 9.4.1.3.

11.2.1.6 Stakeholder(s)

Described in section to 8.2.3.2.

11.2.1.7 Release Planning Schedule

Described in section 8.6.3.1.

11.2.1.8 Identified Risks

Described in section to 8.4.3.4.

11.2.1.9   Dependencies

Described in section 9.3.3.3

11.2.1.10   Scrum Guidance Body Recommendations

Described in section 8.1.1.12

In the *Demonstrate and Validate Sprint* process, Scrum Guidance Body Recommendations may include best practices about how to conduct Sprint Review Meetings and evaluate results from Earned Value Analysis. Also, there may be guidance about how to share experiences with other persons in the Scrum Core Team and also with other Scrum Teams in the project.

11.2.2   Tools

11.2.2.1   Sprint Review Meeting*

The Scrum Core Team members and relevant Stakeholder(s) participate in Sprint Review Meetings to accept the deliverables which meet the User Story Acceptance Criteria and reject unacceptable deliverables. These meetings are convened at the end of every Sprint. The Scrum Team demonstrates the achievements from the Sprint, including the new functionalities or products created. This provides an opportunity for the Product Owner and Stakeholder(s) to inspect what has been completed so far and to determine if any changes should be made in the project or processes in subsequent Sprints.

11.2.2.2   Earned Value Analysis

Described in section 4.6.1

11.2.2.3   Scrum Guidance Body Expertise

Described in section 8.4.2.7.

In the *Demonstrate and Validate Sprint* process, Scrum Guidance Body Expertise could relate to documented best practices about how to conduct Sprint Review Meetings. There may also be some experts who could help provide guidance on how to better facilitate a Sprint Review Meeting.

11

11.2.3   Outputs

11.2.3.1   Accepted Deliverables*

Deliverables which meet the User Story Acceptance Criteria are accepted by the Product Owner. The objective of a Sprint is to create potentially shippable deliverables, or product increments, which meet the Acceptance Criteria defined by the customer and Product Owner. These are considered Accepted Deliverables that may be released to the customer if they so desire. A list of Accepted Deliverables is maintained and updated after each Sprint Review Meeting. If a deliverable does not meet the defined Acceptance Criteria, it is not considered accepted and will usually be carried forward into a subsequent Sprint to rectify any issues. This is highly undesirable because the objective of every Sprint is for the deliverables to meet the criteria for acceptance.

11.2.3.2   Rejected Deliverables

If Deliverables do not meet the Acceptance Criteria, such Deliverables are rejected. User Stories associated with such Rejected Deliverables get added to the Prioritized Product Backlog so that such deliverables may be considered as part of a subsequent Sprint.

11.2.3.3   Updated Risks

Described in section to 8.4.3.4.

11.2.3.4   Earned Value Analysis Results

Described in section 4.6.1.

11.2.3.5   Updated Release Planning Schedule

Described in section to 10.3.3.2.

11.2.3.6   Updated Dependencies

Described in section to 9.3.3.3.

11.3 Retrospect Sprint

Figure 11-7 shows all the inputs, tools, and outputs for *Retrospect Sprint* process.

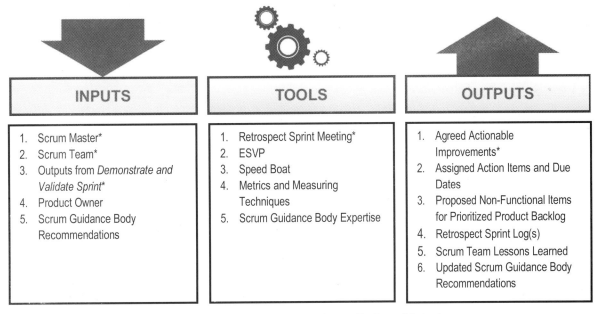

Figure 11-7: Retrospect Sprint—Inputs, Tools, and Outputs

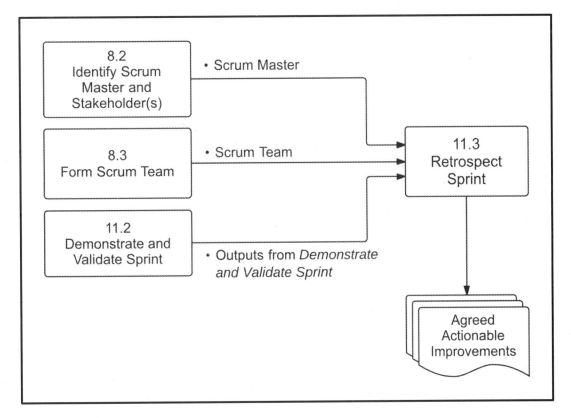

Figure 11-8: Retrospect Sprint—Data Flow Diagram

Note: Asterisks (*) denote a "mandatory" input, tool, or output for the corresponding process.

11.3.1   Inputs

11.3.1.1   Scrum Master*

Described in section to 8.2.3.1.

11.3.1.2   Scrum Team*

Described in section 8.3.3.1.

11.3.1.3   Outputs from Demonstrate and Validate Sprint*

Described in section 11.2.3.

The outputs from the *Demonstrate and Validate Sprint* process provide valuable insight while performing the process *Retrospect Sprint.*

11.3.1.4   Product Owner

Described in section 8.1.3.1.

11.3.1.5   Scrum Guidance Body Recommendations

The Scrum Guidance Body may provide guidelines for conducting Retrospect Sprint Meetings, including suggestions for tools to be utilized and documentation or deliverables expected from the meetings.

11.3.2   Tools

11.3.2.1   Retrospect Sprint Meeting*

The Retrospect Sprint Meeting is an important element of the 'inspect-adapt' Scrum framework and it is the final step in a Sprint. All Scrum Team members attend the meeting, which is facilitated or moderated by the Scrum Master. It is recommended, but not required for the Product Owner to attend. One team member acts as the scribe and documents discussions and items for future action. It is essential to hold this meeting in an open and relaxed environment to encourage full participation by all team members. Discussions in the

Retrospect Sprint Meeting encompass both what went wrong and what went right. Primary objectives of the meeting are to identify three specific items:

1) Things the team needs to keep doing: best practices
2) Things the team needs to begin doing: process improvements
3) Things the team needs to stop doing: process problems and bottlenecks

These areas are discussed and a list of Agreed Actionable Improvements is created.

11.3.2.2 Explorer—Shopper—Vacationer—Prisoner (ESVP)

This is an exercise that can be conducted at the start of the Retrospect Sprint Meeting to understand the mindset of the participants and set the tone for the meeting. Attendees are asked to anonymously indicate which best represents how they feel regarding their participation in the meeting.

- Explorer—Wants to participate in and learn everything discussed in the retrospective
- Shopper—Wants to listen to everything and choose what he takes away from the retrospective
- Vacationer—Wants to relax and be a tourist in the retrospective
- Prisoner—Wants to be elsewhere and is attending the retrospective because it is required

The Scrum Master then collates the responses, prepares, and shares the information with the group.

11.3.2.3 Speed Boat

Speed boat is a technique that can be used to conduct the Retrospect Sprint Meeting. Team members play the role of the crew on a speed boat. The boat must reach an island, which is symbolic of the project vision. Sticky notes are used by the attendees to record engines and anchors. Engines help them reach the island, while anchors hinder them from reaching the island. This exercise is Time-boxed to a few minutes. Once all items are documented, the information is collated, discussed, and prioritized by way of a voting process. Engines are recognized and mitigation actions are planned for the anchors, based on priority.

11.3.2.4 Metrics and Measuring Techniques

Various metrics can be used to measure and contrast the team's performance in the current Sprint to their performance in previous Sprints. Some examples of these metrics include:

- Team velocity—Number of story points done in a given Sprint
- Done success rate—Percentage of story points that have been Done versus those committed
- Estimation effectiveness—Number or percentage of deviations between estimated and actual time spent on tasks and User Stories

- Review feedback ratings—Feedback can be solicited from Stakeholder(s) using quantitative or qualitative ratings, providing a measurement of team performance.
- Team morale ratings—Results from self-assessments of team member morale
- Peer feedback—360 degree feedback mechanisms can be used to solicit constructive criticism and insight into team performance
- Progress to release or launch—Business value provided in each release, as well as value represented by the current progress towards a release. This contributes to the motivation of the team and to the level of work satisfaction.

11.3.2.5   Scrum Guidance Body Expertise

Also described in section 8.4.2.7.

In the *Retrospect Sprint* process, Scrum Guidance Body Expertise could relate to the best practices about how to conduct Retrospect Sprint Meetings. There may also be some experts who could help provide guidance on how to use the tools in the *Retrospect Sprint* process to deliver Agreed Actionable Improvements for the future Sprints.

11.3.3   Outputs

11.3.3.1   Agreed Actionable Improvements*

Agreed Actionable Improvements are the primary output of the *Retrospect Sprint* process. They are the list of actionable items that the team has come up with to address problems and improve processes in order to enhance their performance in future Sprints.

11.3.3.2   Assigned Action Items and Due Dates

Once the Agreed Actionable Improvements have been elaborated and refined, action items to implement the improvements may be considered by the Scrum Team. Each action item will have a defined due date for completion.

11.3.3.3   Proposed Non-Functional Items for Prioritized Product Backlog

When the initial Prioritized Product Backlog is developed, it is based on User Stories and required functionalities. Often, non-functional requirements may not be fully defined in the early stages of the project and can surface during the Sprint Review or Retrospect Sprint Meetings. These items should be added to the Prioritized Product Backlog as they are discovered. Some examples of non-functional requirements are response times, capacity limitations, and security related issues.

11.3.3.4   Retrospect Sprint Log(s)

The Retrospect Sprint Log is a record of the opinions, discussions, and actionable items raised in a Retrospect Sprint Meeting. The Scrum Master could facilitate creation of this log with inputs from Scrum Core Team members. The collection of all Retrospective Sprint Logs becomes the project diary and details project successes, issues, problems, and resolutions. The logs are public documents available to anyone in the organization.

11.3.3.5   Scrum Team Lessons Learned

The self-organizing and empowered Scrum Team is expected to learn from any mistakes made during a Sprint. These lessons learned help the teams improve their performance in future Sprints. These lessons learned may also be documented in Scrum Guidance Body Recommendations to be shared with other Scrum Teams.

There may be several positive lessons learned as part of a Sprint. These positive lessons learned are a key part of the retrospective, and should be appropriately shared within the team and with the Scrum Guidance Body, as the teams work towards continuous self-improvement.

11.3.3.6   Updated Scrum Guidance Body Recommendations

As a result of a Retrospect Sprint Meeting, suggestions may be made to revise or enhance the Scrum Guidance Body Recommendations. If the Guidance Body accepts these suggestions, these will be incorporated as updates to the Scrum Guidance Body documentation.

11

11.4 Phase Data Flow Diagram

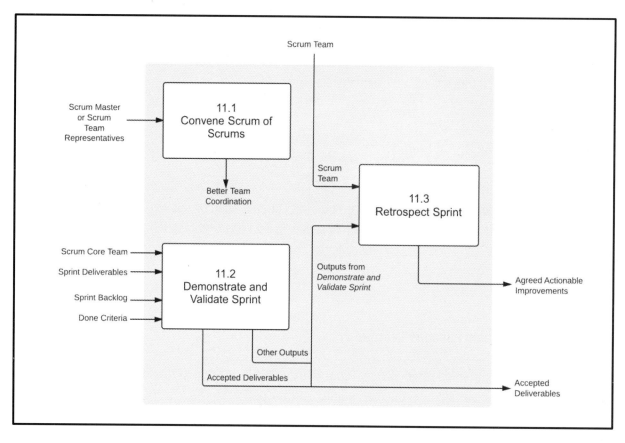

Figure 11-9: Review and Retrospect Phase—Data Flow Diagram

12. RELEASE

The Release phase emphasizes delivering the Accepted Deliverables to the customer and identifying, documenting, and internalizing the lessons learned during the project.

Release, as defined in *A Guide to the Scrum Body of Knowledge* (*SBOK™ Guide*), is applicable to the following:

- Portfolios, programs, and/or projects in *any* industry
- Products, services, or any other results to be delivered to stakeholders
- Projects of any size or complexity

The term "product" in the *SBOK™ Guide* may refer to a product, service, or other deliverable. Scrum can be applied effectively to any project in any industry—from small projects or teams with as few as six team members to large, complex projects with up to several hundred team members.

To facilitate the best application of the Scrum framework, this chapter identifies inputs, tools, and outputs for each process as either "mandatory" or "optional." Inputs, tools, and outputs denoted by asterisks (*) are mandatory, whereas those with no asterisks are optional.

It is recommended that the Scrum Team and those individuals being introduced to the Scrum framework and processes focus primarily on the mandatory inputs, tools, and outputs; while Product Owners, Scrum Masters, and other more experienced Scrum practitioners strive to attain a more thorough knowledge of the information in this entire chapter. It is also important to realize that although all processes are defined uniquely in the *SBOK™ Guide*, they are not necessarily performed sequentially or separately. At times, it may be more appropriate to combine some processes, depending on the specific requirements of each project.

This chapter is written from the perspective of one Scrum Team working on one Sprint to produce potentially shippable Deliverables as part of a larger project. However, the information described is equally applicable to entire projects, programs, and portfolios. Additional information pertaining to the use of Scrum for projects, programs, and portfolios is available in chapters 2 through 7, which cover Scrum principles and Scrum aspects.

12

Figure 12-1 provides an overview of the Release phase processes, which are as follows:

12.1 Ship Deliverables—In this process, Accepted Deliverables are delivered or transitioned to the relevant stakeholders. A formal Working Deliverables Agreement documents the successful completion of the Sprint.

12.2 Retrospect Project—In this process, which completes the project, organizational stakeholders and Scrum Core Team members assemble to retrospect the project and identify, document, and internalize the lessons learned. Often, these lessons lead to the documentation of Agreed Actionable Improvements, to be implemented in future projects.

12.1 Ship Deliverables	12.2 Retrospect Project
INPUTS 1. Product Owner* 2. Stakeholder(s)* 3. Accepted Deliverables* 4. Release Planning Schedule* 5. Scrum Master 6. Scrum Team 7. User Story Acceptance Criteria 8. Piloting Plan 9. Scrum Guidance Body Recommendations **TOOLS** 1. Organizational Deployment Methods* 2. Communication Plan **OUTPUTS** 1. Working Deliverables Agreement* 2. Working Deliverables 3. Product Releases	**INPUTS** 1. Scrum Core Team(s)* 2. Chief Scrum Master 3. Chief Product Owner 4. Stakeholder(s) 5. Scrum Guidance Body Recommendations **TOOLS** 1. Retrospect Project Meeting* 2. Other Tools for *Retrospect Project* 3. Scrum Guidance Body Expertise **OUTPUTS** 1. Agreed Actionable Improvements* 2. Assigned Action Items and Due Dates* 3. Proposed Non-Functional Items for Program Product Backlog and Prioritized Product Backlog 4. Updated Scrum Guidance Body Recommendations

Figure 12-1: Release Overview

12

Note: Asterisks (*) denote a "mandatory" input, tool, or output for the corresponding process.

Figure 12-2 below shows the mandatory inputs, tools, and outputs for processes in Release phase.

12.1 Ship Deliverables

INPUTS
1. Product Owner*
2. Stakeholder(s)*
3. Accepted Deliverables*
4. Release Planning Schedule*

TOOLS
1. Organizational Deployment Methods*

OUTPUTS
1. Working Deliverables Agreement*

12.2 Retrospect Project

INPUTS
1. Scrum Core Team(s)*

TOOLS
1. Retrospect Project Meeting*

OUTPUTS
1. Agreed Actionable Improvements*
2. Assigned Action Items and Due Dates*

Figure 12-2: Release Overview (Essentials)

Note: Asterisks (*) denote a "mandatory" input, tool, or output for the corresponding process.

12.1 Ship Deliverables

Figure 12-3 shows all the inputs, tools, and outputs for *Ship Deliverables* process.

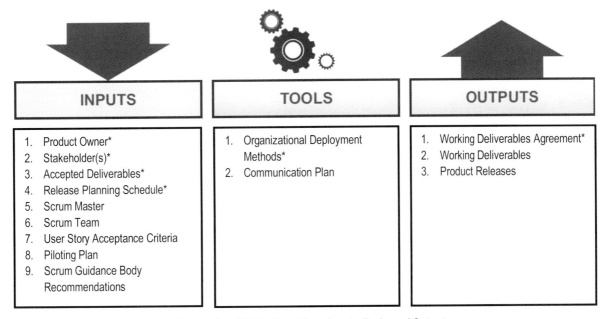

INPUTS

1. Product Owner*
2. Stakeholder(s)*
3. Accepted Deliverables*
4. Release Planning Schedule*
5. Scrum Master
6. Scrum Team
7. User Story Acceptance Criteria
8. Piloting Plan
9. Scrum Guidance Body Recommendations

TOOLS

1. Organizational Deployment Methods*
2. Communication Plan

OUTPUTS

1. Working Deliverables Agreement*
2. Working Deliverables
3. Product Releases

Figure 12-3: Ship Deliverables—Inputs, Tools, and Outputs

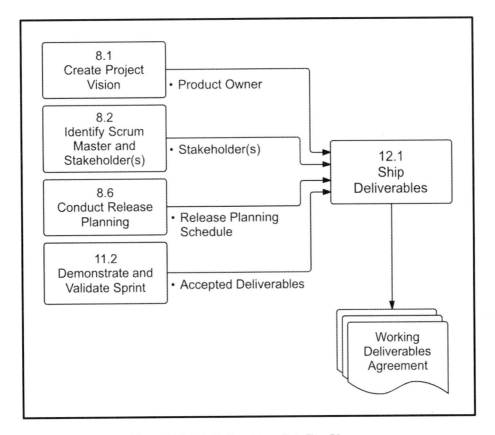

Figure 12-4: Ship Deliverables—Data Flow Diagram

Note: Asterisks (*) denote a "mandatory" input, tool, or output for the corresponding process.

12.1.1 Inputs

12.1.1.1 Product Owner*

Described in section 8.1.3.1.

12.1.1.2 Stakeholder(s)*

Described in section 8.2.3.2.

12.1.1.3 Accepted Deliverables*

Described in section to 11.2.3.1.

12.1.1.4 Release Planning Schedule

Described in section 8.6.3.1.

12.1.1.5 Scrum Master

Described in section 8.2.3.1.

12.1.1.6 Scrum Team

Described in section 8.3.3.1.

12.1.1.7 User Story Acceptance Criteria

Described in section 9.1.3.2.

12.1.1.8   Piloting Plan

A Piloting Plan is an optional input that can be used to map out a pilot deployment in detail. The scope and objectives of the deployment, the target deployment user base, a deployment schedule, transition plans, required user preparation, evaluation criteria for the deployment, and other key elements related to the deployment are specified in the Pilot Plan and shared with stakeholders.

12.1.1.9   Scrum Guidance Body Recommendations

Described in section 8.1.1.12.

In the *Ship Deliverables* process, the Scrum Guidance Body can provide recommendations and guidelines regarding the deployment of products. These are best practices that should be taken into account when deploying a product to the customer in order to maximize the value delivered.

12.1.2   Tools

12.1.2.1   Organizational Deployment Methods*

The deployment mechanisms of each organization tend to be different based on their industry, target users, and positioning. Depending on the product being delivered, deployment can take place remotely or may involve the physical shipping or transition of an item. Because deployment tends to involve a high level of risk, organizations normally have well-defined and established deployment mechanisms, with detailed processes in place to ensure compliance with any applicable standards and quality assurance measures. These might include sign-offs by specific management representatives, user approval mechanisms, and guidelines regarding minimum functionality for a release.

12.1.2.2   Communication Plan

In many projects, a Communication Plan exists. This plan specifies the records that must be created and maintained throughout the project. A variety of methods are used to convey important project information to stakeholders. The Communication Plan defines these methods as well as who is responsible for various communication activities. As Deliverables are tested, the status of the testing activities is communicated as per the Communication Plan as determined by the Product Owner and sponsor. A common communication mechanism is a visual display depicting important information in an easy-to-interpret format, posted in an accessible location, and kept up-to-date with the most current information.

12.1.3   Outputs

12.1.3.1   Working Deliverables Agreement*

Deliverables that meet the Acceptance Criteria receive formal business sign-off and approval by the customer or sponsor. To get formal customer acceptance is critical for revenue recognition and the responsibility for obtaining it will be defined by the company policies and is not necessarily the responsibility of the Product Owner.

12.1.3.2   Working Deliverables

This output is the final shippable Deliverable for which the project was sanctioned. As new product increments are created, they are continually integrated into prior increments, so there is a potentially shippable product available at all times throughout the project.

12.1.3.3   Product Releases

The Product Releases should include the following:

- Release Content—This consists of essential information about the deliverables that can assist the Customer Support Team.
- Release Notes—Release Notes should include external or market facing shipping criteria for the product to be delivered.

12.2 Retrospect Project

Figure 12-5 shows all the inputs, tools, and outputs for *Retrospect Project* process.

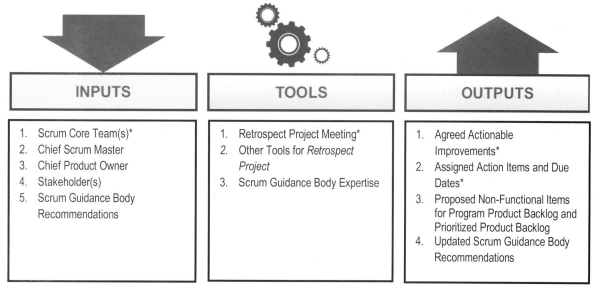

Figure 12-5: Retrospect Project—Inputs, Tools, and Outputs

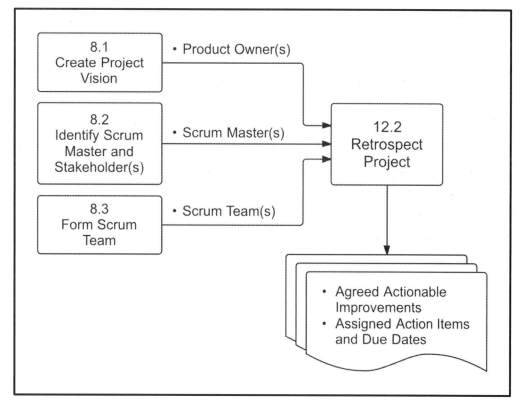

Figure 12-6: Retrospect Project—Data Flow Diagram

Note: Asterisks (*) denote a "mandatory" input, tool, or output for the corresponding process.

12.2.1 Inputs

12.2.1.1 Scrum Core Team(s)*

Described in section 8.4.1.1.

12.2.1.2 Chief Scrum Master

Described in section 8.2.1.6.

12.2.1.3 Chief Product Owner

Described in section 8.1.1.5.

12.2.1.4 Stakeholder(s)

Described in section 8.2.3.2.

12.2.1.5 Scrum Guidance Body Recommendations

Described in section 8.1.1.12.

In the *Retrospect Project* process, Scrum Guidance Body Recommendations can include a repository of internal templates that support the future projects and guidance for conducting the Retrospect Project Meeting. The guidance provided can relate to administrative procedures, audits, evaluations, and project transition criteria. Often, they also include how the organization will maintain the knowledge base of lessons learned and information from all projects.

12.2.2 Tools

12.2.2.1 Retrospect Project Meeting*

The Retrospect Project Meeting is a meeting to determine ways in which team collaboration and effectiveness can be improved in future projects. Positives, negatives, and potential opportunities for improvement are also discussed. This meeting is not Time-boxed and may be conducted in person or in a virtual format. Attendees include the Project Team, Chief Scrum Master, Chief Product Owner, and Stakeholder(s). During the meeting, lessons learned are documented and participants look for opportunities to improve processes and address inefficiencies.

12.2.2.2 Other Tools for Retrospect Project

Some of the tools used in the *Retrospect Sprint* process can also be used in this process. Examples include:

- Explorer—Shopper—Vacationer—Prisoner (ESVP) exercise
- Speed Boat
- Metrics and Measuring Techniques

12.2.2.3 Scrum Guidance Body Expertise

Discussed in section 8.4.2.7.

In the *Retrospect Project* process, the primary responsibility of the Scrum Guidance Body is to ensure that the lessons learned in each project are not lost and are embedded in the organization.

Additionally, a guidance body may provide expertise in various areas, including Quality, HR, and Scrum, that may be helpful in the *Retrospect Project* process. Also, there may be suggestions in the Scrum Guidance Body Recommendations concerning how the Retrospect Project Meeting should be conducted.

12

12.2.3 Outputs

12.2.3.1 Agreed Actionable Improvements*

Described in section 11.3.3.1.

12.2.3.2 Assigned Action Items and Due Dates*

Described in section 11.3.3.2.

12.2.3.3 Proposed Non-functional Items for Program Product Backlog and Prioritized Product Backlog

When the initial Program Product Backlog or Prioritized Product Backlog are developed, they are based on User Stories and required functionalities. Often, non-functional requirements may not be fully defined in the early stages of the project and can surface during the Sprint Review, Retrospect Sprint or Retrospect Project Meetings. These items should be added to the Program Product Backlog (for the program) and Prioritized Product Backlog (for the project) as they are discovered. Some examples of non-functional requirements are response times, capacity limitations, and security related issues.

12.2.3.4 Updated Scrum Guidance Body Recommendations

Described in sections 8.1.1.12 and 11.3.3.5

12.3 Phase Data Flow Diagram

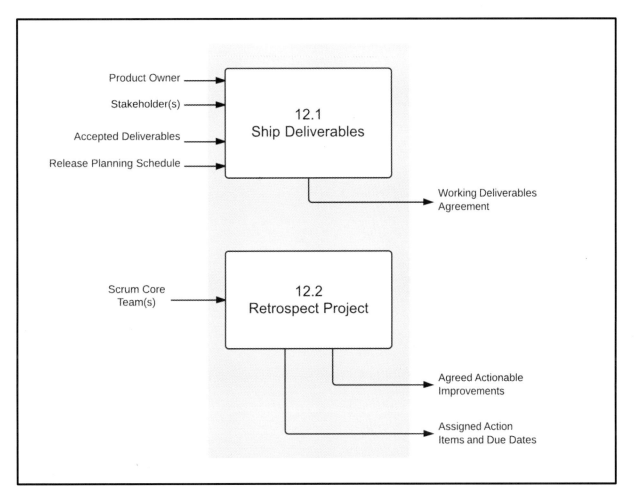

Figure 12-7: Release Phase—Data Flow Diagram

12

APPENDIX A. OVERVIEW OF AGILE

A.1 Introduction

This appendix intends to familiarize readers with the concept of Agile development and the various Agile methodologies.

The following sections are included:

A.2 Overview—This section discusses the definition of and the factors behind the rise of Agile.

A.3 Agile Manifesto—This section presents *The Agile Manifesto*, its principles, and *The Declaration of Interdependence* to provide the historical context of Agile.

A.4 Agile Methods—This section provides a brief overview of specific Agile methodologies including:

- Lean Kanban
- Extreme Programming
- Crystal Methods
- Dynamic Systems Development Methods
- Feature Driven Development
- Test Driven Development
- Adaptive Software Development
- Agile Unified Process
- Domain Driven Development

A.2 Overview

The term "agile" generally refers to being able to move or respond quickly and easily; being nimble. In any kind of management discipline, agile as a quality should therefore be a good thing to aim for. Agile project management specifically, involves being adaptive during the creation of a product, service, or other result.

It is important to understand that while Agile development methods are highly adaptive, it is also necessary to consider stability in their adaptive processes.

A.2.1 The Rise of Agile

Rapid changes in technology, market demands, and expectations have rendered increased challenges to developing products and services using traditional project management models. This paved the way for the conceptualization and implementation of Agile methods and values in many organizations. Agile development models addressed the shortcomings associated with traditional project management models in meeting the ever-growing environmental demands and expectations that organizations were facing. Since traditional project management models generally emphasize extensive upfront planning and conforming to the plan once it is baselined, such models were not successful in meeting the reality of frequent environmental changes.

Agile relies on adaptive planning and iterative development and delivery. It focuses primarily on the value of people in getting the job done effectively. Though adaptive and incremental methodologies have existed since the 1950's, only methodologies that conform to *The Agile Manifesto* are generally regarded as truly "agile".

A.3 The Agile Manifesto

In February, 2001, a group of 17 computer gurus, software developers, and managers held a retreat to discuss lightweight software development methods. They formed the *Agile Alliance* and the discussions at those meetings later resulted in a *Manifesto for Agile Software Development*. The Manifesto was authored by Fowler and Highsmith (2001) and then signed by all participants to establish the basic guidelines for any Agile methodology.

The purpose of *The Agile Manifesto* was laid out as follows:

We are uncovering better ways of developing software by doing it and helping others do it. Through this work we have come to value:

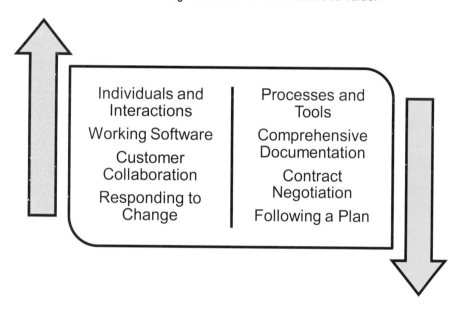

Individuals and Interactions	Processes and Tools
Working Software	Comprehensive Documentation
Customer Collaboration	Contract Negotiation
Responding to Change	Following a Plan

That is, while there is value in the items on the right, we value the items on the left more.

Kent Beck	James Grenning	Robert C. Martin
Mike Beedle	Jim Highsmith	Steve Mellor
Arie van Bennekum	Andrew Hunt	Ken Schwaber
Alistair Cockburn	Ron Jeffries	Jeff Sutherland
Ward Cunningham	Jon Kern	Dave Thomas
Martin Fowler	Brian Marick	

Permission to copy provided by the above authors by notice on http://agilemanifesto.org/.

The four trade-offs emphasized by The Agile Manifesto are elaborated as follows:

1. **Individuals and interactions over processes and tools**

   Although processes and tools help in successfully completing a project, it is the individuals who undertake, participate in, implement a project, and determine which processes and tools to use. The key actors in any project are therefore individuals, so the emphasis should be on them and their interactions, rather than complicated processes and tools.

2. **Working software over comprehensive documentation**

   While documentation is necessary and useful for any project, many teams focus on collecting and recording qualitative and quantitative descriptions of deliverables, when the real value delivered to the customer is primarily in the form of working software. Therefore, the Agile focus is on delivering working software in increments throughout the product lifecycle rather than detailed documentation.

3. **Customer collaboration over contract negotiation**

   Traditionally, customers have been seen as outside players who are involved mainly at the start and end of the product lifecycle and whose relationships were based on contracts and their fulfillment. Agile believes in a shared value approach in which customers are seen as collaborators. The development team and customer work together to evolve and develop the product.

4. **Responding to change over following a plan**

   In the current market in which customer requirements, available technologies, and business patterns are constantly changing, it is essential to approach product development in an adaptive manner that enables change incorporation and fast product development lifecycles rather than emphasizing on following plans formed with potentially outdated data.

A.3.1 Principles of the Agile Manifesto

The 12 principles of the Agile Manifesto by Fowler and Highsmith (2001) are:

1. Our highest priority is to satisfy the customer through early and continuous delivery of valuable software.

2. Welcome changing requirements, even late in development. Agile processes harness change for the customer's competitive advantage.

3. Deliver working software frequently, from a couple of weeks to a couple of months, with a preference for the shorter timescale.

4. Business people and developers must work together daily throughout the project.

5. Build projects around motivated individuals, give them the environment and support they need and trust them to get the job done.

6. The most efficient and effective method of conveying information with and within a development team is face-to-face conversation.

7. Working software is the primary measure of progress.

8. Agile processes promote sustainable development. The sponsors, developers and users should be able to maintain a constant pace indefinitely.

9. Continuous attention to technical excellence and good design enhances agility.

10. Simplicity—the art of maximizing the amount of work not done—is essential.

11. The best architectures, requirements and designs emerge from self-organizing teams.

12. At regular intervals, the team reflects on how to become more effective, then tunes and adjusts its behavior accordingly.

A.3.2 Declaration of Interdependence

The Agile project management *Declaration of Interdependence* was written in early 2005 by a group of 15 project leaders as a supplement to *The Agile Manifesto*. It enumerates six management values needed to reinforce an Agile development mentality, particularly when managing complex, uncertain projects.

The declaration highlights that project teams, customers, and other stakeholders are interdependent and connected and must recognize this to be successful. The values themselves are also interdependent.

We ...

increase return on investment *by making continuous flow of value our focus.*

deliver reliable results *by engaging customers in frequent interactions and shared ownership.*

expect uncertainty *and manage for it through iterations, anticipation and adaptation.*

unleash creativity and innovation *by recognizing that individuals are the ultimate source of value and creating an environment where they can make a difference.*

boost performance *through group accountability for results and shared responsibility for team effectiveness.*

improve effectiveness and reliability *through situationally specific strategies, processes and practices.*

Anderson. D., Augustine, S., Avery, C., Cockburn, A., Cohn, M., et al. 2005

A.4 Agile Methods

A number of Agile methodologies originated and gained traction in the 1990's and the early 2000's. While they differ in a variety of aspects, their commonality stems from their adherence to *The Agile Manifesto*.

The following Agile methods are briefly discussed below:

1. Lean Kanban
2. Extreme Programming (XP)
3. Crystal Methods
4. Dynamic Systems Development Methods (DSMD)
5. Feature Driven Development (FDD)
6. Test Driven Development (TDD)
7. Adaptive Software Development (ASD)
8. Agile Unified Process (AUP)
9. Domain-Driven Design (DDD)

A.4.1 Lean Kanban

The Lean concept optimizes an organization's system to produce valuable results based on its resources, needs, and alternatives while reducing waste. Waste could be from building the wrong thing, failure to learn, or practices that impede the process. Because these factors are dynamic in nature, a lean organization evaluates its entire system and continuously fine tunes its processes. The foundation of Lean is that the reduction of the length of each cycle (i.e., an iteration) leads to an increase in productivity by reducing delays, aids in error detection at an early stage, and consequently reduces the total amount of effort required to finish a task. Lean software principles have been successfully applied to software development.

Kanban literally means a "signboard" or "billboard" and it espouses the use of visual aids to assist and track production. The concept was introduced by Taiichi Ohno considered to be the father of the Toyota Production Systems (TPS). The use of visual aids is effective and has become a common practice. Examples include task cards, Scrumboards, and Burndown Charts. These methods gained attention due to their practice at Toyota, a leader in process management. Lean Kanban integrates the use of the visualization methods as prescribed by Kanban along with the principles of Lean creating a visual incremental evolutionary process management system.

A.4.2 Extreme Programming

Extreme Programming (XP), which originated in Chrysler Corporation, gained traction in the 1990's. XP makes it possible to keep the cost of changing software from rising radically with time. The key attributes of XP include incremental development, flexible scheduling, automated test codes, verbal communication, ever-evolving design, close collaboration, and tying in the long- and short-term drives of all those involved.

XP values communication, feedback, simplicity, and courage. The different roles in the XP approach include customer, developer, tracker, and coach. It prescribes various coding, developer, and business practices as well as events and artifacts to achieve effective and efficient development. XP has been extensively adopted due to its well defined engineering practices.

A.4.3 Crystal Methods

Crystal methodologies of software development were introduced by Alistair Cockburn in the early 1990s. Crystal methods are intended to be people-centric, lightweight, and easy to adapt. Because people are primary, the developmental processes and tools are not fixed but are rather adjusted to the specific requirements and characteristics of the project. The color spectrum is used to decide on the variant for a project. Factors such as comfort, discretionary money, essential money, and life play a vital role in determining the "weight" of the methodology, which is represented in various colors of the spectrum. The Crystal family is divided into Crystal Clear, Crystal Yellow, Crystal Orange, Crystal Orange Web, Crystal Red, Crystal Maroon, Crystal Diamond, and Crystal Sapphire.

All Crystal methods have four roles—executive sponsor, lead designer, developers, and experienced users. Crystal Methods recommend various strategies and techniques to achieve agility. A Crystal project cycle consists of chartering, delivery cycle, and wrap-up.

A.4.4 Dynamic Systems Development Methods (DSDM)

The Dynamic Systems Development Methods (DSDM) framework was initially published in 1995 and is administered by the DSDM Consortium. DSDM sets quality and effort in terms of cost and time at the outset and adjusts the project deliverables to meet set criteria by prioritizing the deliverables into "Must have," "Should have," "Could have," and "Won't have" categories (using the MoSCoW prioritization technique). DSDM is a system-oriented method with six distinct phases—Pre-project; Feasibility; Foundations; Exploration and Engineering; Deployment; and Benefit Assessment.

A later version of DSDM known as DSDM Atern, was introduced in 2007, focuses on both prioritization of deliverables and consistent user or customer collaboration. The newest version is inspired by an Arctic Tern, making it a developer-centric software development framework for on-time and in-budget delivery of user-valued and quality-controlled project features.

A.4.5 Feature Driven Development (FDD)

Feature Driven Development (FDD) was introduced by Jeff De Luca in 1997 and operates on the principle of completing a project by breaking it down into small, client-valued functions that can be delivered in less than two weeks' time. FDD has two core principles—software development is a human activity and software development is a client-valued functionality.

FDD defines six major roles—Project Manager, Chief Architect, Development Manager, Chief Programmers, Class Owners, and Domain Experts with a number of supporting roles. The FDD process is iterative and consists of developing an overall model, building a feature list, and then planning, designing, and building by feature.

A.4.6 Test Driven Development (TDD)

Sometimes known as Test-First Development, Test Driven Development was introduced by Kent Beck, one of the creators of Extreme Programming (XP). Test Driven Development is a software development method that involves writing automated test code first and developing the least amount of code necessary to pass that test later. The entire project is broken down into small, client-valued features that need to be developed in the shortest possible development cycle. Based on clients' requirements and specifications, tests are written. The tests designed in the above stage are used to design and write the production code.

TDD can be categorized into two levels: Acceptance TDD (ATDD) requiring a distinct acceptance test and Developer TDD (DTDD) involving writing a single developer test. TDD has become popular because of the numerous advantages it offers like rapid and reliable results, constant feedback, and reduced debugging time.

A.4.7 Adaptive Software Development (ASD)

Adaptive Software Development (ASD) grew out of the rapid application development work by Jim Highsmith and Sam Bayer. The highlights of ASD are constant adaptation of processes to the work at hand, provision of solutions to problems surfacing in large projects, and iterative, incremental development with continuous prototyping.

Being a risk-driven and a change-tolerant development approach, ASD believes a plan cannot admit uncertainties and risks as this indicates a flawed and failed plan. ASD is feature-based and target-driven. The first phase of development in ASD is Speculate (as opposed to Planning) followed by the Collaborate and Learn phases.

A.4.8 Agile Unified Process (AUP)

Agile Unified Process (AUP) evolved from IBM's Rational Unified Process. Developed by Scott Ambler, AUP combines industry-tried-and-tested Agile techniques such as Test Driven Development (TDD), Agile Modeling, agile change management, and database refactoring, to deliver a working product of the best quality.

AUP models its processes and techniques on the values of Simplicity, Agility, Customizability, Self-organization, Independence of tools, and focus on high-value activities. The AUP principles and values are put into action in the phases of Inception, Elaboration, Construction, and Transition.

A.4.9 Domain-Driven Design (DDD)

Domain-driven design is an Agile development approach meant for handling complex designs with implementation linked to an evolving model. It was conceptualized by Eric Evans in 2004 and revolves around the design of a core domain. "Domain" is defined as an area of activity to which the user applies a program or functionality. Many such areas are batched and a model is designed. The model consists of a system of abstractions that can be used to design the overall project and solve the problems related to the batched domains. The core values of DDD include domain-oriented, model-driven design, ubiquitous language, and a bounded context.

In DDD, ubiquitous language is established and the domain is modeled. Then design, development, and testing follow. Refining and refactoring of the domain model is done until it is satisfactory.

APPENDIX B. AUTHORS AND REVIEWERS OF THE *SBOK*™ *GUIDE*

This appendix lists the names of those individuals who contributed to the development and production of the *SBOK*™ *Guide*.

SCRUMstudy™ is grateful to all these individuals for their continuous support and acknowledges their contributions towards the development of the *SBOK*™ *Guide*.

B.1 Lead Author

Tridibesh Satpathy

B.2 Coauthors and Subject Matter Experts

R-A Alves

Winfried Hackmann

Quincy D. Jordan

Gaynell Malone

J. Drew Nations

Buddy Peacock

Karen Lyncook

Jaimie M. Rush

Elizabeth Lynne Warren

Ruth Kim

Mehul Doshi

Gaurav Garg

Ajey Grandhem

Sayan Guha

Vinay Jagannath

Deepak Ramaswamy

Ahmed Touseefullah Siddiqui

B.3 Reviewers and Edit Team

Corey T. Bailey

Sohini Banerjee

Vince Belanger

Bobbie Green

Magaline D. Harvey

Ravneet Kaur

Robert Lamb

Mimi LaRaque

Melissa Lauro

Richard Mather

Lachlan McGurk

Madhuresh Kumar Mishra

Neha Mishra

Yogaraj Mudalgi

Jose Nunez

Obi Nwaojigba

Bryan Lee Perez

James Pruitt

Charles J. Quansah

Frank Quinteros

Nadra Rafee

Tommie L. Sherrill

Barbara Siefken

Sandra A. Strech

Frances Mary Jo Tessler

Chrys Thorsen

Mike Tomaszewski

Ron Villmow

REFERENCES

Anderson, D., Augustine, S., Avery, C., Cockburn, A., Cohn, M., DeCarlo, D., Fitzgerald, D., Highsmith, J., Jepsen, O., Lindstrom, L., Little, T., McDonald, K., Pixton, P., Smith, P., and Wysocki, R. (2005) "Declaration of Interdependence," accessed September 2013, http://www.pmdoi.org/.

Beck, K., Beedle, M., van Bennekum, A., Cockburn, A., Cunningham, W., Fowler, M., Grenning, J., Highsmith, J., Hunt, A., Jeffries, R., Kern, J., Marick, B., Martin, R.C., Mellor, S., Schwaber, K., Sutherland, J., and Thomas, D. (2001) "Manifesto for Agile Software Development," accessed September 2013, http://agilemanifesto.org/.

Fellers, G. (1994) *Why Things Go Wrong: Deming Philosophy In A Dozen Ten-Minute Sessions*. Gretna, LA: Pelican Publishing.

Greenleaf, R. K. (1977) *Servant Leadership: A Journey into the Nature of Legitimate Power and Greatness*. Mahwah, NJ: Paulist Press.

Kano, N., Seraku, N., Takahashi, F., and Tsuji, S. (1984) "Attractive Quality and Must Be Quality." *Quality*, 14 (2): 39–48.

Leffingwell, D. and Widrig, D. (2003) *Managing Software Requirements: A Use Case Approach, 2nd ed.* Boston: Addison-Wesley.

Maslow, A. H. (1943) "A Theory of Human Motivation." *Psychological Review*, 50 (4): 370–396.

McGregor, D. (1960) *The Human Side of Enterprise*. New York: McGraw-Hill.

Patton, J. (2005) "It's All in How You Slice." Better *Software*, January: 16–40.

Spears, L. C. (2010) "Character and Servant Leadership: Ten Characteristics of Effective, Caring Leaders." *The Journal of Virtues & Leadership*, 1 (1): 25–30.

Takeuchi, H. and Nonaka, I. (1986) "The New New Product Development Game." *Harvard Business Review*, January–February: 137–146.

GLOSSARY

100-Point Method

The 100-Point Method was developed by Dean Leffingwell and Don Widrig (2003). It involves giving the customer 100 points they can use to vote for the features that they feel are most important.

Accepted Deliverables

Deliverables which meet the User Story Acceptance Criteria are accepted by the Product Owner. These are considered Accepted Deliverables that may be released to the customer if they so desire.

Adaptation

Adaptation happens as the Scrum Core Team and Stakeholder(s) learn through transparency and inspection and then adapt by making improvements in the work they do.

Affinity Estimation

Affinity Estimation is a technique used to quickly estimate a large number of User Stories using categories. The categories can be small, medium, or large, or they may be numbered using story point values to indicate relative size. Some key benefits of this approach are that the process is very transparent, visible to everyone, and is easy to conduct.

Agreed Actionable Improvements

Agreed Actionable Improvements are the primary output of the *Retrospect Sprint* process. They are the list of actionable items that the team has come up with to address problems and improve processes in order to enhance their performance in future Sprints.

Approve, Estimate, and Commit User Stories

In this process the Product Owner approves User Stories for a Sprint. Then, the Scrum Master and Scrum Team estimate the effort required to develop the functionality described in each User Story. Finally, the Scrum Team commits to deliver the customer requirements in the form of Approved, Estimated, and Committed User Stories.

Approved Change Requests

Approved Change Requests are changes that have been approved to be included in the Prioritized Product Backlog. At times, Approved Change Requests may originate from the program or portfolio managers and would be inputs to be added to the list of approved project changes for implementation in future Sprints.

Approved, Estimated, and Committed User Stories

The User Stories which are an input to this process have high level estimates from the *Create Prioritized Product Backlog* and *Create User Stories* processes. These estimates are used by the Product Owner to approve User Stories for the Sprint. Once approved, the User Stories are estimated by the team using various estimation techniques. After estimation, the team commits to a subset of approved and estimated User Stories that they believe they can complete in the next Sprint. These User Stories are Approved, Estimated, and Committed User Stories, which will become part of the Sprint Backlog.

Assertive Leader

Assertive leaders confront issues and display confidence to establish authority with respect.

Assigned Action Items and Due Dates

Once the Agreed Actionable Improvements have been elaborated and refined, action items to implement the improvements may be considered by the Scrum Team. Each action item will have a defined due date for completion.

Autocratic Leader

Autocratic leaders make decisions on their own, allowing team members little, if any involvement or discussion before a decision is made. This leadership style should only be used on rare occasions.

Automated Software Tools

Automated Software Tools are software tools used for scheduling, information collection, and distribution.

Better Team Coordination

The Scrum of Scrums Meeting facilitates coordination of work across multiple Scrum Teams. This is especially important when there are tasks involving inter-team dependencies. Incompatibilities and discrepancies between the work and deliverables of different teams are quickly exposed. This forum also gives teams the opportunity to showcase their achievements and give feedback to other teams.

Brainstorming

Sessions where relevant stakeholders and members of the Scrum Core Team openly share ideas through discussions and knowledge sharing sessions, which are normally conducted by a facilitator.

Business Justification

Business Justification demonstrates the reasons for undertaking a project. It answers the question "Why is this project needed?" Business justification drives all decision making related to a project.

Business Needs

Business needs are those business outcomes that the project is expected to fulfill, as documented in the Project Vision Statement.

Business Requirements

Business Requirements define what must be delivered to fulfill business needs and provide value to stakeholders. The sum of all the insights gained through various tools such as user or customer interviews, questionnaires, JAD sessions, Gap Analysis, SWOT Analysis, and other meetings, helps get a better perspective about the business requirements and helps in creating the Prioritized Product Backlog.

Change Request(s)

Request for changes are usually submitted as Change Requests. Change Requests remain in an unapproved status until they are formally approved.

Chief Product Owner

In the case of large projects, the Chief Product Owner prepares and maintains the overall Prioritized Product Backlog for the project. He or she coordinates work among the Product Owners of the Scrum Teams. The Product Owners, in turn, manage their respective parts of the Prioritized Product Backlog.

Chief Scrum Master

In case of large projects, the Chief Scrum Master is responsible for moderating the Scrum of Scrums (SoS) Meeting and removing impediments that affect multiple teams.

Coaching/Supportive Leader

Coaching and supportive leaders issue instructions and then support and monitor team members through listening, assisting, encouraging, and presenting a positive outlook during times of uncertainty.

Collaboration

Collaboration in Scrum refers to the Scrum Core Team working together and interfacing with the stakeholders to create and validate the deliverables of the project to meet the goals outlined in the Project Vision. Collaboration occurs when a team works together to play off each other's contributions to produce something greater.

Collaboration Plan

Collaboration is an extremely important element in Scrum and the Collaboration Plan outlines how the various decision makers, stakeholders and team members engage and collaborate with each other.

Colocation

Colocation is having all Scrum Core Team members located in the same work place leveraging the advantages of better coordination, problem-solving, knowledge sharing, and learning.

Communication Plan

This plan specifies the records that must be created and maintained throughout the project. A variety of methods are used to convey important project information to stakeholders. The Communication Plan defines these methods as well as who is responsible for the various communication activities.

Company Mission

The Company Mission provides a framework for formulating the strategies of a company or organization that guides their overall decision making.

Company Vision

Understanding the Company Vision helps the project keep its focus on the organization's objectives and the future potential of the company. The Product Owner can take guidance and direction from the Company Vision to create the Project Vision Statement.

Conduct Daily Standup

Conduct Daily Standup is a process in which a highly focused, Time-boxed meeting is conducted every day. This meeting is referred to as a Daily Standup Meeting, which is a forum for the Scrum Team to update each other on their progress and any impediments they may be facing.

Conduct Release Planning

In this process, the Scrum Core Team reviews the high-level User Stories in the Prioritized Product Backlog to develop a Release Planning Schedule, which is essentially a phased deployment schedule that can be shared with the Stakeholder(s). The Length of Sprints is also determined in this process.

Conflict Management

Conflict Management techniques are used by team members to manage any conflicts that arise during a Scrum project. Sources of conflict often include schedules, priorities, resources, reporting hierarchy, technical issues, procedures, personality, and costs.

Continuous Improvement

Continuous Improvement is a Scrum approach in which the team learns from experience and stakeholder engagement to constantly keep the Prioritized Product Backlog updated with any changes in requirements.

Continuous Value Justification

Continuous Value Justification refers to assessment of business value regularly to determine whether the justification or viability of executing the project continues to exist.

Convene Scrum of Scrums

In this process the Scrum Master(s) or Scrum Team representatives convene for the Scrum of Scrums Meetings at predetermined intervals, or whenever required to collaborate and track their respective progress, impediments, and dependencies across teams.

Core Role(s)

Core Roles are those roles which are mandatorily required for producing the product of the project, are committed to the project, and ultimately are responsible for the success of each Sprint within the project and of the project as a whole.

Create Deliverables

Create Deliverables is the process in which the Scrum Team works on the tasks in the Sprint Backlog to create Sprint Deliverables.

Create Prioritized Product Backlog

In this process, Epic(s) are refined and elaborated, then prioritized to create a Prioritized Product Backlog for the project. The Done Criteria are also established at this point.

Create Project Vision

In this process, the Project Business Case is reviewed to create a Project Vision Statement that will serve as the inspiration and provide focus for the entire project. The Product Owner is identified in this process.

Create Sprint Backlog

In this process, the Scrum Core Team holds Sprint Planning Meetings where the group creates a Sprint Backlog containing all tasks to be completed in the Sprint.

Create Tasks

In this process, the Approved, Estimated, and Committed User Stories are broken down into specific tasks and compiled into a Task List. Often a Task Planning Meeting is held for this purpose.

Create User Stories

In this process, User Stories and their related User Story Acceptance Criteria are created. User Stories are usually written by the Product Owner and are designed to ensure that the customer's requirements are clearly depicted and can be fully understood by all stakeholders.

Cumulative Flow Diagram (CFD)

A Cumulative Flow Diagram (CFD) is a useful tool for reporting and tracking project performance. It provides a simple, visual representation of project progress at a particular point in time. It is usually used to provide a higher level status of the overall project and not daily updates for individual Sprints.

Customer

The Customer is an individual or the organization that acquires the project's product, service, or other result. For any organization, depending on the project, there can be both internal customers (i.e., within the same organization) or external customers (i.e., outside of the organization).

Customer Value-based Prioritization

Customer Value-based Prioritization places primary importance on the customer and strives to implement User Stories with the highest value first. Such high value User Stories are identified and moved to the top of the Prioritized Product Backlog.

Daily Standup Meeting

The Daily Standup Meeting is a short daily meeting, Time-boxed to 15 minutes. The team members gather to report their progress by answering the following three questions:

1. What did I complete yesterday?
2. What will I complete today?
3. What impediments or obstacles (if any) am I currently facing?

Decomposition

Decomposition is a tool whereby high-level tasks are broken down into lower level, more detailed tasks. The User Stories are decomposed into tasks by members of the Scrum Team. Prioritized Product Backlog User Stories should be sufficiently decomposed to a level that provides the Scrum Team adequate information to create deliverables from the Tasks mentioned in the Task List.

Delegating Leader

Delegating Leaders are involved in the majority of decision making; however, they delegate some planning and decision-making responsibilities to team members, particularly if they are competent to handle tasks. This leadership style is appropriate in situations where the leader is in tune with specific project details and when time is limited.

Demonstrate and Validate Sprint

In this process, the Scrum Team demonstrates the Sprint Deliverables to the Product Owner and relevant stakeholders in a Sprint Review Meeting.

Dependency Determination

Once the Scrum Team has selected User Stories for a given Sprint, they should then consider any dependencies, including those related to the availability of people as well as any technical dependencies. Properly documenting dependencies helps the Scrum Teams determine the relative order in which tasks should be executed to create the Sprint Deliverables. Dependencies also highlight the relationship and interaction between tasks both within the Scrum Team working on a given Sprint and with other Scrum Teams in the project.

Design Patterns

Design Patterns provide a formal way of recording a resolution to a design problem in a specific field of expertise. These patterns record both the process used and the actual resolution, which can later be reused to improve decision making and productivity.

Develop Epic(s)

In this process, the Project Vision Statement serves as the basis for developing Epics. User Group Meetings may be held to *Develop Epic(s)*.

Development in Phases Contract

This contract makes funding available each month or each quarter after a release is successfully completed. It gives incentive to both customer and supplier and ensures that the monetary risk of the customer is limited to that particular time period since unsuccessful releases are not funded.

Directing Leader

Directing Leaders instruct team members regarding what tasks are required and when and how they should be performed.

Discretionary Dependencies

Discretionary Dependencies are dependencies that are placed into the workflow by choice. Typically, discretionary dependencies are determined by the Scrum Team based on past experiences or best practices in a particular field or domain.

Done Criteria

Done Criteria are a set of rules that are applicable to all User Stories. A clear definition of Done is critical, because it removes ambiguity from requirements and helps the team adhere to mandatory quality norms. This clear definition is used to create the Done criteria that are an output of the *Create Prioritized Product Backlog* process. A User Story is considered done when it is demonstrated to and approved by the Product Owner who judges it on the basis of the Done Criteria and the User Story Acceptance Criteria.

Earned Value Analysis

Earned Value Analysis analyzes actual project performance against planned performance at a given point in time. It measures current variances in the project's schedule and cost performance and forecasts the final cost based on the determined current performance.

Effort Estimated Task List

The Effort Estimated Task List is a list of tasks associated with the committed User Stories included in a Sprint. Estimated effort is expressed in terms of the estimation criteria agreed upon by the team. The Effort Estimated Task List is used by the Scrum Team during Sprint Planning Meetings to create the Sprint Backlog and the Sprint Burndown Chart.

Empirical Process Control

An Empirical Process Control model helps make decisions based on observation and experimentation rather than on detailed upfront planning. It relies on the three main ideas of transparency, inspection, and adaptation.

Epic(s)

Epic(s) are written in the initial stages of the project when most User Stories are high-level functionalities or product descriptions and requirements are broadly defined. They are large, unrefined User Stories in the Prioritized Product Backlog.

Estimate Range

Estimates for projects should be presented in ranges. Precise figures may give an impression of being highly accurate when in fact they may not be. In fact, estimates by definition are understood not to be precisely accurate. Estimate ranges should be based on the level of confidence the team has in each estimate.

Estimate Tasks process

In this process, the Scrum Core Team, in a Task Estimation Workshop, estimates the effort required to accomplish each task in the Task List. The output of this process is an Effort Estimated Task List.

Estimation Criteria

The primary objective of using Estimation Criteria is to maintain relative estimation sizes and minimize the need for re-estimation. Estimation Criteria can be expressed in numerous ways, with two common examples being story points and ideal time.

Expected Monetary Value

This is a risk assessment technique where the potential financial impact of a risk is determined based on its Expected Monetary Value (EMV). EMV is calculated by multiplying the monetary impact by the risk's probability, as approximated by the customer.

Explorer—Shopper—Vacationer—Prisoner (ESVP)

This is an exercise that can be conducted at the start of the Retrospect Sprint Meeting to understand the mind-set of the participants and set the tone for the meeting. Attendees are asked to anonymously indicate which best represents their outlook in the meeting.

External dependencies

External dependencies are those related to tasks, activities, or products that are outside the scope of the work to be executed by the Scrum Team, but are needed to complete a project task or create a project deliverable. External dependencies are usually outside the Scrum Team's control.

Fist of Five

Fist of Five is a simple and quick mechanism to achieve consensus in a group and drive discussion. After initial discussion on a given proposal or pending decision, the Scrum Team members are each asked to vote on a scale of 1 to 5 using their fingers.

Focus Group Meetings

Focus groups assemble individuals in a guided session to provide their opinions, perceptions, or ratings of a product, service, or desired result. Focus group members have the freedom to ask questions to each other and to get clarifications on particular subjects or concepts. Through questioning, constructive criticism, and feedback, focus groups lead to a better quality product and thereby contribute to meeting the expectations of the users.

Form Scrum Team

The Scrum Team members are identified during this process. Normally the Product Owner has the primary responsibility of selecting team members, but he or she often does so in collaboration with the Scrum Master.

Forming Stage

Forming Stage is the first stage of team formation, often considered a fun stage because everything is new and the team has not yet encountered any difficulties with the project.

Four Questions per Team

A set of questions asked in each Scrum of Scrums (SoS) Meeting. Each Scrum Team representative will provide updates from his or her team which are usually provided in the form of answers to four specific questions.

1. What has my team been working on since the last meeting?
2. What will my team do until the next meeting?
3. What were other teams counting on our team to finish that remains undone?
4. What is our team planning on doing that might affect other teams?

Gap Analysis

Gap Analysis is a technique used to compare the current, actual state with some desired state and to determine how to bridge the gap between them.

Groom Prioritized Product Backlog

Groom Prioritized Product Backlog is a process in which the Prioritized Product Backlog is continuously updated and maintained.

Identify Scrum Master and Stakeholder(s) process

In this process, the Scrum Master and the stakeholders are identified using specific Selection Criteria.

Impediment

An impediment is any hindrance or hurdle that reduces the productivity of the Scrum Team.

Implement Phase

The Implement Phase includes processes related to the execution of the tasks and activities to create a project's product.

Incentive and Penalty Contract

This contract is based on the agreement that the supplier will be rewarded with a financial incentive, if the project's products are delivered on time, but will incur financial penalties, if the delivery is late.

Incremental Delivery Contract

This contract includes inspection points at regular intervals. It helps the customer or stakeholders make decisions regarding product development periodically throughout the project at each inspection point. The customer can either accept the development of the product, decide to stop the development of the product, or request product modifications.

Index Cards

Index cards, often described as Story Cards, are used to track the User Stories throughout the project. This increases visibility and transparency and facilitates early discovery of any problems that may arise.

Initiate phase

This phase is composed of the processes related to initiation of a project: Create Project Vision, Identify Scrum Master and Stakeholder(s), Form Scrum Team, Develop Epic(s), Create Prioritized Product Backlog, and Conduct Release Planning.

Inspection

Inspection refers to the monitoring required to follow empirical process control, to ensure that the project deliverables conforms to the requirements.

Internal Dependencies

Internal dependencies are those dependencies between tasks, products, or activities that are under the control of the Scrum Team and within the scope of the work to be executed by the Scrum Team.

Internal Rate of Return (IRR)

Internal Rate of Return (IRR) is a discount rate on an investment in which the present value of cash inflows is made equal to the present value of cash outflows for assessing a project's rate of return. When comparing projects, one with a higher IRR is typically better.

Issues

Issues are generally well-defined certainties that are currently happening on the project, so there is no need for conducting a probability assessment as we would for a risk.

Iterative Delivery

Iterative delivery is the phased delivery of value to the customer.

JAD Sessions

A Joint Application Design (JAD) session is a requirements gathering technique. It is a highly structured facilitated workshop which hastens the *Create Project Vision* process as it enables the Stakeholder(s) and other decision makers to come to a consensus on the scope, objectives, and other specifications of the project.

Joint Venture Contract

This contract is generally used when two or more parties partner to accomplish the work of a project. The parties involved in the project will both achieve some Return on Investment because the revenues or benefits generated will be shared between the parties.

Kano Analysis

Kano Analysis was developed by Noriaki Kano (1984) and involves classifying features or requirements into four categories based on customer preferences:

1. Exciters/Delighters
2. Satisfiers
3. Dissatisfiers
4. Indifferent

Laissez Faire Leader

A leadership style, where the team is left largely unsupervised and the leader does not interfere with their daily work activities. This often leads to a state of anarchy.

Length of Sprint

Based on the various inputs including business requirements and the Release Planning Schedule, the Product Owner and the Scrum Team decide on the length of the Sprints for the project. Once determined, the length of the Sprint is usually fixed for the project.

Length of Sprint is the duration of the Sprints determined for a project.

Risks

Risks include any uncertain or unplanned events that may affect the project positively or negatively.

Mandatory Dependencies

These dependencies are either inherent in the nature of the work, like a physical limitation, or may be due to contractual obligations or legal requirements.

Market Study

Market Study refers to the organized research, gathering, collation, and analysis of data related to customers' preferences for products. It often includes extensive data on market trends, market segmentation, and marketing processes.

Minimum Acceptance Criteria

Minimum Acceptance Criteria are declared by the business unit. They then become part of the Acceptance Criteria for any User Story for that business unit. Any functionality defined by the business unit must satisfy these Minimum Acceptance Criteria, if it is to be accepted by the respective Product Owner.

Mitigated Risks

Mitigated Risks refer to the risks that are successfully addressed or mitigated by the Scrum Team during the project.

Monopoly Money

Monopoly Money is a technique that involves giving the customer "monopoly money" or "false money" equal to the amount of the project budget and asking them to distribute it among the User Stories under consideration. In this way, the customer prioritizes based on what they are willing to pay for each User Story.

MoSCoW Prioritization

The MoSCoW Prioritization scheme derives its name from the first letters of the phrases "Must have," "Should have," "Could have," and "Won't have". The labels are in decreasing order of priority with "Must have" features being those without which the product will have no value and "Won't have" features being those that, although they would be nice to have, are not necessary to be included.

Net Present Value (NPV)

Net Present Value (NPV) is a method used to determine the current net value of a future financial benefit, given an assumed inflation or interest rate.

Non-core role

Non-core roles are those roles which are not mandatorily required for the Scrum project. They may include team members who are interested in the project, who have no formal role on the project team, may interface with the team, but may not be responsible for the success of the project.

Norming stage

The third stage of team formation when the team begins to mature, sort out their internal differences, and find solutions to work together. It is considered a period of adjustment.

Number of Stories

Number of Stories refers to the number of User Stories that are delivered as part of a single Sprint. It can be expressed in terms of simple count or weighted count.

Opportunities

Risks that are likely to have a positive impact on the project are referred to as opportunities.

Opportunity Cost

Opportunity cost refers to the value of the next best business option or project that was discarded in favor of the chosen project.

Organizational Deployment Methods

The deployment mechanisms of each organization tend to be different based on industry, target users, and positioning. Depending on the product being delivered, deployment can take place remotely or may involve the physical shipping or transition of an item.

Organizational Resource Matrix

The Organizational Resource Matrix is a hierarchical depiction of a combination of a functional organizational structure and a project organizational structure. Matrix organizations bring together team members for a project from different functional departments such as information technology, finance, marketing, sales, manufacturing, and other departments - and create cross-functional teams.

Paired Comparison

Paired Comparison is a technique where a list of all the User Stories in the Prioritized Product Backlog is prepared. Next, each User Story is taken individually and compared with the other User Stories in the list, one at a time. Each time two User Stories are compared, a decision is made regarding which of the two is more important. Through this process, a prioritized list of User Stories can be generated.

Pareto Analysis

This technique of assessing risk involves ranking risks by magnitude. It helps the Scrum Team address the risks in order of their potential impacts on the project.

PDCA/PDSA cycle

The Plan-Do-Check-Act Cycle—also known as the Deming or Shewhart Cycle—was developed by Dr. W. Edwards Deming, considered the father of modern quality control and Dr. Walter A. Shewhart. Deming later modified Plan-Do-Check-Act to Plan-Do-Study-Act (PDSA) because he felt the term "Study" emphasized analysis rather than simply inspection, as implied by the term "Check." Both Scrum and the Deming/Shewhart/PDCA Cycle are iterative methods that focus on continuous improvement.

Performing stage

The final stage of team formation when the team becomes its most cohesive and operates at its highest level in terms of performance. The members have evolved into an efficient team of peer professionals who are consistently productive.

Personas

Personas are highly detailed fictional characters, representative of the majority of users as well as other stakeholders who may not directly use the end product. Personas are created to identify the needs of the target user base.

Piloting Plan

A Piloting Plan can be used to map out a pilot deployment in detail. The scope and objectives of the deployment, the target deployment user base, a deployment schedule, transition plans, required user preparation, evaluation criteria for the deployment, and other key elements related to the deployment are specified in the Pilot Plan and shared with stakeholders.

Plan and Estimate phase

The Plan and Estimate phase consists of processes related to planning and estimating tasks, which include *Create User Stories*; *Approve, Estimate, and Commit User Stories*; *Create Tasks*; *Estimate Tasks*; and *Create Sprint Backlog*.

Planning for Value

Planning for Value refers to justifying and confirming the project value. The onus for determining how value is created falls on the stakeholders (sponsor, customers, and/or users), while the Scrum Team concentrates on what is to be developed.

Planning Poker

Planning Poker, also called Estimation Poker, is an estimation technique which balances group thinking and individual thinking to estimate relative sizes of User Stories or the effort required to develop them.

Points for Cost Estimating

Cost estimation can be accomplished through the use of relative units (e.g., effort estimates) rather than absolute units (i.e., actual costs incurred). In order to estimate the cost to implement a User Story, the Scrum Team can use story points. When this is done, the cost estimated for each task will be in the form of story points, rather than monetary units.

Portfolio

A portfolio is a group of related programs, with the objective to deliver business outcomes as defined in the Portfolio Vision Statement. The Prioritized Portfolio Backlog incorporates the Prioritized Program Backlogs for all the programs in the portfolio.

Portfolio Product Owner

The Portfolio Product Owner defines the strategic objectives and priorities for the portfolio.

Portfolio Scrum Master

The Portfolio Scrum Master solves problems, removes impediments, facilitates, and conducts meetings for the portfolio.

Prioritization

Prioritizing can be defined as determining the order of things and separating what will be done now, from what can be done later.

Prioritized Product Backlog

The Prioritized Product Backlog is a single requirements document that defines the project scope by providing a prioritized list of features of the product or service to be delivered by the project.

Probability Impact Grid

A grid where Risks are assessed for probability of occurrence and for potential impact on project objectives. Generally, a numerical rating is assigned for both probability and impact independently. The two values are then multiplied to derive a risk severity score, which can be used to prioritize risks.

Probability Trees

Potential events are represented in a diagram with a branch for each possible outcome of the events. The probability of each outcome is indicated on the appropriate branch, and these values can be used to calculate the overall impact of risk occurrence in a project.

Product

The term "product" in the *SBOK™ Guide* may refer to a product, service, or other deliverable that provides value to the customer.

Prioritized Product Backlog Review Meeting

A Product Backlog Review Meeting (also referred to as a Prioritized Product Backlog Grooming Session) is a formal meeting during the *Groom Prioritized Product Backlog* process, which helps the Scrum Team review and gain consensus about the Prioritized Product Backlog.

Product Owner

The Product Owner is the person responsible for maximizing business value for the project. He or she is responsible for articulating customer requirements and maintaining business justification for the project.

Program

A program is a group of related projects, with the objective to deliver business outcomes as defined in the Program Vision Statement. The Prioritized Program Backlog incorporates the Prioritized Product Backlogs for all the projects in the program.

Program and Portfolio Risks

Risks related to a portfolio or program that will also impact projects that are part of the respective portfolio or program.

Program Product Owner

The Program Product Owner defines the strategic objectives and priorities for the program.

Program Scrum Master

The Program Scrum Master solves problems, removes impediments, facilitates, and conducts meetings for the program.

Project

A project is a collaborative enterprise to either create new products or services or to deliver results as defined in the Project Vision Statement. Projects are usually impacted by constraints of time, cost, scope, quality, people and organizational capabilities.

Project Benefits

Project benefits include all measurable improvements in a product, service or result which could be provided through successful completion of a project.

Project Budget

The project budget is a financial document which includes the cost of people, materials, and other related expenses in a project. The project budget is typically signed off by the sponsor(s) to ensure that sufficient funds are available.

Project Charter

A project charter is an official statement of the desired objectives and outcomes of the project. In many organizations, the project charter is the document that officially and formally authorizes the project, providing the team with written authority to begin project work.

Project Costs

Project costs are investment and other development costs for a project

Project Reasoning

Project reasoning includes all factors which necessitate the project, whether positive or negative, chosen or not (e.g., inadequate capacity to meet existing and forecasted demand, decrease in customer satisfaction, low profits, legal requirement etc.)

Project Timescales

Timescales reflect the length or duration of a project. Timescales related to the business case also include the time over which the project's benefits will be realized.

Project Vision Meeting

A Project Vision Meeting is a meeting with the Program Stakeholder(s), Program Product Owner, Program Scrum Master, and Chief Product Owner. It helps identify the business context, business requirements, and stakeholder expectations in order to develop an effective Project Vision Statement.

Project Vision Statement

The key output of the *Create Project Vision* process is a well-structured Project Vision Statement. A good Project Vision explains the business need and what the project is intended to meet rather than how it will meet the need.

Proposed Non-Functional Items for Product Backlog

Non-functional requirements may not be fully defined in the early stages of the project and can surface during the Sprint Review or Retrospect Sprint Meetings. These items should be added to the Prioritized Product Backlog as they are discovered.

Quality

Quality is defined as the ability of the completed product or Deliverables to meet the Acceptance Criteria and achieve the business value expected by the customer.

Quality Assurance

Quality assurance refers to the evaluation of processes and standards that govern quality management in a project to ensure that they continue to be relevant. Quality assurance activities are carried out as part of the work.

Quality Control

Quality control refers to the execution of the planned quality activities by the Scrum Team in the process of creating deliverables that are potentially shippable. It also includes learning from each set of completed activities in order to achieve continuous improvement.

Quality Management

Quality management in Scrum enables customers to become aware of any problems in the project early and helps them recognize if a project is going to work for them or not. Quality management in Scrum is facilitated through three interrelated activities:

1. Quality planning
2. Quality control
3. Quality assurance

Quality Planning

Quality Planning refers to identification and definition of the product required from a Sprint and the project along with the Acceptance Criteria, any development methods to be followed, and the key responsibilities of Scrum Team members in regards to quality.

Refactoring

Refactoring is a tool specific to software projects. The aim of this technique is to improve the maintainability of the existing code and make it simpler, more concise, and more flexible. Refactoring means improving the design of the present code without changing how the code behaves. It involves the following:

- Eliminating repetitive and redundant code
- Breaking methods and functions into smaller routines
- Clearly defining variables and method names
- Simplifying the code design
- Making the code easier to understand and modify

Rejected Deliverables

Rejected Deliverables are the deliverables that do not meet the defined Acceptance Criteria. A list of Rejected Deliverables is maintained and updated after each Sprint Review Meeting with any deliverables that were not accepted.

Relative Prioritization Ranking

Relative Prioritization Ranking is a simple listing of User Stories in order of priority. It is an effective method for determining the desired User Stories for each iteration or release of the product or service.

Relative Sizing/Story Points

In addition to being used for estimating cost, Story Points may also be used for estimating the overall size of a User Story or feature. This approach assigns a story point value based on an overall assessment of the size of a User Story with consideration given to risk, amount of effort required, and level of complexity.

Release Content

This consists of essential information about the deliverables that can assist the Customer Support Team.

Release Notes

Release Notes should include external or market facing shipping criteria for the product to be delivered.

Release Planning Schedule

A Release Planning Schedule is one of the key outputs of the *Conduct Release Planning* process. A Release Planning Schedule states which deliverables are to be released to the customers, along with planned intervals, and dates for releases. There may not be a release scheduled at the end of every Sprint iteration.

Release Planning Sessions

The major objective of Release Planning Sessions is to create a Release Plan Schedule and enable the Scrum Team to have an overview of the releases and delivery schedule for the product they are developing, so that they can align with the expectations of the Product Owner and relevant Stakeholder(s).

Release Prioritization Methods

Release Prioritization Methods are used to develop a Release Plan. These methods are industry and organization specific and are usually determined by senior management in an organization.

Resolved Issues

In Scrum of Scrums Meetings, Scrum Team members have the opportunity to transparently discuss issues impacting their project. This timely discussion and resolution of issues in the Scrum of Scrums Meeting greatly improves coordination between different Scrum Teams and also reduces the need for redesign and rework.

Retrospect Project

In this process, which completes the project, organizational stakeholders and Scrum Core Team members assemble to retrospect the project and identify, document, and internalize lessons learned. Often, these lessons lead to the documentation of Agreed Actionable Improvements, to be implemented in future projects.

Retrospect Project Meeting

The Retrospect Project Meeting is a meeting to determine ways in which team collaboration and effectiveness can be improved in future projects. Positives, negatives, and potential opportunities for improvement are also discussed. This meeting is not Time-boxed and may be conducted in person or in a virtual format.

Retrospect Sprint

In this process, the Scrum Master and Scrum Team meet to discuss the lessons learned throughout the Sprint. The lessons learned are documented and can be applied to future Sprints.

Retrospect Sprint Log(s)

The Retrospect Sprint Log is a record of the opinions, discussions, and actionable items raised in a Retrospect Sprint Meeting. The Scrum Master may facilitate creation of this log with inputs form Scrum Core Team members.

Retrospect Sprint Meeting

The Retrospect Sprint Meeting is Time-boxed to 4 hours for a one-month Sprint and conducted as part of the *Retrospect Sprint* process. The length may be scaled up or down relative to the length of the Sprint. During this meeting, the Scrum Team gets together to review and reflect on the previous Sprint in terms of the processes followed, tools employed, collaboration and communication mechanisms, and other aspects relevant to the project.

Return on Investment (ROI)

Return on Investment (ROI), when used for project justification, assesses the expected net income to be gained from a project. It is calculated by deducting the expected costs or investment in a project from its expected revenue and then dividing this (net profit) by the expected costs in order to get a return rate.

Risk

Risk is defined as an uncertain event or set of events that can affect the objectives of a project and may contribute to its success or failure.

Risk Appetite

Risk appetite refers to how much uncertainty a stakeholder or organization is willing to take on.

Risk Assessment

Risk assessment refers to evaluating and estimating identified risks.

Risk Attitude

Essentially, the Risk Attitude of the Stakeholder(s) determines how much risk the Stakeholder(s) consider acceptable. This is a determining factor in when they will decide to take actions to mitigate potential adverse risks.

Risk Averse

Risk Averse is one of the categories of Utility Function. It refers to a Stakeholder being unwilling to accept a risk no matter what the anticipated benefit or opportunity.

Risk Breakdown Structure

In this structure, risks are grouped based on their categories or commonalities. For example, risks may be categorized as financial, technical, or safety related.

Risk Burndown Chart

A chart that depicts cumulative project risk severity over time. The likelihood of the various risks are plotted on top of each other to show cumulative risk on the y-axis. The initial identification and evaluation of risks and the creation of the Risk Burndown Chart are done early in the project.

Risk Checklists

Risk Checklists include key points to be considered while identifying risks, common risks encountered in Scrum projects, or even categories of risks that should be addressed by the team.

Risk communication

Risk Communication involves communicating the findings from the first four steps of Risk Management to the appropriate Stakeholder(s) and determining their perception regarding the uncertain events.

Risk Identification

Risk Identification is an important step in Risk Management which involves using various techniques to identify all potential risks.

Risk Meeting

Risks can be more easily prioritized by the Product Owner by calling a meeting of the Scrum Core Team and optionally inviting relevant Stakeholders to the meeting.

Risk Mitigation

Risk Mitigation is an important step in Risk Management that involves developing an appropriate strategy to deal with a risk.

Risk Neutral

Risk Neutral is one of the categories of Utility Function that refers to a stakeholder being neither risk averse nor risk seeking; any given decision is not affected by the level of uncertainty of the outcome. When two possible scenarios carry the same level of benefit, the risk neutral stakeholder will not be concerned if one scenario is riskier than the other.

Risk Prioritization

Risk Prioritization is an important step in Risk Management that involves prioritizing risks to be included for specific action in the Prioritized Product Backlog.

Risk Prompt Lists

Risk Prompt Lists are used in stimulating thoughts regarding the source from which risks may originate. Risk Prompt Lists for various industries and project types are available publicly.

Risk Seeking

Risk Seeking is one of the categories of Utility Function that refers to a stakeholder being willing to accept risk even if it delivers a marginal increase in return or benefit to the project.

Risk threshold

Risk Threshold refers to the level at which a risk is acceptable to the stakeholder's organization. A risk will fall above or below the risk threshold. If it is below, the stakeholder or organization is more likely to accept the risk.

Risk tolerance

Risk tolerance indicates the degree, amount, or volume of risk the stakeholders will withstand.

Risk-Based Spike

Risk-Based Spikes are basically experiments that involve research or prototyping to better understand potential risks. In a spike, an intense two to three-day exercise is conducted (preferably at the beginning of a project before the *Develop Epic(s)* or *Create Prioritized Product Backlog* processes) to help the team determine the uncertainties that could affect the project.

Scope

The scope of a project is the total sum of all the product increments and the work required for developing the final product.

Scrum Guidance Body

The Scrum Guidance Body (SGB) is an optional role. It generally consists of a group of documents and/or a group of experts who are typically involved with defining objectives related to quality, government regulations, security, and other key organizational parameters.

Scrum Guidance Body Expertise

Scrum Guidance Body Expertise relates to documented rules and regulations, development guidelines, or standards, and best practices.

Scrum Master

The Scrum Master is one of the Scrum Core Team roles. He or she facilitates creation of the project's deliverables, manages risks, changes, and impediments during the *Conduct Daily Standup, Retrospect Sprint,* and other Scrum processes.

Scrum of Scrums Meeting

The Scrum of Scrums (SoS) Meeting is an important meeting when scaling Scrum to large projects with representatives from all teams attending. This meeting is usually facilitated by the Chief Scrum Master and is intended to focus on areas of coordination and integration between the different Scrum Teams. This meeting is conducted at predetermined intervals or when required by the Scrum Teams.

Scrum Team

The Scrum Team is one the Scrum Core Team roles. The Scrum Team works on creating the deliverables of the project and contributes to realizing business value for all stakeholders and the project.

Scrum Team Lessons Learned

The self-organizing and empowered Scrum Team is expected to learn from mistakes made during a Sprint and these lessons learned help the teams improve their performance in future Sprints.

Scrum Team Representatives

A representative nominated by the team to represent them in the Scrum of Scrums (SoS) Meetings based on who can best fulfill the role depending on current issues and circumstances.

Scrumboard

Scrumboard is a tool used by the Scrum Team to plan and track progress during each Sprint. The Scrumboard contains four columns to indicate the progress of the estimated tasks for the Sprint: a To Do column for tasks not yet started, an In Progress column for the tasks started but not yet completed, a Testing column for tasks completed but in the process of being tested, and a Done column for the tasks that have been completed and successfully tested.

Self-organization

Scrum believes that employees are self-motivated and seek to accept greater responsibility. Hence, they deliver much greater value when self-organized.

Servant Leader

Servant leaders employ listening, empathy, commitment, and insight while sharing power and authority with team members. Servant leaders are stewards who achieve results by focusing on the needs of the team. This style is the embodiment of the Scrum Master role.

Ship Deliverables

In this process, Accepted Deliverables are delivered or transitioned to the relevant Stakeholder(s). A formal Working Deliverables Agreement documents the successful completion of the Sprint.

Simple Schemes

Simple Schemes involve labeling items as Priority "1", "2", "3" or "High", "Medium" and "Low" and so on. Although this is a simple and straightforward approach, it can become problematic because there is often a tendency to label everything as Priority "1" or "High".

Skills Requirement Matrix

The skills requirement matrix, also known as a competency framework, is used to assess skill gaps and training requirements for team members. A skills matrix maps the skills, capabilities, and interest level of team members in using those skills and capabilities on a project. Using this matrix, the organization can assess any skill gaps in team members and identify the employees who will need further training in a particular area or competency.

Speed Boat

Speed Boat is a technique that can be used to conduct the Retrospect Sprint Meeting. Team members play the role of the crew on a Speed Boat. The boat must reach an island, which is symbolic of the Project Vision. Sticky notes are used by the attendees to record engines and anchors. Engines are things which help them reach the island, while anchors are things that are hindering them from reaching the island. This exercise is time-boxed to a few minutes.

Sponsor

The sponsor is the individual or the organization that provides resources and support for the project. The sponsor is also the stakeholder to whom everyone is accountable in the end.

Sprint

A Sprint is a time-boxed iteration of one to six weeks in duration during which the Scrum Team works on and creates the Sprint deliverables.

310 © 2013 SCRUMstudy™. *A Guide to the Scrum Body of Knowledge (SBOK™ Guide)*

Sprint Backlog

Sprint Backlog is a list of the tasks to be executed by the Scrum Team in the upcoming Sprint.

Sprint Burndown Chart

Sprint Burndown Chart is a graph that depicts the amount of work remaining in the ongoing Sprint.

Sprint Deliverables

Sprint Deliverables refer to product increments or deliverables that are completed at the end of each Sprint.

Sprint Planning Meeting

Sprint Planning Meeting is conducted at the beginning of a Sprint as part of the *Create Sprint Backlog* process. It is Time-boxed to eight hours for a one-month Sprint and is divided into two parts - Objective Definition and Task Estimation.

Sprint Review Meeting

The Sprint Review Meeting is time-boxed to four hours for a one-month Sprint and can be scaled according to the length of the Sprint. During the Sprint Review Meeting, the Scrum Team presents the deliverables of the current Sprint to the Product Owner, who may accept or reject the deliverables.

Sprint Tracking Tools

Sprint Tracking Tools are used to track the progress of a Sprint and to know where the Scrum Team stands in terms of completing the tasks in the Sprint Backlog. A variety of tools can be used to track the work in a Sprint, but one of the most common is a Scrumboard, also known as a task board or progress chart.

Sprint Velocity

Sprint Velocity is the rate at which the team can complete the work in a Sprint. It is usually expressed in the same units as those used for estimating, normally story points or ideal time.

Stakeholder(s)

Stakeholder(s) is a collective term that includes customers, users, and sponsor who frequently interface with the Product Owner, Scrum Master and Scrum Team to provide inputs and facilitate creation of the project's product, service, or other results.

Storming stage

The second stage of team formation where the team begins trying to accomplish the work. However, power struggles may occur and there is often chaos or confusion among team members.

Story Mapping

Story Mapping is a technique to provide a visual outline of the product and its key components. Story Mapping, first formulated by Jeff Patton (2005), is commonly used to illustrate product roadmaps. Story maps depict the sequence of product development iterations and map out which features will be included in the first, second, third, and subsequent releases.

Sustainable Pace

Sustainable Pace is the pace at which the team can work and comfortably maintain. It translates to increased employee satisfaction, stability, and increased estimation accuracy, all of which ultimately leads to increased customer satisfaction.

SWOT Analysis

SWOT is a structured approach to project planning that helps evaluate the strengths, weaknesses, opportunities, and threats related to a project. This type of analysis helps identify both the internal and the external factors that could impact the project.

Target Customers for Release

Not every release will target all stakeholders or users. The Stakeholders may choose to limit certain releases to a subset of users. The Release Plan specifies the Target Customers for the Release.

Task Estimation Workshop

Task Estimation Workshop enable the Scrum Team to estimate the effort required to complete a task or set of tasks and to estimate the people effort and other resources required to carry out the tasks within a given Sprint.

Task List

This is a comprehensive list that contains all the tasks to which the Scrum Team has committed to for the current Sprint. It contains descriptions of each task.

Task Planning Meeting

In a Task Planning Meeting, the Scrum Team gets together to plan the work to be done in the Sprint and the team reviews the committed User Stories at the top of the Prioritized Product Backlog. To help ensure that the group stays on topic, this meeting should be Time-boxed, with the standard length limited to two hours per week of Sprint duration.

Task-Oriented Leader

Task-Oriented Leaders enforce task completion and adherence to deadlines.

Team Building Plan

Since a Scrum Team is cross-functional, each member needs to participate actively in all aspects of the project. The Scrum Master should identify potential issues that could crop up with team members and try to address them diligently in the Team Building Plan in order to maintain an effective team.

Team Calendar

A Team Calendar contains information regarding availability of team members including information related to employee vacation, leaves, important events, and holidays.

Team Expertise

Team Expertise refers to the expertise of the Scrum Team members to understand the User Stories and Tasks in the Sprint Backlog in order to create the final deliverables. Team Expertise is used to assess the inputs needed to execute the planned work of the project.

Technical Debt

Technical Debt (also referred to as design debt or code debt) refers to the work that teams prioritize lower, omit, or do not complete as they work towards creating the primary deliverables associated with the project's product. Technical Debt accrues and must be paid in the future.

Theory X

Theory X leaders assume that employees are inherently unmotivated and will avoid work if possible, warranting an authoritarian style of management.

Theory Y

Theory Y leaders assume that employees are self-motivated and seek to accept greater responsibility. Theory Y involves a more participative management style.

Threats

Threats are risks that could affect the project in a negative manner.

Three Daily Questions

Three Daily Questions used in Daily Standup Meetings which are facilitated by the Scrum Master, where each Scrum Team member provides information in the form of answers to three specific questions:

- What did I complete yesterday?
- What will I complete today?
- What impediments or obstacles (if any) am I currently facing?

Time-boxing

Time-boxing refers to setting short periods of time for work to be done. If the work undertaken remains incomplete at the end of the Time-box, it is moved into a subsequent Time-box. Time-boxes provide the structure needed for Scrum projects, which have an element of uncertainty, are dynamic in nature, and are prone to frequent changes.

Transparency

Transparency allows all facets of any Scrum process to be observed by anyone. Sharing all information leads to a high trust environment.

Unapproved Change Requests

Request for changes are usually submitted as Change Requests. Change Requests remain unapproved until they get formally approved.

Updated Program Product Backlog

A Program Product Backlog that undergoes periodic grooming to incorporate changes and new requirements.

User

Users are the individuals or the organization that directly uses the project's product, service, or other results. Like customers, for any organization, there can be both internal and external users. In some cases, customers and users may be the same.

User Group Meetings

User Group Meetings involve relevant Stakeholder(s), primarily users or customers of the product. They provide the Scrum Core Team with first-hand information about user expectations. This helps in formulating the Acceptance Criteria for the product and provides valuable insights for developing Epics.

User Stories

User Stories adhere to a specific, predefined structure and are a simplistic way of documenting the requirements and desired end-user functionality. The requirements expressed in User Stories are short, simple, and easy-to-understand statements resulting in enhanced communication among the stakeholders and better estimations by the team.

User Story Acceptance Criteria

Every User Story has associated Acceptance Criteria. User Stories are subjective, so the Acceptance Criteria provide the objectivity required for the User Story to be considered as Done or not Done during the Sprint Review providing clarity to the team on what is expected of a User Story.

User Story Workshops

User Story Workshops are held as part of the *Develop Epic(s)* process. The Scrum Master facilitates these sessions. The entire Scrum Core Team is involved and at times it is desirable to include other Stakeholder(s).

User Story Writing Expertise

The Product Owner, based on his or her interaction with the stakeholders, own business knowledge and expertise, and inputs from the team, develops User Stories that forms the initial Prioritized Product Backlog for the project.

Utility Function

Utility Function is a model used for measuring stakeholder risk preference or attitude toward risk. It defines the Stakeholder(s)' level or willingness to accept risk.

Value Stream Mapping

Value Stream Mapping uses flowcharts to illustrate the flow of information needed to complete a process and may be used to streamline a process by helping to determine non-value-adding elements.

Vendor

Vendors include external individuals or organizations that provide products and services that are not within the core competencies of the project organization.

Voice of the Customer (VOC)

The Voice of the Customer (VOC) can be referred to as the explicit and implicit requirements of the customer, which must be understood prior to the designing of a product or service. The Product Owner represents the Voice of the Customer.

War Room

War Room is the commonly used term to describe the location where all Scrum Team members working are located. Normally, it is designed in such a way that team members can move around freely, work, and communicate easily because they are located in close proximity to each other.

Wideband Delphi Technique

Wideband Delphi is a group-based estimation technique for determining how much work is involved and how long it will take to complete. Individuals within a team anonymously provide estimations for each feature and the initial estimates are then plotted on a chart. The team then discusses the factors that influenced their estimates and proceed to a second round of estimation. This process is repeated until the estimates of individuals are close to each other and a consensus for the final estimate can be reached.

Working Deliverables

This output is the final shippable deliverable for which the project was sanctioned.

Working Deliverables Agreement

Deliverables that meet the Acceptance Criteria receive formal business sign-off and approval by the customer or the sponsor.

INDEX

1

100-point method, 171

A

Acceptance Criteria, 86
Accepted Deliverables, 248
Actual Cost, 77
Adaptability, 4
Adaptation, 24
Affinity Estimation, 195
Agile Expert Certified (AEC™), 6
Agile Manifesto, 29
Agreed Actionable Improvements, 252
Applicable Contracts, 161
Appropriation, 29
Approve, Estimate, and Commit User Stories, 17, 182
   inputs, 193
   outputs, 196
   tools, 193
Approved Change Requests, 99, 160
Approved Changes, 166
Approved, Estimated, and Committed User Stories, 196
Articulation, 29
Aspects, 7
Assertive, 61
Assigned Action Items and Due Dates, 252
Autocratic, 61
Awareness, 29

B

Back-up Persons, 157
Better Team Coordination, 243
Brainstorming, 121
Budget at Completion, 77
Business case, 70
Business Justification, 13, 65
Business needs, 69
Business Requirements, 169
Business value, 85
Business value delivered, 208

C

Change, 14, 97, 98
Change approval process, 99
Change Requests, 15, 99
Chief Product Owner, 12, 45, 140
Chief Scrum Master, 12, 47, 147
Coaching, 61
Collaboration, 10, 21, 29
Collaboration Plan, 157
Collective ownership, 4
Colocated Teams, 31
Colocation, 31
Communication Plan, 261
Communication Techniques, 231
Company Vision, 141
Conduct Daily Standup, 18, 212
   inputs, 223
   outputs, 225
   tools, 224
Conduct Release Planning, 17, 134
   inputs, 176
   outputs, 178
   tools, 177
Confirm benefits realization, 71, 80
Conflict Management, 59
   Techniques, 59
Continuous delivery of value, 4
Continuous feedback, 4
Continuous improvement, 4, 14
Continuous integration, 92, 106
Continuous value justification, 70, 76
Convene Scrum of Scrums, 5, 18, 236
   inputs, 240
   outputs, 243
   tools, 241
Core roles, 11, 40
Cost Performance Index, 77
Cost Variance, 77
Create Deliverables, 18, 212
   inputs, 217
   outputs, 220
   tools, 219
Create Prioritized Product Backlog, 17, 134
   inputs, 169